CW00548877

RIDING THE TOSH HORSE

Ethel M. Dell, A Written Life

First published 2024
Copyright © David Tanner 2024

The right of David Tanner to be identified as the author of this work has been
asserted in accordance with the Copyright, Designs & Patents Act 1988.

All rights reserved. No part of this book may be reproduced, stored in a retrieval
system, or transmitted in any form or by any means, digital, electronic, electrostatic,
magnetic tape, mechanical, photocopying, recording or otherwise, without the
written permission of the copyright holder.

Published under licence by Brown Dog Books and The Self-Publishing Partnership
Ltd, 10b Greenway Farm, Bath Rd, Wick, nr. Bath BS30 5RL, UK

www.selfpublishingpartnership.co.uk

ISBN printed book: 978-1-83952-720-3
ISBN e-book: 978-1-83952-721-0

Cover design by Kevin Rylands

Printed and bound by CPI Group (UK) Ltd, Croydon, CR0 4YY

This book is printed on FSC® certified paper

MIX
Paper | Supporting
responsible forestry
FSC
www.fsc.org   FSC® C013604

RIDING THE TOSH HORSE

Ethel M. Dell, A Written Life

DAVID TANNER

BROWN
DOG
BOOKS

'You know the meaning of solitude and prejudice.
They always go together – the twin goalers'.[1]

1 Ethel M. Dell, The Quest (London, Ernest Benn), p. 167.

This is dedicated to the memory of Penelope Dell, and to Jackie, Rachel, Clare, Charlotte P., Thalia P., Lily P. and Poppy J.

CONTENTS

Acknowledgements

Unusually, posthumous thanks are of course due to Ethel M. Dell herself. Without her reclusiveness this would not have been the exciting challenge that it turned out to be. Also, of course, her immense wealth enabled her sister Ella to live a lifestyle that enabled her to adopt my mother, Penelope Dell, and provide Penelope with a financially secure and a very unusual background. No one person provided an encompassing resource, but I am very grateful for the advice, insight and guidance from many who might have seemed just ancillary to this work but who provided the essential framework and academic insight. My thanks to, among many, Professor Mary Hammond, Dr. Simon Frost, Judith Wright, Calista Lucy, Lucie Dutton, Dr. Nathalie Morris, Dr. Nicola Wilson, Dr. Mary Gifford, Tony Selman, the archivists at the University of North Carolina, New York Public Library, Boston Public Library, Northwestern University, The Mitchel Library Glasgow and the very patient librarians at the British Library, Amoret Tanner, Katie Devine, David Bowley, Dr. Chris Pawson and Rose Collis.

Images shown for the Edwardian parlour games were selected from the Amoret Tanner Ephemera collection.

The cover image is from Ethel M. Dell's *The Hundredth Chance*, New York, Grosset & Dunlap, 1917. Drawn by E. L. Crompton. 'With the utmost gentleness he laid his hand again upon hers. "Are you afraid to say it?" He said'. Other illustrations are from the author's own collection or are in the public domain, and where possible origins have been stated. Every effort has been made to trace copyright holders and to obtain permission for the use of copyright material. Apologies are given for any errors or omissions and notification is requested so that errors can be corrected in future editions of this book.

Extracts and précises from this book were published in *The Book World, Selling and Distributing British Literature, 1900–1940*, edit. Nicola Wilson, Brill, Leiden 2016

Nomenclatures

Given the plethora of Dells in this biographical anthology, and in order to avoid confusion and repetition, the following discipline has been employed:
- Ethel M. Dell is always referred to as Ethel except for the first mention.
- For the first mention of all other Dell family members the first/given name and the surname will be used, and for all other mentions only the first/given name will be used.
- For all other participants in this narrative both first/given name and surname will be used at the first mention, and only the surname for all other subsequent mentions.

List of Photographs and Drawings

Ethel and Ella Dell a 'society' photograph

A sombre and exhausted Ethel

Ethel, Jimmy, Ella and Penelope Dell

Ethel with Nora and Gerald Savage

Ella and her Alberts

The Dell gypsies

Ethel's brother Reggie Dell

Sister Alphonsine Dell O.S.B.

Violet Ebsworth

Violet Vanburgh

Edith de Wolf

Violet Ebsworth, Mary Bastard and Penelope

Preface

Why has a biographical study of Ethel M. Dell (1881–1939) been written? In 1918 Ethel's *Greatheart* was noted as #6 in Publisher's Weekly list of bestsellers, in 1920 Ethel appeared in the top twelve bestsellers in America and a digital analysis of her press mentions at 557,000 is more than double that of Edith Wharton. In today's values she was earning about £4M per annum at the peak of her popularity. By 1929, seven of her titles, excluding her seminal work *The Way of an Eagle* (1910), had combined print runs of 2.2M. *The Way of an Eagle* itself underwent forty-two impressions by 1920 [1]. These statistics of course exclude the circulation and readership of magazines which were a critical part of her marketing effort. Ethel published ninety-eight titles in total, which were sold throughout Europe, the British 'Empire' and in the United States. Yet despite this she was vilified by George Orwell and lampooned by P.G. Wodehouse among others. Ethel had a very high profile, but she was a mystery. Very little is known about her, yet her output was both substantial and influential on both her contemporary and future generations of women writers. It will be a surprise to some that globally Ethel featured very prominently in both book sales and libraries.

1. Background to a Recluse

To date, in the main, academic literary analysis tends to focus on the perceived literary merit of the written word, not on financial success nor in relation to reader numbers. For the author a success is volume and money in the bank. A wonderful review of a book that does not move off the shelves provides a degree of self-satisfaction for the author and maybe praise from his or her peers, but little else. This is a study of a very successful romantic novelist who was lampooned and vilified by her peers whose works did move off the shelf in volume.

Was Ethel's writing a reflection of her own life, and can one detect what her stimuli were? She published between 1898 and 1939, a period of significant social and political change and changes in security of empire. Can these changes be aligned to the content of her writing? Yes, without doubt. Were changes in book distribution patterns contributory to her success? Yes, without doubt. Her marketing mix that created such apparent wealth for A.P. Watt, her final literary agent, the publishers Fischer Unwin and herself was also instrumental in this wealth generation. Her writing can, in many instances, be seen as self-denigrating and self-deprecating. This work will attempt to unravel this peculiar feature of this romantic novelist's persona. Ethel's writing includes pietistic epigraphs, some written by herself. Was the inclusion of these a moralistic counter to the content? Almost certainly. Florence Barclay, however, believed that a high Anglican framework was the best way of gratifying that need, a backlash against the excesses of the fin de siècle.[1] Who read her books and why did Ethel write the way that she did?

It is these questions to which an answer is sought and has only been achieved through an analysis of Ethel's life and an almost forensic analysis and a deep reading of what she wrote. Ethel's written excesses, which I detail later, however, continued until 1939.

Her 'non-literary' style and plots that skirted on the edge of acceptability meant that there were really no comparatives, so she did not fit into the accepted genre of female romantic novelists. This, combined with her financial and volume success, produced an incomparable author. In 1936 the *Daily Express* newspaper published *Great Stories of Love and Romance*. The editors chose thirty-three authors, of whom only thirteen were women. Of these thirteen only Diver, Ethel Mannin, Katherine Mansfield and Ethel have had any sticking power. Only Ethel, however, can claim to be a success if one acknowledges high readership volume as a criteria for success.

2. The Biographical Environment

The slippery art of biography[1]

As a historian the author has to show his hand. My mother Penelope Tanner (née Dell) was adopted by Ethel's unmarried and unattached sister Irene Elizabeth (Sissie). This is, however, not an unfettered analysis by a family acolyte nor a hagiography, but hopefully it will be seen as an objective assessment, warts and all. There has been a conscious effort not to become too entangled in any emotional barbed wire, of which there is so much. What initially seemed a task fraught with a lack of data turned out to be an iceberg of source material with so much available if one looked below the surface. This source data collection and analysis has, however, taken many years.

Penelope wrote the only known 'biography' of Ethel (*Nettie and Sissie*, 1997). Both in the introduction to this work and later in the body of the narrative I raise serious questions about the veracity of Penelope's work. Ethel was a recluse, she shunned publicity, did not correspond with other authors, and seemingly little with her friends, and what if anything she did write has not been sought by universities. Ethel, similar to Kenneth Grahame (*Wind in the Willows*, 1908), did not keep a diary, but on Grahame's death his wife destroyed all his letters as a result of a reported unhappy marriage. Did Ethel write letters, and could this have happened to Ethel as well? We will never know. Grahame's wife then proceeded to publish a hagiography of her late husband. This, however, is not a hagiography of my great aunt.

Penelope's papers reveal very little research, but substantial use of her 'memory', and at many times her imagination. Ralph Tanner, Penelope's husband, has reported that in forty years of marriage Penelope never mentioned

Ethel, and neither did Ethel's sister Ella. My father, Ralph Tanner, and I in *Burma 1942, Memories of a Retreat* (2006) question the validity of memory as a reliable historical tool not only since it can be proven to be inaccurate, but also the reality that self-perception can have an unduly heavy hand at biasing what might have happened. Memory is autobiographical and therefore subject to bias. The autobiography has of course the same failings, and to some extent *Nettie and Sissie* has some of the hallmarks of an autobiography, which is always prey to the subjectivity of self, and one has to ask why that book was written. Within the context of the insecurity of background of those who have been adopted, this work without doubt became an important marker for Penelope, and it is believed that she was encouraged to undertake the work, which she undertook in partial seclusion, by Iris Murdoch, her neighbour and friend. Dame Iris Murdoch DBE, an Irish and British novelist and philosopher, is best known for her novels about good and evil, sexual relationships, morality and the power of the unconscious. Not too dissimilar an environment to Ethel's perspectives.

It is hoped that this work will go some way to set Ethel's record straight as it is clear that *Nettie and Sissie,* tainted as it is with fiction, failed in providing the historically essential objectivity of a biography. Penelope's work was neither critical nor a study. As a caution to the literary analyst, Penelope was a creative writer in her own right, and this author holds volumes of her unpublished fiction, but she was no literary historian. Michael Holroyd has, however, suggested that 'we call novels creative writing which I believe them to be, and biography and history as re-creative writing because they re-created the past'.[2] Re-creating the past, yes, but from a factual basis. If there is relevant empirical data or facts then these are the cornerstones of a biography. Biography is dependent on information and not as Peter Ackroyd has stated that 'Fiction required truth-telling, whereas in a biography one can makes things up.'[3] This is of course not correct as the biography then becomes a work of fiction, which by its nature it should not be.

Barbara Cartland (1901–2000) commented in a review of Penelope's book that 'It is a pity that she [Penelope] did not confine herself to facts about her adopted aunt'.[4] A novel is just fiction even if it is based on an element of fact. Jane Hodge commented in her biography of Georgette Heyer that 'Her portrait of the Duke of Wellington, based on his own letters and reported speech, is masterly'.[5] Importantly his reported speech, not what he said. Penelope in her 'biography' refers to detailed conversations within her family held before she was born or when she was before the age of reason or away at boarding school. Those conversations might have been reported to Penelope but they are not fact. In 1975 Penelope wrote that 'When I think that Ella (who adopted me) never had much to do with her Dell relations … Ethel of course was quite different, gentle, kind, emotional and retiring. I loved what I saw of her which was very limited, as Ella became very jealous of my affections for anyone but herself'.[6] The 'factoid' as Norman Mailer cleverly coined the elision of fact and fiction in his biography of Marilyn Monroe is a regrettable truth in most historical writing that does not have to pass academic scrutiny.[7] In *Nettie and Sissie* Penelope created an entertaining factoid, and a very significant and important social history, but it is not a biography. But Penelope was writing in the postmodernist style of mixing up fact and fiction, history and invention.

Biographies are of both historical, and in this case, of literary importance and it is a perverse reality that if little is known about the subject of the biography then what little is written is of perhaps greater significance than that of someone about whom there is a volume of biographical data. There is a tight focus on the little, and a general focus on the mass. The biographies of T.E. Lawrence are a case in point. There was a very great disparity between the biographies written by prominent historians, military and student colleagues, friends and comments from his family, and of course his own autobiography.

Richard Aldington wrote in relation to Lawrence that there were 'untruths', and 'systematic falsifications'.[8] However, overall, one understood who and what he was. For Ethel there has been regrettably only one inaccurate narrative and this has been and is used as a reference for her life. The printed word becomes factual. It is not therefore a question of just sweeping up the bits of inaccurate narrative but perforce a need to remedy the inaccuracies, factually, and where such facts are not available and surmise is used to clearly state that this is the case. Ethel deserves no less. Because of her reclusiveness and the dearth of correspondence I have sought to understand her, unusually, and to a very large extent, by what she wrote. We do not know what Ethel thought, as she corresponded very little. One can, however, interpret her published narratives, but this is then my interpretation of her written word.

Penelope died in 1985 and regrettably left little research material to support her publication. She was, however, an assiduous letter writer and Ella kept some of her letters which are an important resource. The intimacy of these letters gives confidence that despite being sent to a boarding school aged nine, and Penelope clearly very lonely, on their travels on the grand tour and other holidays Ella would have shared confidences with her as there was no one else in whom Ella could confide. This to some extent underwrites the probable veracity of the non-authenticated comment, however, it is of significance that Penelope would have had an extremely limited time within Ethel's orbit. Up to the age of four she lived in the same domestic environment as Ethel, but after the latter's marriage she would only have had contact during her holidays from school on visits to Ethel and a significant amount of this holiday time was spent in Menton and other locations in the south of France, or on holidays with Ella in Dorset when the latter played Gypsy complete with caravan or at the 'hut' that Ella owned. We can see Ella's romantic Gypsy holidays mirrored in *The Knight Errant*, where the heroine leads a Gypsy-like existence to escape the advances of an Indian prince. Penelope's drawing of Ella dressing-up as a Gypsy is an idealised middle-class interpretation of simple living.

Throughout *Nettie and Sissie* we are left with the impression that Ella conducted all business matters and typed correspondence and manuscripts for Ethel, and undertook to manage her business affairs. There is, however, empirical evidence to the contrary. All seen correspondence to Watt, and Ethel's manuscripts, are in her own hand. Also, the content of Ethel's correspondence demonstrated that she had a very shrewd business mind. Lastly there is no evidence that Ethel referred to her sister Ella as Sissie. To the contrary there is again empirical evidence that she referred to her as Elizabeth. Ethel was, however, Nettie. Such inaccuracies regrettably put into question the veracity of Penelope Dell's book. Perhaps Penelope had been reading about Rebecca West, who was known to her family as Cissie, or even Elisabeth the high-profile empress of Austria and queen of Hungary (1837–1898) who was known as Sisi or Sissi, who was assassinated with her husband Emperor Franz Joseph. But not Ethel. Penelope was clearly guilty of palpable fabrication in a very readable story that masqueraded as a biography written as the result of a distant association with the subject of this work. The historian, in documenting, has a responsibility or the record becomes indelibly incorrect. Penelope failed this test. The written and published word can suffer from the accretion of myth, as has hers.

The excitement of a biographical anthology is that it poses so many questions before the reader even gets involved in the many facets of the discourse. In this case it is who is she, and perhaps even for the sceptic, why bother to write about her? Ethel does not even warrant an entry in one biographical dictionary of women, and little is known about her.[9] In a tight academic environment with a focus on romantic literature one British university offers an undergraduate course 'The Evolution of Romance Fiction from 1740 to the Present', and for the period 1900 to the start of the Second World War, a period of significant social, political and reader tastes changes, but only E.M. Hull and Georgette Heyer are required reading as sources of primary data.[10] Ethel, as I uncover, seemed to be a greater influence on the reader universe in this period than Hull.

The anthological challenge is somewhat easier as there is the empirical evidence of what she wrote, but it is the analysis of this, the social domestic and political influences and how Ethel's creativity was delivered in multiple media that provides a fascinating window of analytical opportunity to understand Ethel's success. Because of the nature of Ethel's secretive life this work to a very large extent escapes the established biographical taxonomies, but as can be seen there are moments of enlightenment on what could have been a blank canvas. Not quite holy grails, but almost. We read her works and hope that as a result we can understand her a little better, but what is certain is that we have an image of a personality, something that Ethel tried so hard to hide.

In this work I have allowed the dead to speak, albeit through assumption. Where possible I have tried to portray what might have been Ethel's views and lifestyle. A literary anthology and particularly a biographical anthology should of course be regarded as constructs reflecting the places, the times and the socio/political environments of their creation rather than collections of narratives.

Why, despite being a phenomenally successful romantic novelist, is so very little known about her life, her motivations and inspirations? Literary success is of course subjective. Is an author's success measured by a judgement from peers, by money in the bank or by, as in this case, a volume output as well? Can a novelist be successful and not be considered part of the English literary canon?

This biography addresses the background to the phenomenal financial and volume success of Ethel's romantic fiction. Despite being widely read and of significance in popular culture, her work is generally either largely ignored or forgotten, was lampooned by fellow novelists and vilified in contemporary literary discourse. In contrast Pamela Regis wrote that Hull's *The Sheikh* (1919) 'not only achieved popularity immediately on publication but also influenced the popular romance novel throughout the twentieth century'.[11] This does seem a questionable conclusion when the nature of romantic fiction changed so dramatically after the First World War. Clive Bloom has written that the Hutchinson Famous Author series emblazoned with 'The most popular writer of love stories in the world ...' was presenting the reader with 'a less Christian and more liberated sense of women's role that finally put an end to the work of Ouida and Marie Corelli and opened the way for Ethel M. Dell and Mills and Boon'.[12] This open commercialisation of romance with the Hutchinson 6d paperback series does equate to a commercially driven social shift in both acceptability and demand. Barbara Cartland a dominant personality in twentieth century romantic fiction acknowledged the influence that Ethel had on her own literary career: 'I have copied her formula all my life. What she said was revolutionary – that men were strong, silent, passionate heroes. And my whole life has been geared to that ...'[13]

Hidden in Ethel's *The Unknown Quantity* (1923) is a clear statement of female empowerment and sexuality. She refers to her heroine as having 'It'. This is neither a typesetting nor an editing error. 'It' is uppercase in the middle of a dialogue and describes a lecherous impresario's reaction to seeing his theatre heroine in her costume. With an imperious gesture, 'He swept her aside. "You don't know anything about it. How could you? Besides things look so totally different across the footlights. You've nothing to worry about. You are absolutely It"'.[14] The only other time in all her narratives that she uses upper case in the middle of a sentence is when she is referring to God. This concept was clearly purloined by Elinor Glyn (1864–1943) in her developed concept of *IT* published in 1926, and the subsequent 1927 film with Clara Bow (1905–1965) as the star. 'It' was portrayed as a state of supreme self-confidence and an indifference to what others thought in the quest for relationships. Clara Bow was even nicknamed the 'IT' girl.[15] At the time of the publication of *The Unknown Quantity* Glyn was employed by Lasky, the film producer in the United States, while they were creating Ethel's films.

Glyn had established a very high social profile for herself through affairs with members of the British aristocracy including eleven years with Lord Curzon the former viceroy of India from 1907 to 1918. It can be speculated that this and unwanted publicity related to any legal redress prevented Ethel from pursuing matters for what seemed to be a clear case of plagiarism with commercial gain.

3. Peer Envy, Perhaps

'In a way it is easier for people like Ethel M. Dell
to avoid prostitution than it is for a serious writer'.[1]

Ethel was a recluse, and actively avoided marketing herself as a personality in any way, but her formula was successful. As a romantic novelist, she reached a very large audience. Her plots included a popular and heady mix of heterosexual, implicit same-sex relationships, sexual deviances, gratuitous violence, violence, death and exoticised notions of empire and masculinity. Was her popularity comparable with other romantic novelists like Glyn, Florence Barclay, Ruby Ayres and Marie Corelli, an earlier doyenne of the circulating library? The answer is no as the latter authors by and large did not appeal to a mass reader universe. None of them are mentioned in terms of reader statistics, where Ethel is compared with other not necessarily romantic novelists and rarely measured against other female writers. Measure is here the operative and significant term as literary analysis is qualitative without a monetised value but sales are a quantitative measure. From an academic purist/literary point of view Ethel hardly scored at all, but from a quantitative, and monetised perspective, she was extremely successful. 'so substantial were the sales of Ethel M. Dell's novels that there came a moment when T. Fisher Unwin's auditors reported that they were responsible for half of the then very large turnover of the firm.'[2] But what drove her phenomenal commercial success? Her first title published in book form in Britain, *The Way of an Eagle*, had by 1920 undergone forty-two impressions. Ethel did not speak to the Press, did not release photographs of herself, but became significantly rich. This must be some measure of success but in literary circles at the time she was lampooned and certainly not acknowledged as a scholarly force. Along with many other contemporary women authors she was not scholarly, her letters are not coveted by university libraries, but what she wrote found a very receptive audience and made her publishers and herself very rich. Nicola Beauman refers to her former supervisor at Cambridge as 'being almost too appalled to speak' at the prospect of her former student writing about female novelists who published during the 1920s and 1930s.[3] There was and still is an aura of literary mediocrity for women writers of passionate novels in this period. Rooting around in second-hand book shops is a singular pleasure, but even today over 70 years after her death a request for Ethel's works is often greeted with incredulity ... almost, as if to say, why would anyone want one of *those* books?

Ethel, as I will show, used her narratives to voice her personal feelings. This was not a stream of consciousness imparted to the heroes and heroines of Virginia Woolf, Dorothy Richardson and even James Joyce entering into the minds of their characters, but narratives as vehicles for her personal demons; the writer's internal narratives disguised in fiction. Woolf's *Orlando* (1928) is fiction but labelled as a biography. As such perhaps a comparison with Zelda Fitzgerald (1900–1948) is more apposite. Fitzgerald in her one supposed novel wrote about her personal demons and her relationship with her husband, lightly disguised as fiction.

George Orwell, writing in his *Keep the Aspidistra Flying* (1936) without any subtlety, portrays Ethel's reader as being neither well educated nor sophisticated:

> Mrs. Weaver upset her rush basket and spilled onto the floor a much-thumbed copy of Ethel M. Dell's *Silver Wedding*. Mrs Penn's bright bird-eye lighted upon it. Behind Mrs. Weaver's back she smiled up at Gordon, archly, as highbrow to highbrow. Dell! The lowness of it! And then after a discourse about J.B. Priestly and John Galsworthy between Gordon and Mrs. Penn,

Mrs. Weaver announces, 'I think p'raps I can't do better'n 'ave another Dell,' she said. 'You 'ave got some more Dells 'aven't you? I do so enjoy a good read of Dell, I must say. I says to my daughter, I says, You can keep your Deepings and your Burroughses. Give me a Dell I says.' Later in this dialogue: 'I b'lieve I'll just 'ave *The Way of an Eagle* over again,' said Mrs. Weaver finally. 'You don't never seem to get tired of *The Way of an Eagle*, do you, now?'[4]

Orwell clearly labels Ethel's work as being for the less educated and those lower down the socio-economic scale. Writing in his essay *In Defence of the Novel* (1936), Orwell quotes Hilaire Belloc's opinion that the novel is a 'contemptible form of art', but to Orwell the issue was the novel's 'lapse in prestige'.[5] Ethel, who according to Orwell was a party to this decline in prestige, wrote material that appealed to a lowbrow market. Continuing his critique Orwell castigates the 'lazily eulogistic reviewer as, sinking his standards to a depth at which, say, Ethel M. Dell's *Way of an Eagle* is a fairly good book'.[6] Paul Fussell refers to Orwell as being 'fascinated by the pathology of bad taste and loves to display ironically the names of novelists (Ethel M. Dell, Hugh Walpole, Warwick Deeping) once thought of as attractive as Herman Wouk, Leon Uris and James A. Mitchener'.[7] One has to ask bad taste to whom? This neatly encapsulates the tension and sometimes the polarity between perceived literary success and popular success. But Ethel, who was exposed to and no doubt had an influence on millions of readers globally, is virtually invisible today.

P.G. Wodehouses' character Rosie M. Banks is perhaps modelled on Ethel, but there is some suggestion that Rosie M. Banks could have been Rosie M. Ayres. This, however, seems unlikely given that Ayres did not receive such generally negative press to which Ethel was subjected. The lampooned style and titles of Wodehouse's character seem remarkably similar to Ethel's. In *Carry on Jeeves* (1925) the romantic novelist Rosie M. Banks is referred to as 'author of some of the most pronounced and widely read tripe ever put on the market', and then 'dear sensible girl as she is in ordinary life – the moment she gets in front of a dictating machine she becomes absolutely maudlin!'[8]

Wodehouse's dig at Ethel seems to continue in *The Inimitable Jeeves* with Rosie M. Bank's fictional titles, *All for Love, A Red, Red Summer Rose, Madcap Myrtle, Only a Factory Girl*, and *The Courtship of Lord Strathmorlick*. Ethel's prose style is then satired in a dialogue between the characters, ' ...for I'd hardly reached the bit where their lips met in a long, slow kiss and everything was still but for the gentle sighing of the breeze in the laburnum'.[9]

Nine years after her death Wodehouse was still sticking it to Ethel in his *Uncle Dynamite* (1948); no doubt it was nice to have a creative foil:

> You will behave like the heroes of those novels which were so popular at one time, who went about in riding breeches and were not above giving the girl of their choice a couple with a hunting crop on the spot where it would do some good. Ethel M. Dell. That's the name I was trying to think of. You must comport yourself like the hero of an Ethel M. Dell novel. Buy her works, and study them diligently.[10]

And,

> Little wonder that Hermoine Bostock, as Bill having waggled her about, clasped her to his bosom and showered kisses on her upturned face, felt that he was a man she had been looking for since she first read *The Way of an Eagle*.[11]

Noel Coward also waded in with a stinging comment in the introduction to his *Three Plays* and wrote: 'There will always be a public for the Cinderella story, the same as there will always be a public for Miss Ethel M. Dell and the Girls Companion. In the world of amusement it is essential for someone to cater for the illiterate ...'[12]

Ethel did not assist her literary reputation with her self-deprecating comments in *The Electric Torch* (1934): The heroine, Claire, is keeping a suitor at bay and the suitor refers to this as a 'typical Ethel M Dell moment'.[13] Again, denigrating her own readers in *The Juice of the Pomegranate* (1938), 'Hello! Here's a find! Now we shall see what the brainy Blanche reads in her leisure moments! Something she's none too proud of obviously! [The book has been found behind a cushion.] Great Scott! It's an Ethel M. Dell! That poor fish! Blanche, I'm beginning to know what's the matter with you. You're a snob, and I'm going to punish you for it. I shall put this book where all your highbrow friends will mark and learn – even if they refuse to read. It'll be a terrible exposure for you, but it will damn well serve you right'. To compound the denigration, Diana the exposer of the book cannot find it where she had left it for others to see and in response to a question as to where it is the maid replies in support of Blanche: '"My Lady never leaves a Dell book lying around for visitors to see, madam, so I took it away." "I see. Bad style is she?" There was a mischievous gleam in Diana's glance. "I'm sure I don't know, madam." Enid's tone was repressive. "Ever read them yourself?" asked Diana. "Yes madam," said Enid. "And you like them?" "Yes madam," said Enid again. Diana lighted her cigarette. "I congratulate you, Enid," she said. "We may like bad things, but it isn't all of us who have the courage to say so."' Can this extraordinary self-deprecation be considered as a part of her marketing mix ... the worse they are viewed, the more they will sell?

Jen Shelton has put forward the thesis for consideration that James Joyce modelled Gerty Macdonald's romantic notions of womanhood and marriage in *Ulysses* (1922) on Ethel's style as a counter to Cissy's 'overtly sexualised discourse of a tomboy', but there is, however, no empirical evidence to this effect.[14] Can one say that Gerty's monologues are written in Ethel's style? If this was the case then it would be clear that her literary output reflected part of the social reality that influenced Joyce's vision.

Georgette Heyer, twenty years Ethel's junior, was known to consider that personal publicity did not help sales. She was, like Ethel, intensely private and rarely gave interviews. However, in an interview she gave in 1955, as quoted by A.S. Byatt in 1975, she makes the link to Ethel's standpoint very succinctly, 'There seems to be a pathetic belief today in the power of personal publicity over sales. I don't share it, and before you assume how mistaken I am I beg you to consider the case of the late Ethel M. Dell, about whom the public knew nothing, and whose colossal sales we should all of us be glad to have had ...'[15] In contrast, Glyn after her success with the risqué novel *Three Weeks* (1900) sought the maximum personal exposure, and worked assiduously to keep herself before the public. Her 'Glyn' brand became intimately linked with the concept of 'It' after the success of the 1927 film of the same name starring Clare Bow. But, Glyn's literary works were generally seen as faulty and were challenged in both construction and grammar by the literati of the time. Her brand, however, became synonymous with life and love, not her literary skill. There is a clear parallel to Ethel here: synonymous with life and love and poor style.

Yet in contrast to Orwell's contempt and Wodehouse's mocking, some educated readers could respond to Ethel favourably, after a fashion. The writer Rebecca West, a humorous and penetrating critic, wrote in the *New Statesman* shortly after the publication of Ethel's *Charles Rex*:

I am amazed to find that I can blush. My sensations, interesting as they are in themselves, I shall probably deal with elsewhere under the title of 'A Forgotten Sport'; my point now is their surprising origin. For they are caused by a volume named *Charles Rex*, by a writer named Miss Ethel M. Dell, who has received every sort of acclamation save only the morning stars singing together; and I doubt if one worries about the lack of super-terrestrial recognition when one can sell nearly half-a-million copies of a single novel. It is, moreover, a volume that I was predisposed to regard with affection, because of this paragraph in its first page: 'Saltash turned and surveyed the skyline over the yacht's sail with obvious discontent on his ugly face. His eyes were odd, one black, one grey, giving a curiously unstable appearance to a countenance which otherwise might have claimed to possess some strength. His brows were black and deeply marked. He had a trick of moving them in conjunction with his thoughts, so that his face was seldom in absolute repose. It was said that there was a strain of royal blood in Saltash, and in the days before he had succeeded to the title, when he was merely Charles Burchester, he had borne the nickname of the "merry monarch". Certain wild deeds in a youth that had not been beyond reproach had seemed to warrant this, but of later years a mend has bestowed a more gracious title upon him, and to all who could claim intimacy with him he had become "Charles Rex." The name fitted him like a garment. A certain arrogance, a certain royalty of bearing, both utterly unconscious and wholly unfeigned, characterised him. Whatever he did and his actions were often far from praiseworthy this careless distinction of mien always marked him. He received an almost in-voluntary respect wherever he went.' It is pleasant to say that Charles Rex keeps up his form to the end. He habitually said 'egad' and used 'terrible foreign oaths' and broke into French, though that concussion rarely extends to anything more than the word mais he 'dismissed the waiter with a jerk of his eyebrows'; and when dining at home said to the butler, 'I'm going to smoke on the ramparts,' where his acres lay below him ... took the cigar from his mouth and spoke ironically, grimly, 'There is your kingdom, Charles Rex,' he said. And in every line that is written about him one hears the thudding, thundering hooves of a certain steed at full gallop; of the true Tosh-horse. For even as one cannot walk on one's own trudging, diligent feet if one desires to attain to the height of poetry, but must mount Pegasus, so one cannot reach the goal of best-selling by earnest pedestrianism, but must ride thither on the Tosh-horse. No one can write a best-seller by taking thought. The slightest touch of insincerity blurs its appeal. The writer who keeps his tongue in his cheek, who knows that he is writing for fools and that, therefore, he had better write like a fool, may make a respectable living out of serials and novelettes; but he will never make the vast, the blaring, half-a-million success. That comes of blended sincerity and vitality. It is true that in the past a very great success could be attained by writers who had not this latter qualification ... Miss Dell is a queen. She rides the Tosh-horse hell-for-leather. Positively at the most thrilling moments (of which I prefer the moment when the new Lady Saltash, exceptionally light on her feet owing to early training as a circus-rider, springs out upon the ledge of the family ramparts because she wearies of the way that Lord Saltash has neglected to consummate their marriage and only steps back when he explains that he has pursued this policy because of spiritual awakening caused by a remark the poor girl had thoughtlessly made to the effect that he had made her believe in God) one feels as if one might be ridden down. But I blush, and wonder. This is the story of a middle-aged voluptuary who, when he is cruising about the Mediterranean, comes on an Italian hotel proprietor beating a page-boy, and interrupts the sport. That night he finds the boy concealed as a stowaway on the yacht, and immediately realises though he keeps silence that here is a girl in disguise. For five chapters the story titillates us (us includes, one amazedly estimates, the mass of the population of Surbiton, Bournemouth, and Cheltenham) with a description of the peculiar intercourse that takes place between them in these circumstances. There is a specially pleasing incident when they are playing cards and the girl-boy cheats, and Lord Saltash beats her with a riding-switch. We afterwards learn that she had cheated on purpose that she might have this delicious revelation of the gentleman's quality.[16]

Rebecca West blushed as did many readers as they were transported into a sexual fantasy by an author, Ethel, who herself seemed without any heterosexual relationships until she married at the age of thirty-nine, twenty years after her first published work. There is an assumption here that her marriage late in life was in fact consummated.

Success can be measured by the publication of ninety-eight titles (two stories were subject to a change of title for the American market) with forty-eight novels published in her lifetime in the UK, the then British Empire,

Europe and the United States, many into multiple editions, a book of poetry, twenty-five feature film adaptions of her books, stage plays and stories, some serialised running in fourteen magazines in the UK and the United States. Her work is still being published in the United States, the UK, Germany, Italy and France.

A linear and chronological attempt to understand Ethel, a fascinating character with a seemingly dysfunctional family, a small number of female extra-familial relationships, no male relationships other than her marriage late in life, would seem to miss the point of the 'who' and the 'why'. Clearly the passage of time's influence on experience counts, but it is not the years that count here. There is a wealth of empirical data in the appendices that must not be a distraction in sleuthing for answers to both what drove her creativity and an understanding of the influences on her reclusive life. A non-linear narrative or thematic approach allows greater scope for understanding the person whose lifestyle seemed only marginally to fuel her imagination. Michael Holroyd commented that 'a single life biography can be understood as about more than one life perhaps … Few people live wholly solitary lives, though solitude I think may be part of writing and all arts – you've got to shut a door on social life to work'.[17] Ethel was known to shut herself away and write during anti-social hours, but there is a pattern in her life which does indicate a very solitary and perhaps a disturbed person.

Can one write about it without living it? Jonathan Franzen commented 'I'm convinced that a fiction writer's oeuvre is a mirror of the writer's own character'.[18] This comment was made in the context of the novelist Edith Wharton, who with her formidable character, a desire to see and be seen, seems to have been at a polarity with the reclusive Ethel. In T.S. Eliot's 1940 lecture on W.B. Yeats he refers to the experience of youth being a creative force.[19] Was this the case for Ethel? It appears not. Glyn, remarking on her stimuli said, 'I drew out my imagination, material to satisfy my own unfulfilled longing for romantic love, and so, out of my own poverty, I was able to provide the riches of imaginary fulfilment and pour them out into the love starved lives of those thousands of others whom I do not know'.[20] As has been demonstrated Glyn also drew inspiration from Ethel.

Ethel was no different considering her sheltered early life. Then again, what inspired Jules Verne when his boating horizon was the Loire and one trip to Sweden? As a generality it is hard to agree with Franzen's views, but Ethel's writing does open a window, in some of her diegeses, to her feelings. She chose the public domain of her publications, not in letters to confidants or family, as the medium in which to express herself. Some of her works are revealing to the tutored eye. For example: In *The Electric Torch* there is discourse on an unconsummated marriage (she married in 1922), suggestions of single-sex relationships and significantly a knowledge of drugs. From about the time of the release of this story it must be assumed that Ethel was seriously unwell and under medication, as within six years it is understood that she suffered her first mastectomy for cancer.

The Passer-By (1925) explains the surface reasons for her reclusiveness. The focus of the narrative, Jane Brown, an artist who avoids publicity like the plague, 'some people call it a pose. It probably is. But I suppose she has a right to do as she likes'. Clearly this a reference to her own behaviour out of the public eye. The artist has already been approached but declines to have her portrait taken. "'she is a shy bird - a very shy bird. I imagine that she'll take some catching ... what right have the public to intrude on her?" ... "But why should she mind?" said Guy. She looked at him with almost a glint of scorn in her eyes. "I?" He laughed a little. "I really don't know. Would you?" "Yes. I would mind intensely," she said. "To be recognised wherever one went, pointed at, made conspicuous – oh, I should hate it – hate it!" ...

"And she feels as I do, that to be made a show of would be – quite intolerable. She considers all self-advertisement is vulgar, and she – would never stoop to it.'"[21] Central to this reclusiveness was the reason for not wanting to be seen. Pathologically shy yes, but was this just a psychological condition, and if not, what was the cause? A close examination of the very few photographs of Ethel that survive do indicate a slight malformation of her upper lip, and it is possible that she had had a cleft lip that was repaired, that or some facial trauma that had left a disfigurement. There is a case here to suggest that part of Ethel's reclusiveness was perhaps vanity.

An autobiography cannot remove itself from the subjectivity of the author but there is a challenge in this biographical anthology to avoid the subjective 'family' trap into which Penelope fell and the requirement to draw conclusions relevant to the period. The authorship challenge here is to ask questions relevant to the period and to answer in the same frame, in the context of fact and not fiction. I have chosen to focus this biography laterally on the facets of her personality and output. It is perhaps not the empirical data that is of greatest significance but the emotion and personality that drove it. As such there will be, of necessity, some occasional repetition within this biography.

There are of course no fixed rules as to what is either included or excluded in a work of this nature. There is no biographical formula. Ethel was a very obscure canvas so the biographer has to cast wide to find patterns, trends, answers and motivations. Nothing is off the investigative table. Everything is examined and dissected and challenged. Also, the biographer particularly in this case has to be the writer who has to put himself in Ethel's shoes and to try and formulate understanding. Why such violence? Why the drug use? Why suggestions of flexible sexuality? Why the philosophical musings? Why unhappiness in marriage? Why sentences and words that when examined forensically do not hold together?

In this work I will portray Ethel's life not within a literary genre but through her creativity and output, a life discovered, a life through writing. I will bring Ethel to life through the re-creation of that life from what she wrote and what little is known outside of that. Harold Nicholson made the distinction between scientific and literary biography and saw the future of imaginative literary biography in fiction, whilst what he calls scientific biography focuses on facts. Penelope muddled the two and created disbelief. I have separated the scientific (the facts) from the fiction but importantly the latter is based on reasonable assumptions which are identified in the scientific. To do this each chapter is divided into what I am boldly terming the scientific, with the fiction fed by the former packaged as Ethel talking about herself as 'Ethel's Perspective.' This interpretation is therefore a summation of the information available, assumptions made from empirical data and her own writing. 'Ethel's Perspective' is fiction, but a fiction created from reasonable and rational assumptions.

4. A Remarkably Driven Novelist

'If they can not agree to this there is nothing doing'. [1]
{The imperative in can not and not the use of 'cannot' is very emphatic}

In order to understand both the nature of Ethel's life, her creativity and her productivity it is important to comprehend the sheer volume of Ethel's activity over her writing life. The summary of her 'first published' work provides a very clear demonstration of her astonishing creative output.

This 'first published' data is a measure of her original creativity. It is of course self-evident that 'first published' indicates that the writing and creation of that title is in a prior period. Thirty-one titles were first published by her thirtieth birthday. Thirty in the next ten years. Over her whole writing life, on the assumption that she started writing aged eighteen, her average output was just under three titles per year. This first published output peaked in her forties with an average of just under four per annum and slowed considerably in the years up to her death.

Other than the creative effort of producing new narratives for her reader universe there was the ongoing commercial effort with publishing negotiations, film scripts and deals to be concluded. Working with a secretary who focused mainly on her correspondence with her 'followers' and her literary agents, she accomplished a staggering number of deals during her writing career. A total of 280 different deals were concluded, of which a peak of 35% were accomplished during the years 1914, 17, 19, 21 and 22. In the last two years alone she completed forty-seven deals, married and moved house. As one would expect, her deal-making slowed considerably after this but they still averaged one every two months until the year of her death.

Ethel found her story telling vocation at an early age, and was certainly writing from her late teen years. This demonstrated self-assurance in a Victorian teenage woman, dominated by a controlling parent and dominant sister, to not just write romance and humour but also to go out and sell her work was quite remarkable. Her first story, *The Repentant Rogue,* was published in Britain in December 1899 when she was just eighteen years old, and in the United States three months later. This dichotomy of the creative flair and the commercial drive was one of many such polarities that were a feature of her life. Her appointment of Pinker as her literary agent when she was just twenty was a move that she later regretted, as despite her increased income from royalties and one-off fees, she had been persuaded to part with the copyright to twenty-four of the titles that Pinker had sold. In 1912 Ethel wrote to The Society of Authors that 'I know that my magazine contracts in the past have been deplorable, but what can one do? An unknown author has no choice'. Her comment discussed earlier in *The Electric Torch*, referring to herself, 'By the way, that woman has my sympathy if ever a woman had. She is branded for life on account of her juvenile efforts of umpteen years ago' is perhaps not irony as suggested by the Cambridge University Orlando Project, or as Penelope who wrote *Nettie and Sissie* and who acknowledged that she hardly knew Ethel suggests, that it is as a search for literary acceptance.[2] There is, it seems, no basis for these observations and it is more likely that she regretted her early commercial decisions and she used the vehicle of one of her stories to set the record straight, for posterity. It was, however, these juvenile efforts that put her on the literary map not just as an influential novelist but as a very wealthy woman, and she might have been wealthier if she had not parted with her early copyrights. This was not the only time that Ethel used her stories to put the record straight. In *The Secret Service Man* (1914), totally out of context with the narrative of the story, the hero is castigated by his mentor and reminded that: 'Never answer your critics!

Go straight ahead!'[3] Ethel was subjected to continuous critical reviews and she never responded or reacted to them. As discussed, her critics helped cement her reputation as a marketable commodity.

The commercial opportunities presented to both Ethel and Watt were blighted initially by this sale of her rights, which, over a period of time, were re-purchased. It was surely this naiveté to which she referred and her gullibility to Pinker's influence who de facto did not believe in the commercial opportunity that Ethel presented. Ethel was a diligent and hard worker, putting her writing above everything else. After the death of her mother in 1918 she wrote to Watt on black-edged mourning paper: 'Yes, thank you, our holiday has done us both [Ethel and Ella] good, and I now expect to be very busy with my novel, to make up for lost time'.[4] Ethel was a very driven writer with clear personal deadlines. We can see this drive referenced in *Storm Drift:* 'I've got my devil dances coming on and I shall work and work in a perfect fever while the foul thing goads me; and the worst of it is I shall think I'm really doing something worth doing and superlatively great. But it won't be. Nothing in this world is. It's all a mass of illusion put into us to make us kick the beastly old show along'.[5]

The success of a fiction writer is normally measured by critical acclaim of a work, and the volume of books published. This narrow focus on the medium in which the works are viewed can hide, as it does with Ethel, a huge pool of commercialised creativity. Laurel Brake's comment that 'it is a mistake to construct the nineteenth century book as a stand-alone commodity' continued to apply in the twentieth century.[6] In her lifetime, Ethel published her stories in forty-eight books, many of which went into multiple editions, both in the UK and internationally. This number in fact hides her prodigious output of the ninety-eight titles that she published. These stories appeared within thirty-five different magazine titles 157 times, twenty-three films, three stage plays at ten different venues, three radio broadcasts and of course her 'books'.[7] Her works are still being published.

The year 1917 is another good example of the intensity of her work as the start and stop dates of a manuscript are available. Aged thirty-six, while her mother was still alive and living with her at Chattern House in Kent, Ethel produced the 624-page manuscript of *Greatheart* in exactly eight months. She started on 17 February 1917 and finished the work on 16 October the same year.[8] In this one year alone, agreements were also negotiated and agreed with multiple media, and she released the following other stories for publication:

- *The Man from Heidelberg:* Cassell *Penny Magazine.*
- *The Safety Curtain:* with T. Fisher Unwin (UK) in *The Safety Curtain: And other stories (Collection),* and with Putnam in the United States and Copp Clark in Canada.
- *The Place of Honour:* with T. Fisher Unwin (UK) in *The Safety Curtain: And other stories (Collection),* and with Putnam in the United States and Copp Clark in Canada.
- *The Experiment:* with T. Fisher Unwin (UK) in *The Safety Curtain: And other stories (Collection),* and with Putnam and, Grosset and Dunlap in the United States and Copp Clark in Canada.
- *Those Who Wait: The Experiment:* with T. Fisher Unwin (UK) in *The Safety Curtain: And other stories (Collection),* and with Putnam and, Grosset and Dunlap in the United States and Copp Clark in Canada.
- *The Rose of Dawn:* in the UK with *The Strand Magazine.*
- *The Knave of Diamonds:* with Ernest Benn in the UK.
- *The Hundredth Chance:* as a serialised story in The Red Magazine, as a book with Hutchinsons in the UK and Putnam in the United States.

Having signed with Pinker as her literary agent in 1901, her reader franchise had not been established, as little seems to have happened until the rights to twenty-four titles were sold between 1908 and 1913, and her works published in the Red Book in the UK. It is doubtless correct that Ethel's work ethic meant that she was producing material prior to 1908, which was effectively a bank of material that Pinker eventually sold. It is also probable that Pinker's view of her material was that the only way to achieve publication and a financial return was the sale of her copyrights, which she then regretted. Ethel was clearly in need of a new literary agent, but she still bargained hard and reduced Watt's normal commission from 10% to 7.5%.[9] Watt was, however, initially only appointed agent specifically for *The Way of an Eagle* and *The Knave of Diamonds,* and only started supporting Ethel after she had concluded her publishing relationship with T. Fisher Unwin herself at the age of thirty specifically for *The Way of an Eagle.* The title was already sold both in the United States and the United Kingdom in magazine serial form, so Watt did not have to hedge his bets. He was betting on an established winner.

Ethel's relationship with Watt was not dissimilar to Kipling's description of his relationship with Watt: 'he is very kind and nice and does everything for you except – writing your book'.[10] Ethel dealt personally with all business matters, especially all correspondence with her literary agent Watt. Her letters were hand-written, short and to the point.

The function of a literary agent is to promote the works of their client writer and to this one must ascribe some commercial stimulus for the hard-nosed commerciality that is evident in Ethel's business dealings. We also see deference to Ethel from Watt and Stoll the film producer. They needed and sought her approval for all commercial transactions.

- 13 August 1919. Watt to Putnams [the American publishing house] re *The Sacrifice* (1919) and its publication in Hutchinson's Magazine: 'I expect that Miss Dell will probably wish to include it in her next new volume'.

- 15 June 1921. Stoll to Watt: 'the scenarios for *The Experiment* and *The Nonentity (1911)* will be submitted to Miss Dell during the course of the next two months'.
- 4 December 1927. Ethel to Watt re Amalgamated Press payment of £12.12.0d for *The Friend Who Stood By* (1909), complaining that 'I do not quite see why it is £1.1/- less than its predecessor *The Consolation Prize!*'
- 22 May 1931. Ethel to Watt: 'I am quite willing to accept the Weldon's offer of £40 for *Rosa Mundi*, and I do not object to the change of title ...'
- 19 February 1932. Ethel to Watt: 'I am willing to accept Miss Hammerton's offer of £17.10/.0 for the right to re-print *The Friend Who Stood By*, but only on condition that it is published either under its own proper title ...'
- 23 February 1932. Ethel to Watt: 'As regards the request to call my story "Fair Play" I should suggest that it should be taken as a motto instead of a title! As I said in my last letter, the story may be published either under its own title or under that previously used for the second serial but <u>not</u> by any other'.
- 4 February 1937. Ethel to Watt: 'With regard to my story *Rosa Mundi*, Weldon's seem to have broken my rule in 1931 of never allowing a story to come out under a faked name. It is a trick on the public to which I can never give my approval. If they care to publish it under its own name *Rosa Mundi* I think I might accept the twelve guineas, as it is not a long story, about 12,000 words, I fancy'.[11]

Ethel was acutely aware of the value of a copyright and the dangers of the use of copyrighted material without permission. In 1912, before working with Watt, she requested Kipling's address from the Society of Authors in order to seek permission to use a single verse, the tenth, of one of his poems *To the True Romance* 'in my new novel to be published next year'.[12] [*The Knave of Diamonds* in 1913]. In *The Passer-By* (1900), at a reunion dinner the hero Guy Challoner is persuaded to sing a ballad written by an unknown poet but set to music by Edward Purcell [son of Henry Purcell]. Although not revealed in the text the name of the song as composed by Edward Purcell is *Passing By*. The copyright for this song was only secured in 1944, so Ethel had no qualms about the use of the text.

Apart from monetising considerations Ethel's success can be measured by the sheer volume of her printed material that exists in libraries around the world even today. *The Way of an Eagle* underwent fifty-two editions between 1910 and 2010 and is held in 217 libraries worldwide.

Ethel's Perspective

There were I suppose two very different sides to my life. My personal one and my written public one. I call it written because it was only through my writing that I found that I was able to express myself. My written life had itself two sides, the creation of my stories and the business side of selling and making sure that never again will I be misled like I was by Pinker. I worked on the basis that all commercial proposals had to be challenged to make sure that I was maximising all financial opportunities, but certainly not at the expense of my faithful readers. My agent's responsibility was to sell my titles but only with agreements that I had personally approved. It was, I felt, important to establish my authority with Watt very early on and the first thing that I did was to reduce his normal commission. He knew my potential and if he had not agreed to my terms that I could have sought alternative arrangements. After this initial negotiation he no doubt respected me commercially and we became very close friends. Watt never tried to influence what I wrote and at one stage he was selling my stories before they had even been written. I was very fortunate in having him as my agent and we both made a lot of money as a result of this close collaboration. But deep down I knew that I had to keep writing as well as keep the pressure on Watt.

Writing is necessarily a very solitary existence but I broke from my writing discipline to deal with business issues, which was really very enjoyable and a nice change from being by myself. With business I was dealing with real issues and real outcomes. What a contrast to my fiction! Because of Watt's efforts I was dealing with multiple titles in multiple media here in the UK, the United States, Canada and across Europe.

As a result of my copyright experience, I am very aware of the issues and opportunities that are contingent upon use and ownership. If a copyright demonstrably existed then I of course honoured that ownership but if it did not then I was free to use the material wherever I wanted without any acknowledgement. I have used material slightly altered sometimes to avoid the cost of its use. Edward Purcell for example did not register a copyright for his ballad *Passer By* so, I had no compunction about using the material.

5. A Cloistered, Conflicted and Wealthy Family

'I suppose none of us are ourselves to strangers'[1]

The literary world castigated and lampooned her, but her reading public knew nothing about her. Very few of her letters survive, we simply do not know if in fact she corresponded that much. An examination of her fictional oeuvre does reveal signs of her personality and her conflicts and can be interpreted as revealing relationships with her family and friends. Not a single photograph was ever released by her long-term agent Watt or sourced by the media despite their assiduous efforts to do so. Who was she? Today we would certainly describe Ethel as a recluse. To those that knew her Ethel was a quiet, self-effacing spinster until her marriage late in life, and a very different character to her large, flamboyant and domineering elder sister Ella and her weak brother Reginald. This is not a forum for a nature versus nurture discourse, but it is the nurture that we can examine since this perhaps exacerbated a reticent personality and provided creative fodder.

Ethel was the youngest of Vincent and Irene Dell's three children. The eldest Irene Elizabeth (Ella) was a physically large person with a personality to match and the only son, Reginald Vincent (Reggie), a weak man who never achieved much even with Ethel's financial assistance. Vincent had been a clerk with The Old Equitable Insurance Society since the age of seventeen and was following in the footsteps of his father John Caldicote Dell who had held the senior post of Principle Clerk [today's equivalent of Chief Financial Officer) until his death at the early age of forty-nine. Catholic Vincent joined the firm the year his father died, and stayed in the family home until his marriage to the Anglican Irene Parrot. The significance here is that paternal grandmother Mary Davis was a Catholic and some of her children had been brought up in that faith. John Caldicote Dell's sister Alphonsine Mary Joseph became a Catholic nun in the closed Redemptorist order. His niece, the daughter of his sister Mary Louisa, also became a Catholic nun, Dame Joan McLaughlin OSB of Stanbrook Abbey. Ethel had therefore aunts on her father's side and a cousin who were Catholic and Irene, her mother, who came from a strong Anglican background. Ethel's religious background was thus paternal side Catholic and maternal side Anglican.

On Ethel's paternal grandfather John Caldicote's death, her grandmother Mary, John's wife, stayed in the family home in Clapham. With the knowledge that her son Vincent was only nineteen years old and with their employment of three domestic servants it is evident that The Old Equitable Insurance Society had provided well for their late Chief Clerk. Vincent was too young to have been able to provide such financial cover.

Following Vincent's marriage to Irene Parrot in 1878 at the Anglican St. Nicholas, Church, in Potterspury, near the Parrot family home in Stony Stratford, he and his new wife set up home at Ferndale, Polworth Road Streatham near Vincent's mother, and here, like his mother he employed three servants. Today the nomenclature of Clerk would certainly be seen as a pejorative title, the lowest level of bureaucracy in a commercial organisation, someone without authority or scope for managerial flair. The reality at that time was very different. In 1869 when Vincent joined the firm there were only five select staff and twelve directors. The role of Clerk was a substantial one and by the time of his resignation due to his gout in 1901 he was earning the equivalent today of £300,000 per annum. On his resignation he was awarded an annual honorarium of £200,000. This was clearly an upper middle class and wealthy establishment in which Ethel was brought up.

Having been in authority at The Old Equitable, vile tempered Vincent continued to exercise very Victorian male values, in extremis, for the remaining twelve years of his life. He needed to be in control. Neither Ethel not her elder sister Ella were allowed to go to dances and parties, nor were they allowed to buy their own clothes. Until he died, he chose and bought everything for them. Ella, who had for a time been the governess/tutor to the Bowra brothers (Sir Maurice and Edward), was in 1909 invited to continue to be their governess in China to prepare them for secondary education in the UK. Vincent refused to give permission for his eldest daughter, then aged thirty, to leave the household and undertake this exciting opportunity. Unlike Ethel, Ella was adventurous and would not have a similar adventure until she travelled out to Tanganyika in 1948 to visit Penelope and her family. Having arrived in Africa by ship she then chartered her own single-engine aircraft to complete the journey. In June 1912 Vincent was a party to Ethel's contract with her new literary agent Watt, and Ethel was thirty-one years old. One can surmise that he insisted on being a signatory. Vi Johnston, a friend of the sisters, a frequent house guest and a close friend to Ella up until the time that Ella died, recalled that Ella had a ghastly life with that 'unspeakable father'.[2] We must assume that Ethel had the same experience. In the light of some of Ethel's subject matter it is now possible to assume that what Ethel had experienced might well have been some form of abuse. From where else could the creative stimulus of sexual violence come from? Vi also wrote: 'she had a sad and difficult time with her father before he died as heart trouble made him mentally affected'.[3] This was an impression given and Vincent does seem to have been a domineering parent who lost the affection of his youngest daughter. Vincent became terminally ill in Torquay and Ella and Ella's mother Irene went there to assist. Ethel reported to Watt that, 'We had the worst news from Torquay and my Mother has gone down there'.[4] This comment is coldly inserted at the end of a letter discussing American rights for her title *The Penalty* (1913). If Ella was there with her father, it was probably under instruction, and this is why she is not mentioned by Ethel. This is the first evidence of Ethel's focus and determined nature. She was writing, and this was more important than worrying about her father, towards whom she did not perhaps feel particularly warm, or even had perhaps an active dislike. In contrast, however, when her mother died in 1918 she wrote to Watt with black-bordered note paper noting that she and Ella had had a short break but 'now expect to be very busy with my novel, to make up for lost time'.[5] Can one see any parallels with Woolf here? She was sexually abused by her stepbrother which continued until her breakdown in 1904, and 'It is clear that the early incestuous activity [her stepbrother] had a disturbing effect on Virginia's sexuality'.[6]

Vincent Dell had purchased Elgin House in Knockholt, Kent in 1898 three years before his retirement, when Ella and Ethel were twenty and seventeen years old respectively. Although it is apparent that Vincent would have commuted to The Old Equitable by train, his daughters were now effectively marooned in the country, no longer being at school. Son Reggie, who had attended Dulwich College from September 1893 to July 1896, left the school whilst in the fifth form aged seventeen. Despite specialising in three sciences and mathematics he did not achieve much, and had left the school early. The sisters were apparently educated at The Shrubbery, Streatham College for Girls from when the school started in 1894; the school was demolished in 1933 and all Streatham College for Girls records were regrettably destroyed in the London Blitz during the Second World War, so clearly the school ceased functioning some time before. This circumstantial conclusion on their education is based on the location of the school a few minutes away from the Dell family home in Streatham. There is no record of what education the sisters received prior to this, and despite Ella's musical talents there is no evidence that she had any formal musical training in London, at any time.

Ethel's first story, *The Repentant Rogue* (1898), was published in Britain in the *Royal Magazine* in December 1899 when she was just eighteen years old. It can be assumed therefore that she had been writing for some time before that and corresponding with publications on her own initiative. This early demonstration of both her creativity and commercial acumen is confirmed by her correspondence to her first literary agent James B. Pinker in December 1901 that she had sent three stories to F.V. White & Co. who wanted to publish them but 'the terms were not sufficiently tempting'.[7] In March 1900, the same story appeared, heavily adapted for the American market in the publication *Everybody's Magazine*. Ethel was in good company as Rudyard Kipling published his story *A Burgher of the Free State* in the same magazine in October of that year. Ethel did not, however, share the honour accorded to Kipling of a cover reference at that time. Within twelve years Ethel was sharing the same literary agent as Kipling and Rafael Sabatini, whose work also appeared in *Everybody's* that year.

The Repentant Rogue and *In Her Majesty's Service* were the only story titles that Ethel sold without the help of an agent, but she had primed the commercial pump and gained the interest of one. In 1901 aged just twenty after publishing her first magazine short story in 1899, Ethel signed with the literary agent James B. Pinker (1863–1922), whose clients had included Henry James, Joseph Conrad, Arnold Bennett and, briefly, Oscar Wilde.

At least eighteen magazine stories were published before *The Way of an Eagle* and at least three of these early publications appeared in the United States. Her ground-breaking work *The Way of an Eagle* was first published in the United States in 1910, and fifteen more stories were published in magazines in Britain and one in the United States up until November 1911, when *The Way of an Eagle* was first serialised in *The Red Magazine* in the UK. There would have been increasing income from this writing, but it is probable that the household income at Elgin House was largely still very dependent on Vincent's retirement honorarium. That is until the 1912 runaway success of *The Way of an Eagle* when published in book form in Britain by T. Fisher Unwin. It had previously been published by both A.L. Burt and Putnam Knickerbocker Press in the United States in 1910 and 1911 respectively. Apart from Ella's tutoring of the Bowra brothers and their brother Reggie working for Waldron Smithers in the London Stock Exchange, Smithers was a neighbour at Knockholt, Reggie having apparently been fired from his first job, there was no outside income other than Ethel's. The latter, however, increased dramatically from this time.

On Ethel's father Vincent's death in 1913 aged sixty-one, his estate, valued at £969,000 (current values), was divided between his wife Irene and his brother William. William, like his nephew Reggie, seems to have had a chequered career, having been a tea taster and latterly an employee of a manufacturer of surgical instruments. By the time of the 1911 census he was 'retired' aged forty-eight. This legacy would also have helped his eldest sister Mary Elizabeth with whom William was living. William's apparent failures seem to have continued to his death in 1938 where his estate of £684,000 in today's values was absorbed by the inspector of taxes and his solicitor. It is hard to conceive that in such a large family this bachelor would have died intestate and it is likely that he was seriously indebted for unpaid tax.

In contrast to the Caldicotes and the Dells, Ethel's mother's family, the Parrots, seem to have been a stable middle-class family of solicitors who lived and operated out of Stony Stratford in Buckinghamshire. Her father and two uncles were all solicitors, and her father functioned also as the clerk to the county court. A bachelor uncle was a wealthy brewer, and her maternal grandfather was the Stony Stratford wine merchant, a role greater in local hierarchical significance than the same role today. Additionally, within the

Parrot family there was a clerk to the burial board, a magistrates clerk, a coroner and a member of the board of guardians of Potterspury where Ethel's father and great aunt were married in the same church. Today there are still Parrot solicitors in the area. John Caldicoate Dell, Ethel's grandfather, was born in Aylesbury, and this area of Buckinghamshire proliferates with Dells. The first formal connections between the Parrots and the Dells were the marriages of Ethel's aunt Maria Sarah Dell to her uncle Joseph Parrot, and her uncle Thomas Dell to Louisa Sarah Parrot. The two families were clearly very closely connected even before Ethel's father married Irene Parrot.

Ethel grew up in a financially secure environment with never less than three domestic servants influenced by a dominant and controlling father, a less than successful brother and a dominant sister, and an uncle who died leaving extreme tax liabilities. Her maternal family, the Parrots, were solid upright citizens in visible public positions without any discernible failings. Her mother was a strong Anglican but at least two aunts, an uncle and a cousin were staunch Catholics. The latter being Dame Joan McLaughlin OSB, the mother superior of Stanbrook Abbey (1893–1977).

As Ella and Ethel's mother's health started to fail, it became necessary to provide in-home nursing care and through the family doctor, Dr. Vidler, a connection was made with a Mrs. Talbot (Nursie). Nursie was a fiery red-headed woman with a similar featured daughter who, having been abandoned by her husband, came to live in Ashford. Through Dr. Vidler she was providing help with the doctor's bed-ridden patients and thus the connection was made with the Dells in about 1915. Ella, the large domineering woman, took it upon herself to see if she could secure the assistance of this Mrs. Talbot. The approach was firmly refused as it would have meant putting her daughter Peggy into care. Ethel then made the approach herself and was accepted, and mother and daughter moved into the Dell household.

Reggie was called up for service in the Royal Ordinance Corps, ending the war with the rank of captain, so not unusually between 1914 and 1918, there were no male family members in the household, and until Irene's death the household comprised the two Dell sisters, their mother, Nursie, Peggy Talbot and the household staff. The next year, 1919, Penelope the adoptee 'Dell' joins the household. Ella, a spinster, the adopter, is forty years old and Ethel thirty-eight years old.

Ethel's Perspective

It is simplistic to look at my background and think wealthy and privileged. Yes, I was both of those but this could be considered just a veneer on a what was in reality a very turbulent and dysfunctional family environment. My father Vincent had held a position of seniority in the City but had retired early due to his gout, but this retirement caused little financial hardship as he had been awarded a significant annual honorarium. The family on my father's side were strong Roman Catholics and on my mother Irene's staunch Anglicans. There was religious tension at home until my parents died. I personally used the Catholic Bible but kept a copy of the Book of Common Prayer. My parents were married in an Anglican church and my father's religious inclinations effectively became subsumed into my mother Irene's Protestantism. Having held a very senior role in the City he was retired early as he was ill, and at home any religious inclinations that might have lain dormant disappeared. He was a bitter man with a terrible temper. Reggie my brother had proven to have a weak personality and all this caused Elizabeth and I to have a difficult childhood and young adolescence. We were not even allowed to choose our own clothes. My slight disfigurement was perhaps also a reason for his bitterness and unpleasantness.

My schooling at Streatham College for Girls came to an end when I was seventeen and my father had acquired our house in Kent. Elizabeth was tall, much taller than our father, and she took it upon herself to try and protect me from my father's abuse. I loved her dearly but our relationship came to an abrupt halt when I married in 1922.

It was at the end of my school days that I started to write stories, which were initially as an escape from our terrible home existence, but latterly I realised that my fantasies were an enjoyable way of life and I was writing every day. My first story, written while I was still at school, was published in 1898 in *Royal Magazine* when I was only seventeen. I had no agent so I just posted it off to the magazine and it was accepted. Looking back on the plot that I created some of the names are a little unpolished but the theme of a strong woman was very much as I would like to have been. Australia was very much in the news, especially with a focus on women's rights, and in addition all the pictures that appeared in the *Illustrated London News* helped me to create my story. This gave me such confidence that I continued writing and my second publication was the next year in *Ludgate Magazine*. The terrible and continuing Afghan Wars inspired this story published in 1899. I could not but be aware of the many famous paintings of the conflicts: Piper Findlater earning his VC at the battle of Dargai Heights, Lady Butler's painting of the last survivor after the sacking of Kabul. And then Dr. William Brydon and the wretched scene of the 66th Foot's last stand at Maiwand with the regiment's mascot the dog Bobby. Kipling, with whom I would come to share publications and eventually an agent, famously wrote his poem *The Young British Soldier* (1890) where he had written a poignant last verse:

> *When you're wounded and left on Afghanistan's plains,*
> *And the women come out to cut up what remains,*
> *Jest roll to your rifle and blow out your brains*
> *An' go to your Gawd like a soldier.*[8]

My story was about bravery, but also about the conflict between formal and moral duty and responsibility. I suppose that this story was a surprising one to be written by an eighteen year-old girl but I was deeply moved by all that I read. When does a moral responsibility weigh heavier than an order? I suppose all the time, but perhaps the constrains of military orderliness can prohibit it.

These were the last two stories that I sold by myself in the UK and America. My experience with dealing with American publications was not something that I enjoyed. Having accepted my story, the Americans proceeded to change grammar and spelling and deleted all references to aristocracy. I would have thought that the latter was something to which they would attach a value but perhaps the magazine *Everybody's* was aimed at an audience that would not see this as aspirational. After these two stories I was approached by my new agent James B. Pinker and I signed him up in 1901. It was then a roller coaster of magazine published stories. Very early on I questioned the commercial acumen of my agent as he both encouraged me to sell my copyrights and on one occasion tried to palm me off with unacceptable commercial terms. I did not change him until I was approached by Watt in June 1912. My father was a signatory to my contract with his firm. I was thirty-one years old and my father still tried to manage me.

My father died in 1913 and his estate was divided between my mother and his brother, who like his son had a chequered career, with his share being absorbed by the tax man. As my mother's health started to fail it became necessary to have an in-house nurse. Elizabeth was to some people a threatening person, being both large and domineering, and initially she failed to secure our eventual help. But I persuaded Nursie and her daughter to join us.

Reggie saw out the 1914–18 war in the Royal Ordinance Corps although we saw him on leave from time to time. It was during this time that we had the most extraordinary situation where my sister Elizabeth, a spinster aged forty, suddenly decided to adopt a baby girl who was born in 1918. I of course knew why this adoption took place and why a financial settlement to the mother was made, but I could say nothing. However, I did make a side comment in my *Bars of Iron* (1919) that, 'she [Olive] more closely resembled her father than any of the others ...' So, I made a record of the truth. Poppy's original name on her birth certificate was of course Olive.

What I was now realising was that my own family, being both somewhat dysfunctional, and 'ordinary and established', dependant on which side I considered, was providing me with a vast amount of creative stimulation outside of world dramas as reported in the Press.

6. The Siblings' Stimuli

' ...it's downright disgusting the way we all sponge on you'.[1]

Ethel's life before her marriage aged forty-one revolved within a cloistered dysfunctional vortex and there can thus be no doubt of the influence of her family on her creative oeuvre, both as a foil for the intra-family issues and as a stimulus for her writing. This is evident throughout her works. Her sister Elizabeth was large, flamboyant, musical, an organiser and well read with no financial means of support except those provided by her sister. Standing over six foot, her elder sister by three and a half years was known as either Ella or Elizabeth. Ella was also very numerate and careful with money. She was deeply devoted to Ethel and from a very early age felt the necessity to be her protector.

Ella appears to have had no male friends except Cyril Ebsworth, the brother of Violet Ebsworth, Ethel's secretary, with whom she corresponded until his death. Apparently, there was also one marriage proposal from a retired brigadier whom she turned down as reported by Penelope in *Nettie and Sissie*. She was very musical with a fine contralto voice and a gifted piano player. Ethel was not musical, and the references to three Pièces Pour Piano Aubade À La Fiancée, Piano Op. 141 by Georges Bernard, an esoteric piece of music referenced in *The Rocks of Valpré* (1914), were doubtless gleaned from her sister. As was the reference in *Greatheart* (1918) to 'simple Avue' (Francois Thomé (1850–1909) Simple Avue Op.25). This very romantic and lyrical piece of music was well suited for the occasion in the narrative. In *The Bars of Iron* (1915) the hero Piers plays the soldier's chorus out of Faust, a very irritating piece when played on a piano, especially for someone who is, as they are in the narrative, trying to write a sermon. It is not too difficult to imagine Ethel being irritated by Ella on the piano when she was herself trying to write. Ethel uses the romantic song *My Little Grey Home in the West* (1911) in *Bars of Iron* and also the romantic Handel's *Largo* played on the organ in *Bars of Iron*.

Both sisters lived at home with their parents until their mother Irene died in 1918. Irene died and the next year Ella, as a single woman with no male connections, adopted a child, Penelope. The sisters continued to live together until Ethel's marriage in 1922 just four years after their mother's death and three years after the purchase of a new house (The Greenwood). There is no evidence that Ella provided Ethel any literary, secretarial or commercial assistance at any time, as all correspondence and manuscripts were handwritten by Ethel, and in later years Penelope reported to me that very few of Ethel's books ever graced Ella's bookshelves, as they were not sufficiently toney. One can even question whether Ella even read her sister's works. Maurice Bowra wrote: 'At this time we got a letter from Miss Dell (Ella) saying that her sister Ethel had written a book called *The Way of an Eagle*, which had been refused by seven publishers but had at last been taken by Fisher Unwin – would we read it? We did and, amid some mockery of its excesses, greatly enjoyed it. It was a triumphant best-seller ...'[2] Ella was clearly out of touch with the content of the book and the intended readership by sending the work to two teenage boys. But she was well read herself and as a tutor to the Bowra brothers.

Ella had little income or resources other than those supplied by Ethel and today she would have no doubt seemed a little nouveau riche. She spent the winters of 1925, 1926 and 1927 at the Riviera Palace Hotel in Menton, France. At the time this was a very high-end establishment which had seen eminent guests including the Russian imperial family, the shah of Persia, the king of Belgium, Diaghilev, Nijinsky and Stravinsky. At the hotel Ella participated in all the social functions with a particular favourite being the fancy dress parties. Penelope's memories of these can be seen in the illustration that she drew of Ella dressed as a gypsy. This nouveau rich demeanour was offset by her decision as a forty year-old spinster, without any male in tow, to take on the responsibility of a baby girl, Penelope, in 1919. Expensive cars and houses were purchased and Durrant's Hotel in Mayfair was a frequent base for Ella's shopping expeditions. From the moment of Ethel's marriage to Lt. Colonel Savage in 1922 there was little interaction between the women ever again. This strained relationship is highlighted in *The Lamp in the Desert* (1919) in which Ethel describes a woman not fit to be a mother. The hero of the novel, Monck states, regarding the heroine Stella's friendship with the latter woman's daughter ' …so long as you don't adopt her'.[3] This was published the year after Penelope's birth and the same year as she came to live with the Dells. This would seem to be a very direct message to her sister delivered in a very indirect way. Being shy she could not tell her sister what she felt. Conversely Ella from her reputation would always have told Ethel exactly what she thought and felt.

Ethel provided Ella with a capital sum which allowed her to buy her own first house. It is believed that her brother Reggie also received the same amount but there seemed to be an ongoing funding arrangement for Ethel's brother or whenever Reggie felt short of funds. In *The Rocks of Valpré* we can see this reflected in a continuing theme of indebtedness with Chris asking for Jack's help, and of course Jack comes to the rescue. Families are an easy touch but as Ethel explains in *The Rocks of Valpré* that to the contrary friends have scruples about asking each other for money. In this case Ethel has been creative with the English language and turned scruples a noun into the somewhat delightfully archaic verb to scruple. 'It has always been a puzzle to me' he said, 'why money which is the most ordinary thing in life – is the one thing that friends scruple to accept from each other'.[4]

In *The Passer-By* (1925) Ethel has the hero Guy in action in the trenches and he had 'picnicked' in a shell hole. Referencing his call-up at the start of the First World War Bowra wrote, 'but I did not think that it would be at all pleasant, and even when Miss Dell wrote. "I expect that you are longing to get at the Germans," I found it hard to answer. A little later, when Rupert Brooke's famous war-sonnets were published and acclaimed as proof of a new heroic spirit in England, I felt nothing of the kind'.[5] Ella spent time with the Bowra boys but understood so little about them. Although a VAD nurse Ella demonstrated lack of emotional intelligence in her comment and Ethel seemed naïve in her removal from reality, and Ethel would initially seem to have been influenced by this naiveté. However, by the early 1930s Ethel was writing emotionally about the carnage of the First World War.

> And dead men hurled about in fragments – and others choking
> in their own blood – sound ones driven to frenzy with the horror
> of it and turned into brute beasts such as God never created! ...
> women waiting to bind up the wounded and soother the maniacs
> and comfort the dying, with shells bursting and spreading more
> and more destruction all the time – blowing them to pieces
> along with the men they tried to save.[6]

There is such a dichotomy between the narrational emotion and knowledge displayed in *The Passer-By* and *The Losers*, as above, that it can be assumed that the former was a very early story published some significant time after Ethel had finished the manuscript.

Ethel's Perspective

While my parents were alive my sister was my protector. She was a dominant personality, sensible and very careful with money. She was very talented musically but largely self-taught, and as a result of stimuli at the Streatham College for Girls was very well read. But she never developed any male relationships except one that came as a result of my employment and deep friendship with Violet Ebsworth, who handled all my non-business correspondence. Violet's brother Cyril and Elizabeth maintained a weekly correspondent relationship. Like myself, Elizabeth seemed somewhat ambivalent to male sexuality and enjoyed the company of women.

Elizabeth's musical abilities provided me with much creative stimulus and musical knowledge that I would not have had access to without her. She, however, practised and played at all opportunities and at times it was difficult to concentrate on my writing. A case in point is the soldier's chorus from Faust played on the piano, especially if played slowly. It can grate and ruin concentration.

Elizabeth had the best intentions but was not at all worldly and provided me no help at all at any time as my literary career developed. At one stage she was employed to tutor the Bowra brothers and gave them a copy of my *The Way of an Eagle* to read. She clearly had not read my work but the teenage boys of course thoroughly enjoyed it.

After our mother died Elizabeth had no source of income so I provided for her financially. She enjoyed her new riches, dressed extravagantly and stayed in the best hotels in London and the south of France. We were living together in Kent and when travelling she was staying in hotels frequented by Stravinsky and the shah of Persia. She was I think what could be called 'nouveau riche'. Then the bombshell. The year after our mother died she takes on the care of and eventually adopts a little girl, the daughter of a household help. She put about the thought that the mother of the child worked in the air ministry and that the father was a South African airman. This new parental relationship was consummated with the transaction of British American Tobacco shares. Why? Clearly there was a family connection or why else would a forty year-old spinster risk social approbation by such an act? The conclusion must be that Reggie my brother had created the issue. Elizabeth was kind to take on the child but it was my money that solved the problem.

I was financially supporting both my sister and brother. Elizabeth totally and Reggie when he ever came asking for help which was, regrettably, very frequent. I was the bread winner for the Dell family and the pressure was intense. I of course had the trappings of wealth but no one really understood the pressures that this created as my resources were under threat all the time. Eventually to ease the pressure I made a financial settlement on both of them and that was the end of the demands.

Although Elizabeth worked as a VAD nurse towards the end of the war I do not really think that she fully comprehended the enormity of the issues in play, and certainly did not communicate any concerns to me. She was seeing wounded men and I was cloistered at home writing and all I understood was the glamour of bravery but not the reality of suffering. She was my window into the real world, but we did not talk about such things at that time.

7. Relationships and Wealth

'inspiration won't burn in a cold place'.[1]
'marriage is like the tide. It cuts you off when you aren't looking,
and you can't get back'.[2]
'marriage has such a nasty way of taking the gilt off the gingerbread, and I must
admit I always liked the gilt the best'.[3]

Ethel was a shy, reclusive and gentle spinster (shyness as the antonym of self-assurance), a woman who surrounded herself with women friends without any apparent male relationship(s) until her marriage aged forty-one, a relationship seemingly engineered by her new husband's sister. Even in death Ethel was a loner. It was not her husband nor her sister nor even a friend who cared for her last wishes, but Watt, her literary agent. He kept her original will and inherited her literary estate.[4]

Ethel's financial provision for Ella, Reggie and of course the flights of fancy of her husband Gerald with his model trains and boats was a cause of concern, as she seems to outline in relation to the egoism she faced. In *Storm Drift* Ethel wrote: 'and it was only by a queer perversion of egoism that he could view himself in any other light …Whatever he did, by some unwritten law, he was compelled to fall into line with the needs and circumstances of other people. To strike out for himself was for some reason forbidden. His was the task to place himself at the disposal of all the rest, to be ignored or made use of according to necessity. While everyone else fought and grabbed for what they wanted, he could retain nothing for himself, but must for ever hand on such prizes as came his way'.[5] This is an unequivocal complaint about her family and their selfishness.

Although outwardly living a life of dull gentility, Ethel was under financial pressure from her brother and sister, suffered religious polarity within her family with her father being a Catholic and her mother a fervent Protestant, was perhaps of ambivalent sexuality, suffered a manipulative sister in-law, had a self-image issue and later had to cope with her own and her sister's illnesses and the related knowledge of drug use, which she demonstrated in *Electric Torch*.

Writing a letter to an intimate friend is a personal demonstration of the importance of that relationship. None of Ethel's letters of this nature have been located but what is apparent is that she used her printed works to publicly announce those relationships that she thought important through the dedications to her works. It also conversely perhaps does the opposite and flags those relationships that were less comparatively important.

The success of *The Way of an Eagle* would have brought a sudden inflow of wealth into the Dell household, but there is no evidence that anything changed in the way of life in the family home at Chattern House, Ashford, Kent. Vincent's retirement honorarium would seem to have enabled the family to move from Streatham into Elgin House, Knockholt where the family lived for nine years. After Vincent's death in 1913 and his assets were divided between his wife Irene and his brother William there probably were not yet the accumulated assets from writing to enable Ethel to manage any significant lifestyle changes. When Irene died in 1918 she left her whole estate valued at £891,000 in today's values to Reggie Dell.[6] Yet again Ethel had no capital from her family but in the next year she had acquired her first house, The Greenwood in Guildford. She moved into this her first and very substantial property with Ella, and the next five years were of momentous emotional and perhaps creative significance.

The whole pattern of Ethel's life seems to have changed at this point, with, initially, a series of deep and long-lasting female friendships all of which can be said to have influenced her creativity. One certainly gets the impression of female friendships suddenly appearing with her success. Importantly there is no evidence of any male friendships except that engineered by Norah Savage for her brother Gerald, whom Ethel eventually married. Violet Ebsworth was employed as Ethel's secretary to deal with all non-business correspondence and by 1929 was living in the same house as Ethel and Gerald. Violet with her 'growly voice' had apparently given up her employment in London and worked full time for Ethel.[7] In October 1929 Penelope wrote to Ella that 'I will write to Auntie Ethel and Auntie Violet because they are in the same house'.[8] Although Violet worked with Ethel she acquired a property in London, but Ethel's book dedications in both *Tetherstones* (1922) and *Sown Among Thorns* (1938) would seem to indicate a very close and long-lasting relationship.

Electoral records indicate that Violet had rooms at various addresses in London until 1934 when she acquired a flat in Abercorn Place London NW8 probably funded by the generous Ethel. In 1938 Penelope refers to this property in a letter to Ella. Ethel clearly enjoyed her company, and a photograph has Violet sharing a meal in Ella's first house of her own, 'Blackmoor' in the New Forest. Having found security through her work with Ethel she died in April 1939, leaving an estate of £210,000 in today's values to her brother Cyril (Ella's friend).[9] Violet's cousin writing in 1977 stated that Violet had retired to Felixstowe, and 'built herself a bungalow – naturally – Violet's love of Miss Dell remained'.[10] It is an interesting surmise that Ella's apparently only male friend was perhaps the only non-family recipient of Ethel's money, albeit indirectly.

Once Ethel became independent of her parents she came under the influence and demands of her siblings, female friends and what objectively appears to have been a manipulator, or in contemporary parlance a 'gold digger', posing as a friend. Nora Savage, whose family had strong military connections, appears on the scene sometime before 1919. Nora's father was a colonel in the Corps of

Engineers and she had been brought up in army barracks. Ethel made a personal dedication of *Greatheart* to her: 'With love to Nora from Auntie. Xmas 1919'.[11] The dedication is in Ethel's hand and there was a Nora on the scene, but the honorific of auntie seems strange given their similarity in age, there being only four years separating them. Can one surmise that Ethel was hiding the reality of their relationship? Nora and her brother Gerald Savage had been living in Chester, however, in the 1911 census Nora does not appear. Perhaps she was one of the those influenced to boycott the census as promoted by the Women's Freedom League ... no vote – no census. If this was the case one can surmise that she was a strong-willed woman with decidedly strong opinions and a personality to match. By 1923 Nora and her parents had moved to Guildford, Ethel having lived there from 1919. Gerald was by the end of the 1914–1918 war a brevetted lt. colonel in the Royal Army Service Corps (whilst commanding a heavy repair shop) who had been awarded a DSO, but he only held the substantive rank of a major. There can be little doubt that Nora's introduction of her 'gallant' brother to Ethel had only one purpose. Ethel was forty-one and Gerald thirty-eight, and both were unmarried and Ethel exuded a wealthy potential. Gerald on the other hand was unlikely to receive any substantial inheritance as he had two older brothers, and, as it turned out, had received only a one-sixth share of his father's assets excluding the family 4.5 acre property at Blair's Hill in County Cork, Ireland which was left to his elder brother. The O'Keeffe clan was and is dominant in County Cork. Ethel uses the O'Keeffe family motto, misspelt, in the frontispiece to *The Altar of Honour* (Forti et fidele nil [nihil] difficule) for no apparent reason except perhaps that her sister-in-law Nora had indicated that her husband was connected to the O'Keeffe clan to give him added status, as an added lever for her game plan. He was not of course in anyway connected. Gerald's next eldest brother received a stipend for life because of his war wounds. The colonel, as he liked to be called, with only a major's pension was without doubt in need of financial assistance, and a wife with money would fit the bill. We have now a forceful woman almost certainly promoting her 'gallant' but impoverished brother. The photograph of Nora, Gerald and Ethel (page 250) is very revealing in that Nora and Ethel are arm-in-arm but standing distant from Gerald.

Over a period of five years from 1918 Ethel was exposed to a concentration of divergent and conflicting emotional events. In 1918 her mother Irene died, and that same year Gladys Olive aged three and a half months is collected by Ella reportedly from the John Lewis department store in Oxford Street, London, and named Poppy. Poppy became Penelope. Penelope's mother was Nellie Gladys Hamblin (née Lailey), and her father was shown as Charles Hamblin (Nellie's father) on the birth certificate. Nellie had, not unusually for this time, taken her own father's name as the name for the father of the child, disguising it with the use of his middle name. Nellie signed an agreement with Ella dated 7 March 1919 when Poppy was three and a half months old.[12] The consideration for the transaction was about £71,000 in today's values worth of British American Tobacco preference shares to be held in trust for Penelope. Ella had no private income except what Ethel supplied, one assumes in the form of an allowance at this stage. For Ethel to be suddenly faced with a small child clearly funded by her own money in her own home must have been emotionally challenging. The photograph on page 249 of Ethel and Ella in together is very revealing. One of the sisters proudly shows off a baby, the other has a dog.

An objective observer of Penelope's arrival in the Dell household must question why, at very short notice, a spinster with no recorded close male attachments at any time, chooses to take on a baby, except perhaps that Ella was 39 years old at the time and saw a last opportunity for a child. How did she suddenly locate the child? What was the motive for this momentous decision that doubtless caused malicious gossip with a spinster taking on a baby? In *Bars of Iron*, in referring to the child called Olive (Penelope was born Gladys Olive) Ethel states 'she more closely resembled her father than other members of her family'.[13] Penelope was born in 1918, and there have always been doubts about the identity of her father. But in *The Knave of Diamonds* Ethel states, 'I don't believe one person in a million cares a rap about what his parents were'.[14] Circumstantial evidence suggests that this comment hid a knowledge and was not just a comment 'en passant'. Was Ethel letting it be known that she knew the truth and all was not coincidental?

In none of the correspondence between Penelope and Ella was there any indication of Ella's maternal instinct, and it could have been seen to have been quite the opposite. Penelope wrote to Ella in 1963 stating that she was not being treated as a daughter. It is very hard to imagine tall, flamboyant, not very maternal Ella canvassing wayward mother homes looking for a baby. Ella must have realised that for a mature spinster in 1918 to have a baby, however acquired, she would be open to severe approbation. Ethel's maternal instincts also seemed somewhat incongruous when she gave the just three year-old Penelope a copy of *Hymns Ancient and Modern* inscribed 'Poppy Dell with best love from Auntie Ethel Christmas 1922'. There is of course the possibility that this gift and inscription was just a ritualistic formality, or even a Machiavellian demonstration of a rejection.

It is a small logical stretch to conclude that Penelope's father was known to the sisters and the decision to take on Penelope was perhaps to avoid a scandal. How many men were known to the sisters or Ella for whom they would make such a huge commitment? Only one close male appears and that is Reggie who, despite receiving his mother's inheritance, was, it is understood, continuously funded by Ethel. Reggie, however, was demobbed at the end of the First World War and a connection with Nellie would have been before the armistice in November 1918, but it is not known if he was at home on leave at that time. The reason for exploring this side to Ethel's life is that there must have been intrigue of some sort. Ella writing in 1963 stated that she thought that Nellie was a clerk in the air ministry and that Penelope's father was a South African airman, a casual acquaintance. Military records for 1918 record no South African airmen in the UK at this time. This was possibly a suitably romantic cover. Nellie is now known to have been in domestic service living in the Paddington area of London, and immediately after the war Reggie also lived in North London. Nora's entry into Ethel's life at the point of Penelope's appearance can only be seen as emotionally fortuitous for Nora and her brother Gerald, as Ella was now settling down with a family, and Ethel had none.

Into this emotional mix we now add Alice Cassan, a local spinster who had made contact with Ethel apparently through fan mail as reported by Penelope and became a close friend. Alice, a trained nurse who had worked at the London Hospital, was born in 1876 and was therefore five years older than Ethel was reported by Penelope as 'The Cassan'. Alice Cassan moved with her mother to Farnham in Surrey, a move from London, in 1919 and stayed in the same house until her marriage to William Warren in spring 1937 aged sixty-one. Alice's mother had died in 1932. Alice died, however, the same year as her marriage, leaving her estate of £1.2M in today's values to her brother and sister. Her brother (Reverend Arthur William Marshall Cassan, Army Chaplains Department, attd. 1st Bn Gloucester Regt. MC) about whom she must have talked to Ethel was the antithesis of her own brother Reggie. Before being called up for the First World War Reggie was employed in the London Stock Exchange as a jobbing clerk. It seems apposite that in *The Sea Urchin and the Prince* (1907) there is a reference to a 'stock Exchange cad'.[15] This was not accolading for her brother's employment. William Cassan's citation for bravery read as follows:

For conspicuous gallantry and devotion to duty during the operations south of Maissemy on September 15th and 16th 1918. This chaplain went forward on both occasions with the advancing troops and worked throughout tending the wounded and burying the dead although exposed to heavy shell and machine-gun fire. His conduct throughout these operations, as also on previous occasions, has been of the highest value and encouragement to the troops.[16]

All of this was a huge resource for Ethel's creativity, as demonstrated in the dedication and quotation at the start of *The Juice of the Pomegranate* (1938), which one can assume to have been concerning 'The Cassan', as no other death related or connected to Ethel around this time has been located. Alice and Ethel had a strong emotional attachment, and Ethel lost her good friend when they both married and the loss was compounded by Alice's death in 1938 just a year before her own death.

Ethel became engaged to Gerald Savage in December 1921, the Press got wind of it in March 1922, and they were married on 21 August that year. Ella and Gerald's father, a real colonel in the Royal Engineers, were witnesses. For the secret wedding by special licence at the Holy Trinity Church in Guildford there were only twelve family and guests attending. There is a significance here in that this church was not in the parish in which she lived, hence the special licence. Her parish church was St. Mary's Shalford where Ella worshipped. The house that the sisters had shared, The Greenwood in Guildford, acquired with Ethel's earnings, was sold and Ella acquired a property on her own in the New Forest. There must have been some financial settlement between the sisters for this to have occurred. In both her titles *The Unknown Quantity* (1923) and *The Real Thing* (1925) Ethel refers to a deed of settlement. The latter is not a commonplace legal activity and it can be surmised that this narrative reference was a creative cue as a result of settlements on Ella and Reggie. Ethel's indebtedness to Nora (h) is evident in the dedication in *The Unknown Quantity*. 'I dedicate this book to NORAH in most loving remembrance of all that she has given me'. She had provided her with a man, Gerald. Ella saw that she had a responsibility for Ethel, and her marriage to Gerald despite the financial settlement would have been a severe blow to both her relationship and her way of life. The financial tap was turned-off. In Ella's papers I discovered a photograph, which had been carefully torn in half with the Ethel part thrown away.

Edith de Wolf was another curious character in the mix: A spinster, she probably met Ella and Ethel sometime before 1910 when Edith's mother Alice who had been living in Cumberland died. Penelope reports that Ella and Ethel met her in the Lake District. Edith never married and from photographs does not seem to have been physically very attractive. She was certainly a long-term part of Ella's and Ethel's circle of women friends as she visited Penelope in hospital during 1932, and Penelope wrote to Ella that, 'Auntie Edie visits every morning'.[17] She is recorded as travelling on the SS *Franconia* first class in 1914 from Boston, presumably having been visiting her Canadian family. With a Canadian-born ship broker father, Edith probably introduced some glamour into the milieu.

Mary Bastard, another of Ethel's very close friends, was also subject to a book dedication in *The Obstacle Race* (1921). 'I Dedicate this book To My Dear "Half-sister" MARY With My Love'. This dedication with Mary in upper case was published a year before Ethel's marriage and when she had started to come under Nora (h) Savage's influence, and seems to indicate a very deep relationship that must have hurt Ella tremendously. Was Mary, born in 1876, and thus being five years older than Ethel, emotionally connected and therefore a fictitious elder half-sister? There is no evidence, however, of any familial or legal connection. Mary Bastard lived in Sussex with her mother Johanna until she died sometime after the 1911 census. Mary continued to live there in her family home until she travelled to East Africa first class on the Deutsche Ost Afrika Linie ship *Tanganyika* in October 1934. Ethel had lost another friend.

Throughout what appears to have been a very turbulent time Penelope was clearly well cared for by those other than Ella her 'auntie'. Whilst in hospital recovering from appendicitis she had frequent visitors and gifts: She was visited by Uncle Reggie who gave 'swank' note paper and three leather-bound books. He sometimes came at night and brought grapes, flowers and books. Ethel sent her four books (*The Girls of St. Olaves, A Handful of Rebels, The Leader of the Lower School, The Golden Story Book for Girls*). These were sensible gifts for a young girl, unlike her brother who demonstrated his excesses. Penelope wrote to Ella: 'Auntie Edie [Edith deWolf] visits every morning. Uncle Gerald [Gerald Savage] visits sometimes in the afternoon'.[18]

Reggie himself had married in 1920 and his first child was stillborn the next year. His son Robin Dell, after Ethel's death, was 'constantly sponging on Ella' as Reggie had done continuously on Ethel.[19] Reggie also had a daughter who required special schooling and a son Jock who was mentally challenged and was institutionalised. Reggie's wife Patricia was seen as an abuser of her children, became an alcoholic and died aged forty-two, two years after Ethel. Her death certificate stated the cause of death as 'Pulmonary and Cerebral Emboli resulting from septic fracture dislocation of the ankle due to a fall in the house'. Reggie married again the same month that Patricia died. Reggie and Patricia were living in separate houses at the time of her death.

The newly married Savages moved to the Sundridge Park Hotel in Bromley, Kent, and to their first permanent house in Dorking the next year where they stayed for two years. The couple lived in a further three houses over the next fifteen years until Ethel's death. In total Ethel lived in eight different houses and locations over a twenty-seven-year period. She appears to have demonstrated restlessness and an inability to settle, maybe even to find happiness despite, or perhaps because of her substantial wealth. This, and with a desire to behave in a conventional heterosexual manner with a husband, but perhaps being asexual or even bisexual combined with her desire to explore adventure through third parties in her novels, yet being shy to a paranoid degree, 'makes the possibility of suggesting definitive Jungian traits or any personality traits an impossibility. Maybe it is sufficient to say that she was beset by both internal and external factors that created a degree of elasticity in any of the traits that she demonstrated'.[20] Madge Churchill reported that 'Miss Dell was a sweet gentle old lady always pleased to see one'. She clearly portrayed an 'old' image but she died aged only forty-nine years old. But then, 'Ethel was full of fun and such a happy person'.[21]

The Philipps sisters, Madge and their younger sibling Patsie became regular visitors to the Dell household after Ella and Reggie met Madge in on holiday in Switzerland just before the 1914/18 war. Madge Philipps invited herself and her sister Patsie to visit them at Chattern House in Ashford. Given that the siblings were on holiday it is likely that this occurred in late 1912 or 1913 as after the death of Vincent Dell they were able to escape his control. Also, this is perhaps the first real evidence of a flush of money from Ethel's writing.

The newfound wealth bought houses, servants and motor cars with chauffeurs. It is perhaps not untypical for newly acquired income to result in unsuitable purchases. This seems to apply to Ethel's first car, a Wolsley 30/98 which was a fast open tourer, and it is easy to imagine her discomfort in such a powerful and relatively uncomfortable vehicle without privacy. Over time she graduated to a Daimler called Martha and then to a pale grey Rolls Royce called Lady Jane Grey with the chauffeur similarly attired in pale grey.[22] Madge Philipps recalls visiting Ethel and going 'for stately drives every afternoon in the pale grey Rolls ...'[23] Ella meanwhile did not resort to a chauffeur but was taught to drive in her new Albert by Barwell, Ethel's chauffeur. This expensive four-seat tourer with a radiator grill not unlike a Rolls Royce has been termed the poor man's Rolls. Ella acquired two versions of this exclusive car all before Ethel's marriage to Gerald, and then the funding stopped. Ethel never drove but Ella was a prodigious driver and owned cars until her death.

Violet (Vi) Johnston the daughter of the barrister Sir Arthur Johnson and Lady Johnston was also a close friend to Ella. The Johnstons lived in aspirational Hampstead and Vi on her marriage in 1937 bought a house that was to become a school, a house that had belonged to Lord Roberts of Indian army fame. Perversely Ethel's apparent need for aspirational social affiliations is demonstrated in *Greatheart* by her reference to a hunt master wearing pink. This might be the perceived colour but it is socially incorrect, as the colour worn is referred to as red or scarlet. The relationship with the Johnstons was close enough for Auntie Violet to send Penelope a puzzle and for Lady Johnston to visit her when she was in hospital. Violet herself married very late in life and became Penelope's life-long mentor. This established upper social hierarchy was a much-coveted connection into higher places for the Dell sisters and a source of Indian romance for Ethel.

The dedications within Ethel's publications are very revealing:

~

· **Female Friends**

Sown among Thorns: '*I dedicate this book to my precious Violet in loving and grateful remembrance of all she has done for me*'. This was the last of Ethel's works written and published when she was dying of breast cancer and had undergone double mastectomies. It is understood that her husband Gerald was with her all the time at this point yet the work is dedicated (the second dedication) to Violet Ebsworth, her secretary and long-term companion.

Tetherstones: '*I dedicate this book to Violet, the dear friend who always stands by, as a token of my ever-loving gratitude for all she has done for me*'. The first dedication for Ebsworth.

Greatheart: '*I dedicate this book to A.G.C. friend of my heart, and to the memory of all the happy days we have spent together* '. A.G.C. would seem to be Ethel's close friend Alice Cassan.

The Juice of the Pomegranate: '*I dedicate this book to the loving memory of one who has passed beyond these earthly shadows whose precious friendship now shines out for me like a beacon from the land of our joyful resurrection*'. This title was published in 1938 the year that the Cassan died. The subtext in the epigraph is significant in this context: 'Our partings never parted us, and so though earthly sight could follow you no further we only said, "Good night!"'

The Obstacle Race: '*I Dedicate this book To My Dear "Half-sister" MARY With My Love*'. This is for Mary Bastard.

A Man under Authority: '*I dedicate this book to my dear friend Violet Vanburgh in loving remembrance of 1921'*. Vanburgh appeared only once in an Ethel production work, the London West End production of *The Knave of Diamonds*, which was played in London and Manchester. Vanburgh's career was at its height in the early 1900s. Divorced in 1917 she along with her sister was described by Sir John Guilgud as: 'The Vanbrugh sisters were remarkably alike in appearance. Tall and imposing, beautifully spoken, they moved with grace. ... They were elegantly but never ostentatiously dressed, entering and leaving the stage with unerring authority. ... Violet never struck me as a natural comedienne, as Irene was'.[24] She was commanded to perform before King George V at Queen Alexandra's birthday party at Sandringham; worked tirelessly for theatrical and other good causes including the Elizabeth Garrett Anderson Hospital for Women in London, made another royal performance before Queen Elizabeth in 1938 and was made a Dame in 1941. Ethel perhaps enjoyed the association with such a public figure and was not shy about putting her full name in the dedication.

~

· Gerald Savage

Charles Rex: *'Dedicate this book to G.T.S in remembrance of a winter's day'.* [Note that the 'I' is missing.]

The Prison Wall: *'I dedicate this book to my husband with my love'.*

The Serpent in the Garden: *'I dedicate this book to my husband for his birthday with my love'.*

~

· Extended Family

The Knave of Diamonds: *'I dedicate this book to my friend and sister in loving remembrance of her sympathy and help'.*

The Lamp in the Desert: *Dedicate this book to my dearly beloved Elizabeth and to the memory of her great goodness when she walked in the desert with me'.* [Note that the 'I' is missing.]

The Unknown Quantity: *'I dedicate this book to Norah in most loving remembrance of all that she has given me'.* Norah had provided Ethel with her husband Gerald.

Bars of Iron: *'I dedicate this book to my brother Reginald with my love'.*

~

· Business

The Hundredth Chance: *'I dedicate this book to my old friend W.S.H. in remembrance of many kindnesses'.* This is probably a reference to Haddock, the accountant that Ethel shared with Kipling.

The Electric Torch: (1924): '*I dedicate this book to my friend A.S. WATT, C.B.E. in grateful remembrance of his many kindnesses'*.

The conclusion here is clear, that perhaps of all her connections and relationships Ethel's women friends played a significant role in her life. Throughout Ethel's writing one can perhaps also see the personalisation of literary metaphors particularly in *The Electric Torch*, where Yvonne is the controlling Norah Savage and Claire is the delicate Ethel.

Ethel's Perspective

It was not really surprising that Elizabeth and I were not recipients of any part of our father's or our mother's estate, but it hurt. There was Reggie, a bit of a reprobate and not holding down a very good job and he gets it all, but then that was the way Edwardian families functioned. Any ill feeling soon disappeared when, through the auspices of Alexander Watt my agent, my first major work *The Way of an Eagle* became such a success, and I had received sufficient royalties that within twelve months of publication I was able to buy my own house. Elizabeth of course came to live with me, but the house was mine.

For the first time I was independent but only really in my earnings. I still had to provide for Elizabeth and Reggie and of course there was the little girl that Elizabeth took on, and paid a considerable amount of money for no doubt for the mother's silence. Again, my money of course. I really cannot imagine a less suitable person to be a mother. I certainly was not at all maternal. Elizabeth demonstrated few if any maternal instincts, but luckily Nursie as she was now no longer looking after our mother provided the care that little Poppy needed and of course Nursie's daughter became a quasi-sister for her.

Violet, my secretary and very close friend on whom I relied so much, eventually worked full time for me and lived with me. Ironically her brother

Cyril and Elizabeth carried on a correspondent relationship but nothing came of it. Violet bought her own house in London with my help but worked for me from before I married Gerald Savage until my very last book when I was so ill with cancer. Violet and I shared so much and also shared a great love. Without Violet's help and support I could not have achieved as much as I did.

Violet's main role was to deal with all my non-business correspondence and this brought me many female admirers. Latterly Norah Savage became a frequent visitor and a very close friend and her brother Gerald eventually joined her on these visits. Norah was a very strong and opinionated woman and supported the Women's Freedom League and refused to comply with the census as women were not allowed to vote. Deep down I'm sure she controlled her brother. Gerald had never married and as far as I know had never had any female relationships himself before he was introduced to me. He was a kind and harmless man and filled a need in my life to be able to project some sort of normalcy. Norah's aim I'm sure all along was to act as a match maker between Gerald and myself. We were not in love but when we were married he helped run my household and I became fond of him. As a penniless brevetted colonel with a pension of a major the Savages clearly saw the opportunities of a relationship with my money. Gerald had no private income or wealth, and a relationship with me provided him with stability status and a way of life that enabled him to pursue his pastime and hobby of model trains and boats. Gerald was a military man with an ego who liked to be called colonel, which of course he wasn't really. He was a very efficient organiser within the Army Service Corps, but never saw action as such. Norah would, however, have been very proud of him when the king presented him with his award at Buckingham Palace. I could not help but make the comparison between Gerald's war service and that of Alice Cassan's brother William, who won the MC for conspicuous bravery. Reggie's war service was unremarkable. In hindsight Norah's arrival on the scene was perhaps fortuitous as I had become involved with Alice Cassan, Mary Bastard and Edith deWolf. This was such a difficult and emotional time for me and the only place that I could express my feelings was in my writing. I loved my friends deeply and after my marriage I was never able to settle and enjoy life. Gerald meant that I now longer had access to the women that I loved. Gerald was a kind man but I was unhappy and just never seemed able to settle down after our marriage. It seems silly but I moved houses eight times in twenty-seven years.

I did not enjoy home life very much and did not want to cope with publicity so rather like Kenneth Grahame's Toad in *The Wind in the Willows* I indulged in motorcars. I did not drive myself but latterly enjoyed immensely being driven around in my Rolls Royce that I called Lady Jane Grey. My chauffeur Barwell taught Elizabeth how to drive and I saw my money spent on her expensive machines that she also clearly enjoyed.

Reggie married before me in 1920 to a trollop called Patricia Cheshire and I knew that this relationship would not work out. She was very fond of drink and sadly their first child was stillborn. A married man, but I still provided for him financially. Retrospection is not always healthy but I wonder what would have happened to Elizabeth and Reggie without my continual and substantial financial support?

It was very sad but my marriage to Gerald was the end of my close relationship with my sister. I made a financial settlement, I sold the house in which we had lived together and we parted company. She did not approve of my husband and was perhaps a little jealous that I had achieved so much and she had achieved so little. In my life she now ceased to exist. What is so sad is that if our father had allowed her to go to China as a tutor for the Bowra boys she would have had her own life, a life of adventure and travel. Sometimes I think that I was a bit harsh, especially my book dedication to Mary Bastard as 'my half-sister' in my 1921 publication *The Obstacle Race*. My sister was hit with this and then my marriage. She had lost me, the focus for her life. The famous actress Violet Vanburgh played the lead role in the stage production of *Knave of Diamonds* and although I dedicated a book to her in 1921 our friendship was very enjoyable but short-lived.

My marriage left me with Gerald, Norah and Violet as my close companions, and I increasingly came to rely on Alexander Watt and his accountant Mr. Haddock as sounding boards. Gerald was of no help to me except in keeping my domestic affairs in order.

8. Health, Sickness and Drugs

'she was done for the moment he taught her the opium habit'.[1]

Ethel died in 1939 after a long battle with breast cancer and the trauma of having to suffer double mastectomies. Drug use, high fevers and delirium are a frequent topic in her narratives. This aspect of the creative stimuli to which Ethel was exposed is the hardest to interpret. From where did she access her knowledge prior to her terminal sickness? What is most surprising is the mention of drug use in her first major success *The Way of an Eagle*, published when she was just twenty-three years old. In this work there is a deep understanding of the effects of opiate use. Muriel the heroine resorts to 'a relief in in a remedy which in her normal senses she would have turned in disgust, opium'.[2] Was there more to the shy young spinster cloistered at home with her female friends that we have not discovered? What is certain is that there was a dramatic change in her physiology as demonstrated in photographs between when she was in a studio situation with her sister and sitting alone in her garden some years later. The fresh-faced young woman has become visibly strained with dark rings around dull eyes. She looks thin, lifeless and without joy.

In *The Keeper of the Door* there is a very insightful description of the effects of a painkiller: 'she felt as if a strange glow were dawning on her brain, a kind of mental radiance, inexpressively wonderful, adsorbing her pain as mist is absorbed by the sun. Gradually it grew till all the pain was gone, swamped, forgotten, in this curious mix of warmth and ecstasy. It was the most marvellous sensation she had ever experienced. Her whole being thrilled responsive to the glow. It was as though a door had been opened somewhere above her and she was being drawn upwards by some invisible means, upwards and upwards, light as gossamer and strangely transcendentally happy, towards the warmth and brightness and wonder that lay beyond'.[3] In the same title we read about effects of drug-induced sleep: 'only the utter weariness that follows the sleep of morphia'.[4] Again, in this title we see evidence of an understanding of drug use: 'That was what made me take to those cigarettes. I never felt it when I was smoking them. They made me so deliriously sleepy. It was terrible when – he – took them away. I felt as if he had pushed me over a deep abyss. I really can't do without them. They make me float when I'm going to sink'.[5] Franzen's views expressed earlier concerning writing from experience must hold a very specific validity here. How could Ethel write this unless she had experienced it? Q.D. Leavis writing in 1932 quoted an un-named successful writer (whose books sell a million copies a year): 'It was my custom as a child, and in fact it has been all my life, to day-dream romantic stories filled with action and adventure. Many of my written stories are based upon these. What suggested them I do not know'.[6] I suggest that Ethel did know. Leavis also makes the wonderfully socially pejorative positioning comment that romantic fiction can be linked to 'the romantic names on suburban gate-posts'. This is of course abject nonsense and undermines the validity of some of her posits. This lack of understanding or interpretation of a writer's stimuli is staggeringly shallow, and demonstrates a blinkered academic focus on reality.

Both male and female drug use in the Victorian era, but less so in the Edwardian, has been the subject of much discourse. In the period Degas painted absinth drinkers as did Viktor Olivia. The following literary luminaries also used drugs: Elizabeth Barrett Browning, George Eliot, Elizabeth Gaskell, Bronte, Bram Stoker. Sarah Bernhardt and Browning freely admitted that the use of laudanum helped their creativity. But the effects of the use of drugs in the narratives of novels in this period with the characters describing these effects in some detail to a lowbrow readership universe was not unique to Ethel.

Marie Corelli focused on absinthe abuse in her work *Wormwood* (1890). There is of course a chasmic difference between a description of the use of drugs to a description of the effects of that use. Ethel focused on the latter surely through her own use. Only in *The Black Knight* (1926) do we see a specific recreational drug cocaine mentioned. This and the shocking revelation, not just in relation to the period but also in relation to the twenty-first century, of the suggestion of drug use and sex trafficking:

> He lent me money and I lost that. In between times there were great orgies when everyone either drank or took cocaine. I had kept out of it till then, but I lost my balance at last. The Silvers said that they were broke, couldn't get me home. So I fell. I took cocaine one night. When the morning came I found I had been made over to him. I was his property ...I thought that he would stay with me, but he found some people he knew – decent people – and– and I was left out. That brought home the awfulness to me more than anything. I had been more or less under the influence of that filthy drug till then, but that night I came out of it. It was like waking up in a crawling quagmire ...[7]

The most significant word there is 'crawling'. The crawling skin sensation is one of the main topical reactions to sudden drug withdrawal. Ethel understood this.

In *The Lamp in the Desert* drug use is fundamental to the cohesiveness of the narrative's structure: A suspicion that opium in cigars had caused an accident, and an assault that was caused by a drug experiment, 'to try a native drug which in its effects was far worse than the fever pure and simple'.[8] The excuse for a sexual assault now moved from the cause being a fever to a drug experiment. This tainted smoking was not a new literary device, as Wilde used it in the *Picture of Dorian Grey* (1890) when Lord Henry smokes opium-tainted cigarettes, and his subsequent seduction of Dorian, persuading Dorian to seek solace in an opium den. Sherlock Holmes was of course portrayed as a cocaine addict.

Ethel died from breast cancer and had no doubt suffered considerable pain for many years and this would have occasioned her use and knowledge of the effect of drugs. But her use before her sickness is a speculative issue. A frequent participant in the Dell household was a Dr. Vidler who provided care for Ella and Ethel's mother and provided a nurse. As the family doctor he must have also treated their father Vincent for his gout. Opiates were used as painkillers for this affliction and Wilkie Collins (*Moonstone* 1868) was known to have used laudanum as a painkiller for his gout. It is highly probable therefore that the doctor also provided 'help' to Ethel for her anxieties and worries. On this assumption Ethel was using a drug or drugs, probably laudanum before her success with *The Way of an Eagle*. How else could she have had the erudition to describe the effects of drug use?

Of the eighty-nine titles that have been located and closely read, 15% contained intimate descriptions of the effects of drug use. In *A Man under Authority* (1925) the young man Gaspard suffers from a mysterious weakness – the implication here is drug addiction – and is looked after by a secretive and hostile man servant who would seem to have been positioned in the narrative as his supplier. The boy suffers an overdose and is forced to keep awake until a doctor arrives. Just nine years before Ethel's death we see in *Storm Drift* (1930) the hero visiting his sister and noting that Harvey his brother-in-law is given tobacco that peacefully lulled his senses: 'I believe that there is opium in it'.[9] His sister was also drugging herself every night. In *Honeyball Farm* (1937) there is also opium in the tobacco. In Ethel's *The Serpent in the Garden* (1932) she describes the effect of the use of injected narcotics with 'The place where it [the needle] entered showed an inflamed circle'.[10]

There is discourse on an unconsummated marriage in *The Electric Torch* (1934) (Ethel married in 1922), of single sex relationships and significantly a knowledge of drugs. From about the time of the release of this story it must be assumed that Ethel was seriously unwell and under medication, as within six years it is understood that she suffered her first mastectomy for cancer. In this same title the heroine drugs her husband and then drugs herself before a difficult interview with a policeman.

At the end of her life Ethel, engages her reader yet again in a startling portrayal of the use of drugs for sexual dominance and this time rape from which the heroine Diana in *The Juice of the Pomegranate* becomes pregnant. She then describes the impression that a drug influenced person portrays:

There was a particular look when his eyes would regard her with pupils so distended that they appeared like pools of blackness that really frightened her. It gave him an insane appearance that was almost diabolical ... she eventually discarded the idea of drink, but she strongly suspected that there was some drug in his possession which he had twice used upon her without her knowledge and which he was in the habit of taking himself when his affairs, whatever they might be, caused him anxiety.[11]

Despite this deviance, it is very easy to fall into the trap of considering drug use in terms of twenty-first century ethics, moral codes of conduct and the law. However, opiate availability was widespread as was its use. Popular patent medicines such as Kendal Black Drop, Batley's Sedative Solution and Dover's Powder were sold over the counter without prescription. 'Chloral hydrate', the first of the popular sedatives, and 'the first rehearsal of the "Prozac" scenario', was synthesised in 1832 and by the 1870s had a great public following as a drug that common symptoms from insomnia to anxiety and the vapours – or melancholia. 'Woolf amongst many others was prescribed it for home use'.[12]

Laudanum was, however, perhaps the most widely used straight opiate. In the likelihood that Ethel was a 'user', she was in good company as stated earlier. Even 'Mrs. Beeton included opium in her list of home remedies in *Mrs. Beeton's Household Management* (1861)'.[13] A close read of Lewis Carroll's *Alice in Wonderland* (1865) details Alice's opiate use although not specifically detailed.

... the substances that Alice consumes in wonderland are never called drugs specifically, but her encounters with mysterious bottles filled with strange substances, cakes imprinted with injunctions to consume them, hookah-smoking caterpillars, and magical mushrooms – all of which appear to Alice in a dreamspace and which distort her sense of her body, space, time and logic – have become associated in the popular imagination (today's at least) with drug consumption.[14]

Very few of Ethel's letters outside of her business dealings exist, but in 1936, three years before her death, she wrote to a Mrs. Blakeney, the wife of the headmaster of King's School Ely: 'I have just finished my twenty fifth novel (4 weeks ago) immediately before undergoing a rather severe operation up at the Sarum B ... [unreadable] Nursing Home. I was there for a fortnight and Gerald was able to be there with me ... They are very pleased with me though naturally I still feel a little shattered! Everybody was so fond of us, and things were made so easy for me'.[15]

All of this hides the possible reality that Ethel was a deeply troubled woman. Escaping into the solitude and inward nature of writing can seem cathartic to the writer but seldom helps to overcome mental stress and perceived demons. L.M. Montgomery the *Anne of Green Gables* (1908) author apparently committed suicide with a prescription drugs overdose at the age of sixty-seven. Montgomery's granddaughter Kate Macdonald Butler stated: 'Despite her great success, it is known that she suffered from depression, that she was isolated, sad and filled with worry and dread for much of her life'.[16] Montgomery wrote about her difficulties in her personal journals, but Ethel wrote no journals but exposed her demons in the very public domain of her narratives.

The Bioscope, an illustrated news magazine which focused on early cinema, reported in June 1925 that the adaption of Ethel's *The Top of the World* featured the acting of James Kirkwood who capably distinguishes the sharply contrasting characters of the two cousins, giving a particularly realistic study of the drug-sodden Guy. Jack Cunningham, the film's screenwriter, understood the significance of drugs to the plot, and kept to the storyline.

Ethel's Perspective

Living at home with the family was a huge strain. My relationship with my father deteriorated once he retired and as he became more and more unwell, the abuse intensified. I was, however, very lucky that once we moved to our new family home in Ashford I had access to Dr. Vidler, who initially came to treat my father and latterly my mother and he also arranged a nurse for her. The strain of living with my father and trying to write was extreme. I could only write when family members were not around and this meant that I did not get much rest. The doctor prescribed laudanum for me, which helped me to relax and sleep. I also found that I needed the drug more and more and really could not function without it. The advertisements for drugs in the Press which were allowed until 1920 presented the good side of opiates. For example: Le Fée Verte, the green fairy, as absinthe was called when I was growing up, was a devilish concoction to which it was easy to become addicted, and even Degas used it as a subject for some of his paintings.

I was addicted and this helped me to cope with my father, my internal conflicts, and I think helped me to be creative. Latterly when I was so ill drugs were essential for me as a pain killer.

9. Dislike of Adventure, Kind and Socially Naïve

'... to be recognised wherever one went, pointed at, made conspicuous – oh, I should hate it – hate it'![1]

I wrote earlier of Ethel lacking in maternal instincts and removed from the reality of children and families when she gave Penelope, aged three, a hymnal. We can see this 'out of reality-ness' again in *Where Three Roads Meet* with a child aged four calling her mother by her Christian name. I would suggest that this was an unheard-of phenomenon during the time of her writing and an impossibility during her own childhood.

One can question whether, other than on her trip to Switzerland, Ethel ever ate out at a restaurant, as she does not appear to understand menu taxonomy. Table d'hote for example is described as a location not a type of menu in *Death's Property*. Again, in the same title we see a fisherman wearing a sou'wester hat indoors. The first thing that a fisherman or sailor who had had the need to wear a sou'wester would do would be to take it off at the earliest opportunity. Does one really put 'the tea pot on the hob', and one wonders if she ever made herself a cup of tea. Kettles, not tea pots go on the hob.[2] Evening drinks are served and the hostess asks if he takes lemon, but we discover that the guest is drinking wine.[3] We have learnt from Maurice Bowra that Ethel served visitors sherry midmorning but was Ethel herself a non-drinker to make such a mistake? She was, however, very au fait with the management of servants. In *Where Three Roads Meet* we see the following comment: 'a good servant neither knows – nor does not know – anything that he ought not to'.[4]

Ethel's shy nature and reclusiveness are well demonstrated in *The Passer-*

By. The American in the narrative wants to secure a portrait of an artist and is willing to pay the hero, who is very down on his luck, $50,000 ($8M in today's values). She is clearly out of touch with reality here. The artist, Jane Brown, an imaginative name for someone that the men have imagined as very unattractive … lank haired, goggle eyed, large feet and shoelaces undone, who avoids publicity like the plague, 'some people call it a pose. It probably is. But I suppose she has a right to do as she likes. [Clearly a reference to her own behaviour in the public eye.] … she's all the rage now. She's taken the public fancy by storm, as you say. But her vogue will pass. It always does. These hot favourites are seldom stayers …'[5] The artist has already been approached but declines to have her photograph taken. 'she is a shy bird – a very shy bird. I imagine that she'll take some catching. What right have the public to intrude on her?'[6] '"Yes. I would mind intensely," she said … "to be recognised wherever one went, pointed at, made conspicuous – oh, I should hate it – hate it!" … And she feels as I do, that to be made a show of would be – quite intolerable. She considers all self-advertisement is vulgar, and she – would never stoop to it."'[7]

A unique feature of Ethel's work was, despite her huge wealth, her demonstration of a lack of confidence in her own abilities, which did not help her literary reputation. Her self-denigration is subject to a huge amount of page space in *The Electric Torch*. The heroine, Claire, is keeping a suitor at bay and the suitor refers to this as a '"typical Ethel M. Dell moment. By the way, that woman has my sympathy if ever a woman had. She is branded for life on account of her juvenile efforts of umpteen years ago." "I don't like her [Ethel]," said Claire. "She portrays a world that is hopelessly out of date." His smile broadened. "But the pendulum swings back. And after all, human nature doesn't vary in the long run. Only customs – like eyebrows and things. She isn't what you would call the sophisticated type. But – can anyone say that sophistication can last?" "I don't know," said Claire "it's nice of you to sympathise with her anyway." "I always sympathise with the downtrodden," he said, "don't you?"[8] This whole dialogue is contextually out of place in the narrative and plays no part in the plot. Why would the hero and the heroine in a very dramatic situation refer to Ethel's critics? She is talking to her reader universe because she has nobody else in whom to confide. This seems to be Ethel complaining that her earlier work has typecast her later work. As discussed earlier in *The Juice of the Pomegranate*, a year before her death, we find the following scene:

Hello! Here's a find! Now we shall see what the brainy Blanche reads in her leisure moments! Something she's none too proud of obviously! [The book has been found behind a cushion.] Great Scott! It's an Ethel M. Dell!'[9]

Then in the next scene, appearing to compound the self-denigration, Ethel writes 'My Lady never leaves a Dell book lying around for visitors to see [the implied bad taste], madam, so I took it away'.[10] Can this self-denigration be considered as part of her marketing mix, demonstrating a disdain for the literary world, or as Nicola Beauman has suggested, a shared joke with the reader?

In *Storm Drift* Ethel refers to Tiggie's perversion of egoism in that he saw himself as an amiable fool. One cannot surmise whether this is a reference to ethical egoism, the doctrine that holds that individuals ought to do what is in their self-interest, or psychological egoism, the doctrine that holds that individuals are always motivated by self-interest. Either way it is Ethel being altruistic. Maurice Bowra wrote, '... and Miss Ethel, who was the gentlest and most self-effacing of women and had a genius of teaching dogs to do elaborate tricks, began to make lots of money. She and Miss Dell (Ella) set up house outside Guildford and shut themselves off from the world by building a massive brick wall around their domain. Edward and I were asked to stay there, and the comforts were such that we had never known, including a glass of sherry and a plum-cake in the middle of the morning'.[11]

The LGBT broadcaster and journalist Nancy Spain saw Ethel as probably the shyest authoress in the world. 'The Garbo of English literature…'[12] Greta Garbo, the late Swedish actress, who never married or had children, was infamous for both her need for secrecy and also her ambivalent sexuality, and lived in isolation apparently thinking of her childhood sweetheart the actress Mimi Pollack until she died. How can one square the shy, reclusive authoress with the purveyor of sensational and sensual romantic fiction? The answer has to be inspiration from her own family's dysfunctionality and a need to express her own frustrations.

Ethel holidayed with The Cassan in the UK, and they both changed their names at the hotels where they were staying. No doubt wishing to avoid public knowledge of Ethel's presence and perhaps the fact that they were holidaying together. Ethel only travelled abroad once to Switzerland and apart from her holiday with Alice Cassan and a honeymoon in England with Gerald it seems than unlike her sister she did not holiday and never went abroad again. It is also possible that her great success compounded her need to be reclusive … the more successful she was the more pressure there was to be seen so Ethel retreated behind her walls and curtains. Ethel's engagement to Gerald Savage in December 1921 was kept from the Press until March 1922, when they got wind of this event, an event that if secured, would be a scoop indeed given the reclusive nature of the target. Ethel wrote to a neighbour Lady Smithers to thank her for her good wishes on her engagement, but '(please don't tell the press!)' and 'We have had a horrible time trying to dodge the reporters. One creature patrolled up and down outside the gates on Sunday for a long time; but at least we managed to baffle him, though it was a very near thing. As they have already surmised the wedding will be a "secret" one. In fact we are thinking of having the ceremony in the coal cellar! But our plans are as yet indefinite'.[13] The paranoia of secrecy surrounding the wedding ceremony on 21 August 1922 extended to the 'happy' couple leaving for the church at 8.30 in the morning to avoid the London Press, and travelling as Mr. and Mrs. Gerald White and removing name tags out of the bride's underclothing.[14] The paranoia of the latter is hard to understand. Anecdotally, however, whilst living in the United States I had contact with a professor from Harvard who, during the Second World War, shared a billet with the American actor Henry Fonda, who never had any underwear as they were all stolen by the laundry ladies as souvenirs, given that they were identified by his name tags. Stranger things do happen.

Ethel hardly ever entertained at home, did not want to be a celebrity and did not at any stage in her career appear in public, give an interview nor release photographs of herself.[15] Thirty-six years after her death this reclusiveness was maintained when a ninety year-old member of her household staff was reluctant to give away personal details, as this was breaking an undertaking. In contrast Philip Waller's reference to Hall Caine's Greeba Castle's formal opening with 'charabanc loads of excursionists who flocked to meet the elderly author' was designed to create a personality for the author as a marketing tool.[16] In contrast Ethel's house was surrounded by a high wall and the curtains of her cars were always drawn. There was certainly mystery surrounding her and the Press tried on numerous occasions to gain access, even attempting to bribe Ethel's staff for a photograph, but without success.

Professor David Smithers, the son of Sir Alfred and Lady Smithers who visited Ethel in The Greenwood frequently, commented that she was a shadowy figure and that the visits were pure Ella. The implication here is that Ella dominated her sister, confirmed by Nursie, who thought that Ella was haughty and Ethel gentle.[17]

Ethel never forgot to send money to the pensioners from her parent's house at Knockholt and was generally soft hearted with poverty of any kind. Ella discovered at some stage that Ethel had been sending a monthly stipend to a man who had written that he was without work and that his wife was ill. It turned out that this was a conman and the payments soon stopped. However, when sent a pile of her own books to sign Ethel, however, just sent them straight back.

Writing is a lonely and anti-social occupation that requires, for most writers, a solitude for thought and creativity. Ethel was no exception and accomplished this by retiring after her evening meal and working at night, in her study which she kept locked. Nursie reported that Ethel's dog woke her at four a.m. everyday so that she could write before the household stirred. The late Victorian household in which Ethel lived her early years was rigid and conformist and would have been a difficult environment in which to write her sensationalist material. This practice of working at night which probably started when her parents were still alive in order that she should not disturb the household routine continued. It is also highly probable that her earlier works were produced in secret away from the influence of her father. There was a polarity between Ethel's work and her life: a possible lack of fulfilment which could have been the spark that ignited her creativity when she escaped into her own world, working through the night in her study which – according to those who worked for and knew her – she kept locked.

What few photographs of her survive show that even before her illness she had a tired drawn face with deep set black shadowed eyes, perhaps demonstrating a degree of sleep deprivation, and, as discussed, drug usage. These photographs also, as discussed earlier, show what seems to be a cleft lip or facial damage of some sort.

The five surviving original manuscripts of her ninety-eight stories written in her large and firm hand show a very clear thought process with remarkably few alterations and changes. It is easy to imagine the quiet and gentle woman of leisure during the day with her imagination racing, finishing her meal quickly – she did not eat much, had little interest in food, wanting it plain but well served – and then rushing off to put her thoughts down.

Ethel's idea of simple food seemed at odds with the exotic environs of her novels; stewed eels with parsley sauce, chocolate blancmange with tinned cream, Petite Beurre biscuits with St. Ivel cheese, and whole Whiting boiled 'tail in mouth' with tomato sauce from a bottle, warmed and served in a gravy boat. Ethel, a very wealthy woman, owned a huge house, had household help, bought expensive cars yet lived a comparatively simple life behind her high walls.[18]

Ethel's Perspective

I know that I have made a lot of money through my writing, and as a result I could do just about anything that I wanted to do. But I am, deep down, a very shy person, and have always been overshadowed by Elizabeth, who has always been loud, glamourous and outspoken. She is well read, plays the piano and sings very well. I just think that I am a bit dull really and I do not enjoy social situations and all the chit chat that is required. She has also always seen the need to look after me. My father abused me, my sister dominated me, and my dissolute brother makes financial demands and the public want to see me and hear me talk. I cannot imagine anything worse than that. What right have the Press to interfere in my life and what on earth can I say to them? My life is my own and private. Yet they try and interfere. We had one man walking up and down outside the house hoping to get a glimpse of me. We also had a reporter try and bribe our staff for a photograph. I am a very shy person by nature but my shyness was initially built around my deformed upper lip so I did not find it easy to meet new people.

My main focus is story writing, which I enjoy so much. The exception to story writing was my book about Afghanistan and the moral dilemma that soldiers face when confronted with the dilemma of obeying an order or doing what is morally correct. I set deadlines and I do my utmost to stick to those. The death of my mother was so sad for me but I was soon back on track, losing myself back in my own fictional world.

From the very beginning I had managed my commercial relationships myself but I deeply regret taking the advice that my first agent Pinker gave me to sell all my copyrights. Looking back, it was naïve of me to accept his advice, but at that time I knew no better of course. He clearly had no confidence in my ability to sustain a writing career. How wrong he was! Writing and publishing were of course not sequential and my second story about Afghanistan was very topical and was accepted very quickly no doubt because of that, but some of my later stories were written some years earlier and I blush sometimes thinking about the content. My readers liked them, however, which was the most important thing.

Elizabeth never reads my books as I think that she considers them too low brow for her tastes, and this makes me worry about the quality of what I write. Some comment is better than no comment. After 1912 my agent Watt provided me with help and encouragement and I listen to his advice. He never tells me what to write but seems to have such a confidence that whatever I produce will sell.

10 The Lampooned Style

'He hated her with the rancorous and cruel hatred of conscious inferiority'.[1]

When debating the levers for success that Ethel employed it is important to set the contemporary literary scene as a benchmark against which her successes were judged. Unlike Florence Barclay who, according to Mary Hammond, with her first work *The Rosary* (1909) 'claimed a new high ground that refused to apologise for the mere fact of popularity', Ethel did not pretend to write art and, as with so much popular fiction, her work was written and read for other reasons and values.[2]

In Nicola Beauman's *A Very Great Profession* (2004), she agrees with Hammond and states that Ethel is seen 'as a pleasure giver pure and simple. She seems to have felt no need for heart searching about her merit or her role as a writer'.[3] Ethel was pathologically shy. She did not speak to the Press nor release photographs of herself, but at the peak of her popularity she was earning about £25,000 a year (approximately £4M pa in today's values).[4] George Orwell writing in 1946 stated that £1,000 (£89,000 at today's values) was the best income for a writer so 'he can live in reasonable comfort'. Later in the same article he wrote that, 'In a way it is easier for people like Ethel M. Dell to avoid prostitution than it is for a serious writer'.[5] This was an acknowledgement of Ethel's financial success but also a very crude and seemingly frustrated swipe at her literary credentials. Her earning power no doubt rankled many contemporary writers. Robert Graves also writing in the same journal (Horizon vol. XIV No. 81 September 1946) that carried Orwell's prostitution comment attacked the definition of and categorisation of a writer very clearly when answering the question, 'Do you think a serious writer can earn this sum (how much do you think a writer needs to live on?) by his writing, and if so how?':

> Robert Graves commented that 'serious writer was, I think a term invented by the young experimental writers of the twenties to distinguish themselves from the commercial, academic, and elder writers whom they lumped together as their common enemies. But if Horizon is using the word in a less provocative sense, it includes such different types as the modern novelist who writes for entertainment but not according to a commercially dictated formula, the literary historian and the poet.[6]

Orwell's pejorative comment appears to have been countered by Robert Graves as Ethel, writing for entertainment, was by this definition a 'serious' writer. Ethel's success without apparent literary merit has also had a continuing residual negativity in literary circles. In Antony Alpers' work *The Stories of Katherine Mansfield* (1984) as reviewed by W.H. New in 1985 the extraordinary conclusion is posited that Mansfield's story *A Cup of Tea* (1922) was dropped from the anthology because it had appeared 'in a pulp magazine called Story-Teller, which also published Ethel M. Dell'.[7] This surely is an absurdity and a demonstration of inadequate research. Mansfield appeared in many magazines both 'pulp' and otherwise both before and after 1922. Was the association really perceived as so negative, or was this just an unthinking continuation of the swipe at Ethel's literary credentials forty-six years after her death? Mansfield used the same magazines as Ethel extensively and *Story-Teller* itself published Kipling two years later.

Ethel has been correctly pigeon-holed as a writer of titillating fiction and her not infrequent mentions in other works or by other authors as a scene setter or as a comparative does give some credence to the exposure that she had:

Dorothy Sayers with *The Unpleasantness at the Bellona Club* (1928) and *Murder Must Advertise* (1933) where Ethel was linked with Philipps Oppenheim and Elinor Glyn in the context of mysteriousness and 'fruity', Gladys Mitchel's *The Saltmarsh Murders* (1932), Winifred Watson *Miss Pettigrew for a Day* (1938), Richard Hughes *In Hazard* (1938), Cornelia Skinner's *Our Hearts were Young and Gay* (1942), John Harrison *The Centauri Device* (1974), and as recently as 2008 John Simpson CBE, the much heralded BBC world affairs editor wrote in his *Strange Places, Questionable People* (2008), a description of meeting Col. Gadaffi the Libyan dictator: '"You should eat," he [Gadaffi] said, and everything became even more Ethel M. Dell than ever'.[8] This was a reference to the unreal situation in which he faced with Gadaffi, which became a Dell moment. Of particular interest is the scene in *In Hazard* where the male engineer of the steamer Archimedes cannot sleep so reads one of Ethel's works. In *The Centauri Device* (Harrison, 1974) a bound copy Ethel's works is displayed at a twenty-fourth century narcotics party as one of a number of 'objets d'art' of the twentieth century.

The New Yorker, the American liberal weekly journal, frequently published derogatory comments concerning Ethel's style. Although the journal did not publish any of her works they carried notes of publications and they frequently carried asides:

- 1932 ... 'Live Bait by Ethel M. Dell published by Putnam – short stories this time, and all about love'.
- 2 March 1927: 'Granite [stage play] by Clemence Dane [Winifred Ashton] is, after all, merely the Ethel M. Dell of near poetic drama'.
- 10 January 1931: Referencing sex appeal and *It* [novel by Elinor Glyn 1927, and film starring Clara Bow]: 'Old fashioned girls, who love to hear tell of the marble of their shoulders and the utter oblivion that stole over the most temporary dancing partner at the mere thought of them, have to read Ethel M. Dell for their romance'.

- 9 December 1950: a comment that the world heavyweight boxing champion Gene Tunney read Ethel.
- 5 September 1964: in a film review, '... and have reduced it to the puerile aesthetic and intellectual level of a novel by Ethel M. Dell ...'
- 30 September 1952: Commenting on Darryl F. Zanuck file of Hemingway's *Snows of Kilimanjaro*, 'This interlude, which is as slow in the unravelling as the collected works of Ethel M. Dell ...'
- 13 October 1952: 'fascists mouth the decadent glorification of blood and the cavemen apparent in the Ethel M. Dells and Hemingways'.
- 8 August 1953: In reviewing Frederick Rolfe's *The Desire and Pursuit of the Whole*, 'the handsome boy-girl servant breaking down the reserve of a fastidious and handsome yachtsman is a throwback to a novel by Ethel M. Dell'.
- 26 September 1964: in a short story, '... and you're frightfully uneducated. You don't know how to punctuate a sentence, and all you've ever read is Floyd Dell, Ethel M. Dell and the Rubaiyat'.

Nancy Spain saw Ethel very differently.

Ethel wrote with passionate unswerving sincerity. She believed in her characters: her ugly, fascinating army officers (all her men are fascinating and marred) in some way her beautiful, wronged women (her women are always beautiful and nearly always wronged), her cads (her cads are more caddish than any other cads in fiction). Second, when her characters spoke, they spoke in character. They used the sort of language that we all understand ... Third, something tremendous – like a seduction or a kiss, or an unmasking of a coward and a poltroon – took place on every single page, sweeping her readers off their feet, gasping and panting, until the end the heroine and the hero look

RIDING THE TOSH HORSE

at each other 'with fire and memory and understanding in their eyes'.[9] This is the last sentence of *The Way of an Eagle*.

Ethel's first title in the UK, *The Repentant Rogue*, can be seen as an immature start to a writing career with a charming almost childlike naiveté and Ethel finding the start of her career's literary theme. This naiveté is perhaps understandable if one assumes that the actual writing of the narrative took place maybe up to two years previously. This story incorporates romance, sexual fantasy (the couple pointedly do not sleep together), female independence, weaknesses, without understanding she admires the culture and ready flow of his talk, and strengths ... the heroine shoots the conman's accomplice. But the conman falls in reciprocated love with his target. She rides a bicycle, plays billiards, hunts, indulges in boating, plays tennis, is 'no ignoramus' of the manly exploits of the conman. The heroine's father has sold out his holding in the Great Poobah Gold Company, and irrelevant to the story and only referred to once, was that he had been a drover (there was perhaps an intended exoticness here). Ethel has lifted the name of the company from The Grand Poobah, the haughty character in Gilbert and Sullivan's *The Mikado* (1885).

The publication of the same story, *The Repentant Rogue*, a year later in the United States (*Everybody's Magazine* March 1900) was a significant achievement but the narrative was subject to considerable editing for the American market. Apart from the obvious changes to currency and spelling, check for cheque for example, jail for gaol, there was wholesale deletion of references to aristocracy and royalty and application of American colloquialisms: shan't becomes sha'n't, aesthetic becomes aesthete, Her Ladyship becomes a mere Mrs., and 'limp heap of clothed flesh and bones' becomes 'a mere limp heap'. This was not just a case of adjusting to the American anathema to hyphens, but significant changes, and not just to idioms. Can one assume that Ethel gave carte blanch editing authority to *Everybody's Magazine* for this market? Probably so, as she would not have had the ability to adjust her copy to American English. Evidence that she did not have a good grasp of American English is evidenced by an American character in *The Passer-By* who addresses his friend and companion, an ex-soldier as 'son'. This is a misunderstanding of the use of the British familiar nomenclature in the United States. To an American it would have seemed pejorative and patronising for a friend to use the phrase. Within British culture the use of 'son' is mainly in the context of a relationship with a generation gap, and is neither paternal nor patronising.

Her Freedom (1908), a short story published in *Grand Magazine* told at a brisk pace, has the hero, a died-in-the-wool, dominant American with a tattoo of the Stars and Stripes on his arm improbably cast as a British viscount who courts the heroine in disguise having been jilted by her. The disguise is a beard and the heroine does not recognise him. The common exclamation 'Great Scott' has been written as 'Great Scotland'. To Ethel it must have sounded about right. 'Great Scotland' appears again in *The Right Man*.

The Australian theme in *A Repentant Rogue* is maintained but India is added as well in *Her Compensation* (1908) published in *Story-Teller Magazine*. In this third title she writes in a very ponderous style and seems not to have found her writer's metier. Thoughts are dysfunctional and narrative links are confusing. This is a difficult story to enjoy or follow as the positioning dialogue is more dominant than the meat of the narrative. The writing style is of a period significantly before the date of publication. There is perhaps an attempt to match the style of writing with the period within which the story is set. There are horse-drawn carriages, mentions of the Crimean War, kissing of hands ... The main characters are, however, set out in the first paragraph of the story but it is still hard to follow because there is also a very confusing style in the use of surnames and Christian names at random for the same person, and given that there are a number of characters with the same surname this is cause for even greater confusion. Religion is used as a character benchmark: a man who honours God and lives a pure life. There is a woman with a past who makes good but also the death of a child, a theme that can be seen in many of her later titles. This is the first example where Ethel demonstrates that there might be a mirror of her own character in her narrative. '... but what of the woman whose life lies in just that one groove, who is set about with limitations and boundaries in every direction? It's not so easy then to break free, is it?'[10] Can we see here the frustration of her environment creating aspirational alter egos in her characters?

Ethel's fourth published work *The Sea Urchin and the Prince* is a revealing source of influence on her writing. Published when she was twenty-eight years old after an unexplained ten year gap in publishing activity, it seems, from the naïve style, to have been written significantly earlier. This work appears to have borrowed, at the very least, the nomenclature of one of the characters, Von Steinwald, from George Macdonald's *Phantastes: A Faerie Romance for Men and Women* (1858).[11] The latter appears as an evident part of Ethel's reading material when she was younger, and one can assume that *The Sea Urchin and the Prince* was written some significant time before it was published. It is just possible that a dormant creativity was assisted by similar works. This would seem to apply to many of her titles, especially the short stories that are in the ambit of fiction's unrealistic realm.

It is tempting to look at the liberating and creative forces at work within the Fin de Siècle and the Art Nouveau movement as grounding influences on her creativity especially given the overlap between her literary start and the quick end of the movement with the jailing of Wilde in 1895. There can be no doubt, however, that she felt at greater liberty to insinuate excess and perhaps unacceptable behaviour in her content because of the movement. But, as her contemporary authors were not shy in pointing out, the style, the tosh that Rebecca West described, was however, both simplistic and uncomplicated.

Simplistic and uncomplicated maybe, but using what pejoratively and idiomatically might be referred to as everything but the kitchen sink in terms of the human condition in the intertextuality of her narrative. Ethel's breakthrough first major work and runaway success, *The Way of an Eagle*, set the style benchmark for her success. There is here a weak, virginal, vulnerable and confused heroine who had an inbuilt pride whose mother died giving birth to her, highlighted by a supporting cast of:

- The hero: Ugly with a gaunt yellow face, slightly built, brave, self-effacing (he turns down a VC), very determined and strong character, unnatural physical strength (he loses an arm in battle), a patronising man in the norms of the twenty-first century but clearly seen as caring in the early twentieth. The advertising slogan used by T. Fisher Unwin stated, 'The Novel with an Ugly Hero'.[12]
- Competitive suitor: A massive man, but a weak character. He is a Victoria Cross recipient, but is not able to make clear and incisive decisions in his personal life, and dies trying to save lives from a shipwreck.
- Second-tier heroine: She has a failing marriage, dallies with a same-sex relationship, loves a male first cousin, loses a baby, but returns to her unselfish hard working unglamorous husband a broken woman.
- Socially dominant woman: A manipulator, who is physically large, a liar and a cheat.

All of this within an environment of notions of empire, the conventions of colonial social strata, drugs, extremes of weather, tribal revolts, scarlet fever, brain fever (this could be any number of conditions from stress to meningitis, a condition that reached the height of its vogue in the nineteenth century, with its literary use by Flaubert in *Madame Bovery*, Bronte in *Wuthering Heights*, Dostoyevsky in *Brothers Karamazov*, and Conan Doyle in the *Complete Sherlock Holmes* among others), assassination, infidelity, unhappy marriage, suggestions of incest, lesbianism, dishonesty and social domineering.[13] Ethel's naïve style was without doubt the cause for the rejection of this story's manuscript by eight publishers before it arrived at T. Fisher Unwin. Stanley Unwin reported that his First Novel Library attracted many promising new authors and he organised one of the first prize competitions for new writers. Manuscripts poured in and among them was one by 'Ethel M. Dell which showed great promise but was unsuitable for publication as it stood ... Suggestions for its improvement were made over and over again; Miss Dell worked away patiently under tuition until eventually *The Way of an Eagle* emerged in its present form, when all of us were confident we had a best seller'.[14] Tom Werner the Fisher Unwin manager, whose sister was the broadcaster and novelist Nancy Spain's partner, thought so little of it that the contract drawn up stated that the first 500 copies should be sold without benefit to the author, and he was of course taking a gamble as Ethel had only sold into magazines prior to the US publication of *The Way of an Eagle*.[15] In *The Way of an Eagle* she demonstrated an ability to mine the extremes of human feeling and frailty albeit with sometimes contradictory emotions in a very compact discourse, without it seeming to be implausible to the narrative; to the reader it could have been possible and believable. A very successful formula that led to thirty-four impressions within four years of first publication, and sixty impressions by 1954.

How can a literary critic take a story seriously where a woman is portrayed as ugly and lank haired, goggle eyed, unattractive, large feet and shoelaces undone and then called Jane Brown, and her protagonist a wealthy and powerful man named Plutarch in *The Passer-By*.[16] The nomenclatures certainly describe the characters, but this naming albeit somewhat onomatopoeic and puerile is surely demeaning to serious readers. The valet in *The Knave of Diamonds* 'has the features of an American Indian with fiery red hair'.[17] Perhaps a superlative too far! Maybe George Orwell had a point here.

It is hard to think that Ethel deliberately talked down to her vast reading universe. For example, her correspondence with Watt does indicate that she cared for them and did not want them to be misled. In writing to Watt regarding the request for a title change for *Rosa Mundi* (1918) from *Weldon's Magazine* Ethel states that 'though I cannot help thinking it is a rather mean trick to play on the public'.[18] Again in 1932 she wrote, 'As regards the request to call my story "Fair Play" I should suggest that it should be taken as a motto instead of a title! As I said in my last letter, the story may be published either under its own title or under that previously used for the second serial but not by any other. I can not consent to having old stories dished up with different titles each time in order to pass them off as new. If they can not agree to this there is nothing doing. It is the meanest frauds upon the public that I ever heard of and I will not be party to it'.[19] The issue had not gone away by 1937: 'With regard to my story "Rosa Mundi", Weldon's seem to have broken my rule in 1931 of never allowing a story to come out under a faked name. It is a trick on the public to which I can never give my approval ...'[20]

Ethel's plots are fun, serious, creative and very often implausible. One can surmise that she just wrote material as stories, not as literature, and when they sold she just kept churning them out, which she was able to do with consummate ease. There was probably very little time spent agonising over syntax and sentence structure. Perhaps the only non-story narratives are those where Ethel, for the record, is making a point about herself as this appears to have been her only method of communicating outside her very small circle of friends and family.

Frequently Ethel used word structures that sounded right if glossed over, but in fact were either meaningless and contextually wrong, or had the opposite real meaning to that intended. She wrote to some extent phonetically. It sounds like the right word or phrase but on analysis it is not the meaning intended. Again, within *The Passer-By*, to 'catch an old guy ratting' is used to describe a man turning up late, however, to 'rat' on someone is to expose them to an authoritative third party.[21] The hero is offered a proposition valued at US$50,000 (US$8M in today's values) and it is suggested that he 'turn it over ...' What she has written sounds plausible and Ethel clearly meant turn it over in his mind/ponder on it/reflect on it but the subject for the turning is missing in her narrative.[22]

In *The Safety Curtain* (1917) she refers to her heroine being compassed with passion. Surely, she meant encompassed! In *The Passer-By* the hero is in action in the trenches and had 'picnicked' in a shell hole. This description of a picnic in the trenches is both naïve and even ill-informed. Ella worked as a part-time VAD nurse in a hospital in Ashford looking after recuperating officers from May 1915 until one assumes the end of hostilities. Ella cannot have talked about it to her sister, or Ethel ignored the reality and stuck to the romance of a picnic, swept up in the glamour of the Edwardian era she simply ignored the very public realities of the war and just glossed over the horrors of the conflict. Given Ella's large personality it seems highly unlikely that what Ella saw and did was not discussed, given that the sisters were living together at the time. Ethel's fiction had been totally removed from reality. Again, as a parallel to Ethel's apparent cloistered naiveté Edith Wharton was publishing articles from the front in *Scribner's Magazine* and *Saturday Evening Post*, magazines that Ethel would herself use later. These articles were later published as *Fighting France* in 1915.[23] Wharton went on to publish extensively with a 'war' focus completing this genre with articles in the *Saturday Evening Post* again and

Woman's Home Companion with the title *Writing a War Story*.

A Debt of Honour (1909) has the first of Ethel's ugly heroes, and he is described as a millionaire, a baboon with a squint. In twenty-first century marketing terms Ethel had established a USP (unique selling point). Heroes were by default dashing and handsome, but this was not her route to riches. Of her first five titles four had ugly heroes, and one title has a very effeminate one who wears perfume, a lady's ring and has a limp handshake.

There is a hidden narrational skill where Ethel uses implication and surmise to wrongfoot her reader. In *The Rocks of Valpré* we are misled into thinking that Chris's brother is paying the blackmail when this is later revealed not to be so. In *Greatheart* Basil is assumed to have died but she creates a hook that allows the reader to see that it might not have been so. There were wrongfootings but also non-sequiturs, inconsistencies, contradictions and sometimes just nonsense, but all sounded believable. In the context of the obnoxious Doctor Max in *The Keeper of the Door* (1914), it is nonsense that the highly infectious diphtheria poison can be sucked out and that there is an operation for the disease. Sal volatile, which is a smelling salt, is drunk, and there are no "red as coral" British moths, and this moth becomes a butterfly later in the narrative. In *Her Freedom* a died-in-the-wool American is a viscount. This contradiction does not seem to matter. In *The Woman of his Dream*, the use of pseudonym is incorrect. There is even no alias in the narrative. Surely this is deliberately wrong-footing the reader, as the pseudonym is in fact the woman of his dreams. In *Greatheart* the reader is wrongfooted as to the sexual inclinations of a character, 'He [Stumpy] complied with almost feminine dexterity'.[24]

Ethel had this ability to write what sounded correct but was in modern parlance a soundbite for the expressed thought. In *The Way of an Eagle* we have a man who is 'headlong'. How can a man be headlong? It is an adverb and an adjective, not a noun. But we know what she means, and it does make

RIDING THE TOSH HORSE

sense. Five pages later 'headlong' is used in the correct grammatical context. But in *The Knave of Diamonds* (1911) we read again 'you are always wise,' she said, 'never headlong.' Ethel means headstrong. There is an analogy here with the modern advertising world where there is no desire to produce beautiful advertising per se but advertising that sells, and these two positions can be mutually exclusive. It looks and sounds terrible but when the products that are supported by this advertising move off the shelves, the advertising has served its purpose. An anathema for the literary purist is that writing does not have to be beautiful or even grammatically correct to move volume off the shelves, if that is the objective of writing. In *The Keeper of the Door* she uses the word 'lounge' as a verb … 'he lounged after her'. One can suspect that this might be a typographical error, but what a wonderful word it is as an elision of lunge and louche (disreputable, sordid, unappealing). The word fits the scene perfectly. It was an unappealing lunge. Sometimes her logic overcame established similes. In *The Hundredth Chance* (1916) we see 'fit as a fiddler'. Etymologically this should have been 'fit as a fiddle', but she was correct as logically fiddles cannot of course be fit.[25] In both *Greatheart* (1919) and *Bars of Iron* (1919) we see 'sleeping like a hog'. The simile that we are accustomed to is to 'sleep like a log'.[26] But, to sleep 'like a hog' is so much more expressive and meaningful in the context of the narratives. 'Hog' paints a wonderful picture of deep noisy and perhaps less than clean sleep. The use of the verb 'board' prior and proximate to 'ship' has the connotation of movement in other words getting 'on board'. In *Storm Drift* (1930) the words 'board-ship friends' are used to mean the more colloquial 'ship-board', as in ship-board friends. Does it matter? No, of course not, as the meaning is perfectly clear and is an acceptable short-hand for friends on board the ship, but it is wrong.[27] In *The Bars of Iron* we read: 'he was trying to muster strength to give the lie to the passion that throbbed in the holding in his arms…'[28] The holding means what he was holding, and holding has become a noun. In *Lamp in the Desert* a character is berated soundly, but Ethel 'rates him soundly'. This has a good sound bite but is in fact nonsense. Again, in *The Knave of Diamonds* we read '... and rated his wife for admitting him'.[29] Ethel's description of an angry barmaid in *Full Measure* carries weight but on analysis means very little. 'He looked at her. She stood like a fury, a being as utterly alien to the business-like automaton of a quarter of an hour before as molten lead to the ore from which it is hewn'.[30]

What Ethel is guilty of is excessive and to the literary purist the unnecessary use of superlatives, malapropisms and sometimes just abject and contradictory nonsense if one takes the time to interpret what is written. The meaning is, however, normally clear, and there is a wonderful freedom of expression, as we can see in the following examples:

- Preparing a bath quickly becomes 'with deft celerity'.[31]
- 'wonderful hair, quite lustreless, so abundant ...'[32] What was the condition of her hair? Wonderful or lustreless?
- 'To take someone seriously is a moral impossibility'.[33] This is abject nonsense, it has a sound bite but means nothing.
- 'It was hard to lead a life without becoming morbid, but Anne was fashioned upon generous lines'.[34] This is, however a reference to moral inclinations and not her shape.
- 'Discretion, Lady Carfax, is but another term for decrepitude'.[35] The meaning here cannot be discerned.
- A pulse rate of 150 is reported as a normal.[36]
- 'she scattered her own greetings broadcast'. But to scatter is of course to broadcast.[37]
- 'If I let you down I shall be underneath'.[38] Does this mean lower than the low?
- 'he's in low water'.[39] Low water in this narrative means down on his luck.

This sounds correct and is a delightful fabricated simile.

- The word cram is used to imply lie or an untruth.[40]
- 'his caresses-though they seemed to strengthen his own proprietary attitude-seemed almost too much for her tottering strength'.[41]
- 'Piet Cradock isn't unreasonable as that if he is a Dutchman'.[42] What is meant is 'if he is a Dutchman'.
- 'head over ears …'[43] This cannot be a typographical error when 'head over heels' is meant.
- '… the first deliberate lie I think that I have told since I came to years of discretion'.[44]
- 'he scouted the idea with a laugh',[45] meaning in this context that he dismissed the idea.
- 'the inspector is not a man likely to be lightly baffled'.[46] The intent here is to say it is not easy to baffle the inspector.
- 'but she won't if you twit her about it'.[47] Ethel uses the word twit as a verb to make someone look foolish.
- In *Death's Property* we see some alarming similes and metaphors. The hero is remembering his childhood by the sea and especially in a fishing smack with his twin sister until 'he had gone forth into the seething sea of life to fight the whirlpools … he had breasted the tide and risen above the billows'.[48]
- A bitchy description of a bride as 'Fautily fautless [sic], icy regular, splendidly null'.[49]
- Then we have an on-the-button description of a teacher as: 'out-at-the-elbows pedagogue'.[50]

There can be little doubt that Ethel had access to and used Roget's Thesaurus as not all the superlatives that Ethel used are the first meaning of a concept.

The use of a foreign language is a much-practised tool for establishing tone, style and location, and when used within English prose the foreign language is normally accompanied by a translation. With Ethel this was not the case. The foreign language text is there and if the reader cannot understand it then perhaps it is not that important to the flow of the narrative and is just there to provide tone given the suspected socio-economic profile of the Ethel reader, and for herself a bit of self-respect in the demonstration of her knowledge, and in the process a demonstration of pretentiousness. In *The Rocks of Valpré* the beach is always the plage, and who would understand ennui. We have 'Preux chavalier', 'mais c'est tres drôle, cela', 'Après cela, – I lay, depuis longtemps', 'il faut que les anglais soinet toujours, toujours les premiers', 'mignonne', 'canaille', 'scélérat', 'chouse', 'perçante'. In *Storm Drift* we have, 'These things are always unequal. Il y a toujours l'un qui baise, et l'autre qui tend le joue … You are a horrid old cynic, Tom.' In *The Knave of Diamonds*, we have: 'manque de mieux…' Being given their marching orders in *The Keeper of the Door* is referred to as 'Congé.' Canaille (scoundrel) is used again in *Charles Rex*, but is developed in *The Juice of the Pomegranate* with 'mais quelle espece de Canaille'. It must be doubted that any of her reader universe would understand this, or even 'coûte qui coûte' should read coûte que coûte … no matter the cost. Was this a typesetting error? But, so what, the reader would not understand it anyway as with most of the use of non-English text, it was just an environment pointer. It is of course regrettable that all Ethel's works were also subject to careless editing and typesetting errors. No doubt caused by the need to publish as quickly as possible.

French is the dominant inserted language but there are instances of 'hein', demonstrating a knowledge of conversational German, or very colloquial French. *The Serpent in the Garden*, which is set in the south of France, has a principal villain who is Italian. The narrative is littered with French, but Ethel injects the Italian's dialogue with Italian exclamations and then mistakenly also in Spanish; 'bueno' is used as is 'quien sabe'. A demonstration of her lack of travel outside of Britain perhaps that the reader would not latch onto. Kipling also used the device of non-English words in italics to create environment and mood, as did Ethel.

Once stylistic prejudices caused by the excesses and superlatives have been overcome one cannot ignore Ethel's ability to paint her non-stereotyped characters with great finesse and a bare minimum of words to create an understanding of the character. The context of the following is a portrait not of the horse but of the rider: 'Edward Weston arrived unexpectedly on a piebald horse – a trampling, uncertain monster that bore him with ease yet chafed like a charger impatient to be gone'.[51] The villain smoking a 'thin' cigar is a portrait of a dangerous and mean man 'dragging his carpet slippers along the floor' with no description other than that but she has described a decrepit old man servant.[52] Nothing else need have been or was said; we know exactly what she meant, and we can almost smell him. 'Emily, a boneless shadow of a woman who moved with stealth and whose uncertain eyes had a strained look as though they perpetually peered round corners'.[53] This woman is clearly untrustworthy. '... very slim, oddly graceful, dressed with an almost Puritanical severity in dark blue with a plain black hat which looked as if it had been designed to carry a badge'. The hat that needs a badge is the small touch that sets this young woman's character in the minds of the reader. She could have perhaps been in the Salvation Army.

Aside from language there was a surprising expectation of Ethel's readers that they, like her, were moderately well read. Very early on in *The Lamp in the Desert* we have 'the fruit of the lotus which assuredly she was eating day by day'.[54] In Greek mythology, lotus eaters were a people represented by Homer as living in a state of dreamy forgetfulness and idleness as a result of eating the fruit of the lotus plant, a people who spend their time indulging in pleasure and luxury rather than dealing with practical concerns. This reach into academia is then ruined by the following incomprehensible sentence, '... the unreality that was allegorically real, she felt it all as a vague accompaniment to the heartache that never left her – the scornful mockery of the goddess that she had refused to worship'.[55]

Ethel's understanding of the human condition though sees many gentle and elegant touches of brilliance. There is a wonderful analogy in *Lamp in the Desert* of a bird calling but receiving no reply, 'a fine example of perseverance'.[56] The major in *A Debt of Honour* (1909), a man who says nothing but has his own views and lets others make the mistakes, states, ' Unprofitable questions ... like ill-timed jests, are better left alone'.[57] And in the same title Ethel no doubt reflecting on her own situation: 'sleep! The very thought of it was horrible to him. It had never struck him before as a criminal waste of the precious hours of life, for Phil was young, and he had not done with mortal existence'.[58] In *Storm Drift* there is a wonderfully evocative description of holding hands: 'A few groups of men sauntering home from the public-houses, but otherwise the street was deserted. The river bridge loomed before them. They sat in silence in the dark taxi, holding hands'.[59] What is so surprising about this simple passage is that it is so simple, so short on superlatives, and most significantly so un-Ethel, except that she is demonstrating being out of touch with reality and the improbability of male pub drinkers holding hands.

Like many authors Ethel borrowed from other works but stayed well clear of potential allegations of plagiarism. In *The Swindler's Handicap* (1910) by misquoting or not even quoting she misses an allegorical comparison with: 'the man who took his hump wherever he went. No, he took his burden'.[60] In Bunyan's *Pilgrim's Progress* the pilgrim has a burden but in Victor Hugo's *The Hunchback of Notre Dame* the hunchback has a hump. Yes, Ethel was nervous of litigation, but was this an example of her nervousness if she made a direct comparison or a quote? One sees Ethel's caution in her request to have permission to use one verse of a Kipling poem. '*Oh Charity, all patiently ...*'

Or more likely it is a combination of the Victor Hugo thought and a heavy leaning on the Bible. 'I dreamed, and behold, I saw a man clothed with rags, standing in a certain place, with his face from his own house, a book in his hand, and a great burden upon his back. (Isa. 64:6; Luke 14:33; Ps. 38:4; Hab. 2:2; Acts 16:30,31)'.

Graham Greene's comment that most writers get to a point where they realise that there is something that they *cannot* do did not apply to Ethel. She did not have this limitation in confidence. Greene, like Evelyn Waugh, wrote to be read with pleasure; like Waugh, he was in earnest about his craft. Greene thought that self-doubt, or at least awareness of one's incapabilities, was the mark of a good novelist.[61] Ethel wrote to give pleasure and she cared about her readers, but there were no limits to what her contemporaries saw as her facileness.

In 1975 the Catholic theological magazine *The Furrow* took exception to the film *The Abdication* concerning a wayward cardinal, stating that the film should be re-titled *Ethel M. Dell Goes to Rome*. Not Mills and Boon or Cartland, but Ethel. There was clearly at that time certainly within the Roman Catholic curia a residual memory of the imagined passion that Ethel created even some thirty-six years after her death.[62]

Leavis examined the secret of commercial success and commented:

There is something else to the great names of popular fiction – Marie Corelli, Florence Barclay, Ethel M. Dell Gene Stratton Porter, Hall Caine – than sympathetic characters, a stirring tale and absence of the disquieting. Even the most critical reader who brings only an ironical appreciation to their work cannot avoid noticing a certain power, the secret of their success with the majority. Bad writing, false sentiment, sheer silliness, and a preposterous narrative are all carried along by the magnificent

vitality of the author, as they are in *Jane Eyre* (1847). Charlotte
Bronte one cannot help but feel after comparing her early work
with modern bestsellers, was only unlike them and fortunate in
her circumstances, which gave her a cultured background, and in
her age in which she lived ...[63]

Victoria Stewart in 2011 quoted Michael Joseph's question as to whether it
is possible 'to teach oneself or to be taught how to produce a successful novel
on [Ethel M. Dell] lines, but he expressed the view that this seems doubtful.
... A curious, albeit, a very valuable instinct seems to be responsible for action
of this character'.[64] As we saw earlier Leavis echoes this view.

I return to the theme of aesthetic versus commercial success later but
Leavis suggests in her *Fiction and the Reading Public* (1939) that works should
be judged on their own merits and successes that as such critics should not try
and categorise themes and subject matter.

If based on theme or subject matter it leads to the fallacious
conclusion that Wells is a greater or better novelist than Henry
James or Jane Austin because he is apparently concerned with
every side of human activity and they with nothing but what
Henry James himself describes as "human passion"; or if on
plot that *Wuthering Heights* (1848) and *Clarissa* (1890) are as
preposterous as the novels of Ethel M. Dell, and so on.[65]

Of course, there was literary nonsense but Ethel's readers saw what they
wanted to see in her work, somewhat Rorschach-like, and an understanding
was perhaps not that important.[66] The essence of the story captivated and
washed over them. In *The Altar of Honour* the frontispiece states 'Forti et fideli

nil difficile'. This is incorrect Latin. It should read nihil not nil, but to the reader it sounds right. As I have surmised earlier this use of the Irish O'Keeffe clan motto was probably a sop to her new sister-in-law. The Irish were a feature of many of Ethel's works.

Like all writers there were good narratives and less good ones. *Tetherstones* is almost incomprehensible and disjointed with the initial hero just disappearing from the text with no explanation. But then a high was achieved latterly in *The Black Knight,* after a gem of character setting comment, 'I hate women who trail their hearts about like pet dogs on the end of a string ...'[67] Hidden within the superlatives and linguistic excesses is a deeply sensitive tale of human frailty, kindness and determination. A young woman with an independent streak leaves home and ends up in the south of France gambling and becoming addicted to cocaine, and is then in effect sex-trafficked to a man hiding behind his war heroics. He tracks her down back in England and tries to force himself on her again and threatens marriage. A local man who is cloyingly helpful and caring 'she felt as if she almost hated him for his gentleness and his mild efficiency in dealing with her' marries her as a prize for beating up the sex trafficker.[68] It transpires that all along he has known of her difficulties and planned to marry her and this is the reason for his caring un-challenging nature. The interplay between her rejection of and his determination to care is very sensitively written.

At the other end of the narrative content spectrum we see a more balanced and mature writer in *The Prison Wall* (1932), a narrative which is somewhat believable, a good tale. Her output has slowed and her writing seems less frenetic. There are no philosophical asides, no leaning on religion, no sexual aberrations and little violence; just a not very complicated but good story, well told. Also, the descriptions of life in Australia are not too unrealistic for the period.

An extrapolation of the qualitative nature of this work is an analysis of the key words that Ethel used throughout her writing career. This analysis shown in Chapter 27 is by definition highly subjective but it does indicate where Ethel's various creative foci lay, and how they varied over her career. By definition because of the multiplicity of foci some of the less dominant qualitative indicators have been left out of this analysis. This is not a quantitative analysis but a subjective qualitative indicator of focus compiled by this author through a forensic reading of all Ethel's narratives.

After a reading of all Ethel's works one is left with a different impression as to the weights that she put on her creativity than this analysis demonstrates. A lack of health, the empire, feminism, abuse, strong men and dysfunctional marriages dominate the foci. These foci were of course routes to a happy heterosexual ending in most cases.

In summary the major foci were as follows, as a percentage of all titles:

Ill health:	39%
Relating to the British Empire	36%
Strong women	34%
Cruelty and violence	33%
Strong men	31%
Death, stillbirth/miscarriage	29%
Dysfunctional marriage	27%

11 An Understanding
of Ethel's Writing

'… the fact that they are not "good literature" does not prevent them from being "good thrillers", "good ghost stories", "good nonsense" …'[1]

There is no evidence to suggest that there was any strategic creative planning of content to her stories, but the formula varied very little. Short and novelette stories are less extreme in terms of sexuality and violence than full-length novels, and in the main there is a polarity of morbid extreme starts and love finishes. There is also of course no attempt to compare Ethel with Joseph Conrad but Kate Symondson writing in 2017 referred to Conrad's style as 'the incomprehensible alliance of irreconcilable antagonisms'.[2] Symondson's comments do seem very apt in relation to Ethel's writing style.

Watt was instrumental in creating demand but the creative content was entirely Ethel's choice, with stories sold in advance of a title or even a synopsis. The key influences on her creative style, which could produce a heady cocktail of creativity, would seem to have been her own dysfunctional and financially demanding family; perhaps an abusive father (Ethel portrays a frighteningly abusive and violent father in *The Live Bait* (1927)). A family that comprised as well a very tall, loud, dominant, single and flamboyant sister whom she also supported financially who adopts a child [Penelope], a dissolute brother with an alcoholic wife and children who were suspected of being maltreated whom she supported financially, religious polarity between the Catholic Church and the Anglican Church within her family, her own apparently ambivalent sexuality, a marriage late in life that, if one links her writing to her personal life, one can draw the conclusion that it was perhaps not consummated, a manipulative sister-in-law who seems to have engineered Ethel's marriage, her own and her sister's illness, personal knowledge of drug use, her own insecurities and notions of masculinity and empire. Ethel only left the British Isles once to visit Switzerland and did not repeat the exercise. The literary formula was so successful both in the UK and the United States that although appearing to self-denigrate it seems clear that Ethel took trouble to market her works to the lower socio-economic parts of society, and as such was marketing what at first sight seems to be a lack of self-esteem. Passmore writing in 1957 stated:

> Thus, my saying of *The Decline and Fall* that it is not literature may be interpreted as a condemnation of that work, which is far from my intent. The works of Ethel M. Dell are literature; the works of Gibbon are not. Accurately to distinguish between literature and other 'works in words' may be difficult ... but it is sufficiently clear that we draw attention, in criticizing Miss Dell, to the absence in her work of properties we find in Shakespeare, not to the absence of the properties we detect in Newton, in Hume or in Gibbon.[3]

It is in this context that we can look at Ethel's constructions.

Given the nature of Ethel's narratives it is difficult to categorise them but there appear to be three phrases in her writing both as she matured, suffered family issues, a marriage and her illness that led to her early death. These I have been arbitrarily called Naiveté, Maturity and Introspection. The other significant issue is therefore can a pattern be discerned to her novel constructions? The narratives are dominated by discourse between the characters who, in the main, lay out the plots within this discourse. Each title is divided into multiple chapters, and in one instance the device of a prologue is used. Each chapter tends to have an explanatory paragraph to scene-set at the beginning. In *The Woman of his Dream* Ethel experimented with a prologue, but the device adds little to the narrative, and it is in effect just another chapter, and was not mused again.

Perhaps the most distinguishing feature of Ethel's style of writing is her multiple, and to some purists, excessive use of superlatives and non-sequiturs as a result of wishing to use lifted third-party or biblical text, or meaningless words that, well, sounded right. There are parallel literary planes in all of Ethel's works; the sexually antagonistic relationships and her knowledge of the Bible and other literary works. The former literally and figuratively steams ahead while Ethel dips into the other with great frequency to find suitable literary conjunctions and scene benchmarks, if the reader understands them as such. The narratives are often extended by this narrational tool, a verbal puffery and literary extender.

Allegory is a frequently used tool, for example, in *Bars of Iron* a dog is choking on his own chain and she cleverly uses this as an allegorical simile to the situation in which one of her characters finds himself. He has killed the first husband of the woman he wants to marry and is burdened with guilt.

Her very earliest works, among them *Sea Urchin and the Prince,* have an almost schoolgirl and irritating naiveté, and then as her writing career progresses we move away from the totally unbelievable into the perhaps possible and see sexual deviance, implicit same-sex relationships, perhaps even homosexual paedophilia, and gratuitous violence. Joseph's contention that,

It is very simple. The novel that sells on the scale of Ethel M. Dell just represents the ordinary human being's idea of a happy dream duly realised. It never does happen in real life; that's why the largest numbers of readers turn to the story that supplies their need.[4]

This is of course true for all readers of fiction but perhaps Ethel was fulfilling a greater need for deviance in a fancy dust jacket. Even putting oneself into the 'between war years' it is still very hard to imagine the credibility of talking about a defrocked doctor in Australia, who is not colonial born as he is not 'rough' and a very ugly aboriginal boy (referred to as a negro) called Beelzebub (one of the fallen angels in Milton's *Paradise Lost*). Ethel's narratives were so powerful that they were able to carry the new concept of an ugly hero. A wrinkled yellow skin and a face like an Egyptian Mummy, but ugly Nick Ratcliffe in *The Way of an Eagle* fulfilled reader's dreams of a kind, decisive and strong man at a time when men were in short supply and emancipation was starting to bite.

The Way of an Eagle displays literary skill in that Ethel leaves a trail of snippets that has the reader wondering and eager to progress with the story, but she never tells the whole story but lets the reader's imagination wander. Clever writing is again demonstrated with: 'You will be false to yourself, false to Grange, false to me, rather than lower that miserable little rag of pride ...'[5] This literary high ground is then somewhat destroyed by the tortuous logic of the hero losing his arm because he stayed behind to avoid going (Ethel says coming) to England to see the heroine. This dialogue is set in India but is therefore related from an English perspective. T. Fisher Unwin surprisingly did not edit out the use of the phrase 'tu quoque'. (Tu quoque means an attempt to defend oneself or another from criticism by turning the critique back against the accuser. This is a classic red herring since whether the accuser is guilty of the same, or a similar wrong is irrelevant to the truth of the original charge.) This could have meant nothing to the average reader.[6]

Sexual symbolism is rampant in *The Way of an Eagle* where the troubled heroine dreams of the man of whom she is afraid as an eagle who will carry her off to a paradise despite her independent use of opium and his eventual administration of the drug to her. At the end of this title it seems that Ethel tried to instil some greater depth to her characters with the last line from Kipling's poem *The First Chantry* (1896), 'Prophet and priestesses we came ...' which is revealed as a quote, but, surprisingly not attributed.[7]

To the thoughtful reader it would seem that religious symbolism is employed in *The Knave of Diamonds*, to a laughable extent: 'In that hour Anne Carfax went down into the Place of Desolation which some call hell and some the bitter place of sorrow ...'[8] Maybe, but it is very removed from the reality of the conflict that surrounds her, and would seem to have been a concept lifted from the Bible (Mathew 24:15–16). Upset, concerned and unhappy becomes a lift from the Bible.

The Rocks of Valpré has its share of literary 'tosh': this work opens with a seventeen-year-old girl with a curvaceous body fascinated by a magic cave on the beach. If this is humour, it almost belittles the reader. It is hard to reconcile the serious side of the narrative with this apparent literary naiveté, but then the story is about naiveté and its perils.

Ethel had never experienced India nor monsoon conditions yet in *The Safety Curtain* she writes with great authority:

The rains set in in earnest, and the reek of the Plains rose like an evil miasma to the turbid heavens. The atmosphere was as the interior of a steaming cauldron. Great toadstools spread like a loathsome disease over the compound. Fever was rife in the camp. Mosquitoes buzzed incessantly everywhere, and rats began to take refuge in the bungalow. Puck Merryon left the mess early, tramping back over the dusty road, convinced that the downpour for which they all yearned was at hand. There was no moonlight that night, only a hot blackness, illumined now and then by a brilliant dart of lightning that shocked the senses and left behind a void indescribable, a darkness that could be felt. [This is a very accurate and clever description of the start of the monsoon season. Graham Greene researched the locales for his novels in depth and he wrote from first hand of the environment and the people, but Ethel never left home ...] There was something savage in the atmosphere, something primitive and passionate that seemed to force itself upon him even against his will. His pulses were strung to a tropical intensity [an overkill that ruins the veracity of the situation] that made him aware of the man's blood in him, racing at fever heat through veins that felt swollen to bursting. He entered his bungalow and flung off his clothes, took a plunge in a bath of tepid water, from which he emerged with a pricking sensation all over him that made the lightest touch a torture, and finally, keyed up to a pitch of sensitiveness that excited his own contempt, he pulled on some pyjamas and went out to his *charpoy* on the veranda.[9]

This is a very accurate description of prickly heat, the bane of tropical living, yet she had never suffered it. What was her source of information? Was there dialogue with Kipling other than to ask permission to publish part of a poem? Most probably.

In *The Keeper of the Door* (1915), the work is divided into two parts. In the first part it is significant that there is no romance but an underlying narrative about drug addiction and the release that death provides for sufferers, and in the second there is of course the romantic novel's requirement of a happy ending. But the very black and disturbing narrative about drug use and death is clearly linked to Vincent Dell's death in 1913 when this work would have been started. The book's dedication is 'to the dear memory of one who waits beyond the door for those he loves'. If this was in fact a dedication to Ethel's father it is surprising, unless there is hidden malice in the concept of waiting for those he loves. It is not loved but loves, as if he is dead then he cannot love anyone. Overall, the work can be viewed as a thesis on some disturbing insights into human frailties. Within the first seventy pages a whole host of characters appear without any anchor as to their identity, unless the reader has read *The Rocks of Valpré* (1914) where their relevance and connection is revealed. There is a significant presumption here that a reader of one will have read the other, but a series has been created.

In *The Electric Torch* we see creative misuse of language. The phrase down and out is used in the context of being depressed in the country and cannot be considered correct. The country does not get one down and out, but it can get one down. This phrase means without money, employment, or a place to live. So Ethel, removed from colloquial dialogue, has heard and not understood the phrase, and then misused it.

Implication and suspense are much in evidence throughout her writing. In *Storm Drift* one can guess that there is a transfusion and that a baby has been lost but we are not told. And in *The Place of Honour* the issue that upsets the heroine is never revealed. Ethel is not shy of the double entendre and in *Debt of Honour* much use is made of the Christian name of the heroine, Hope.

Ethel's Perspective

I escaped into my own fictional world as much as I could get away with without seeming to be either rude or unfair to my husband. Luckily Gerald did have his own interests, so different from mine. Playing with his model boats and trains seems so distant from my fictional world. Once there was an idea I just wrote without faltering. I very rarely had to go back on my manuscripts and change things. Ideas and words just flowed. Deep down I always felt that life was too short and that I had to make the most of my 'awake' time. Although necessary sleep seemed such a waste when I could be writing. One hears words in conversations that one could use and I never felt that I had the luxury of time to check so I very often just phoneticised words.

The cliché of the handsome honest man and the beautiful dedicated woman seemed to me to be so shallow. Love and relationships are not like that generally. Life just is not like that. Just in my family, I saw and experienced abuse, dominance, greed, moral impropriety, drug use and alcoholism for example. I just loved the drama of every page that I wrote, and then had to suffer the Americans changing my work. But being honest I could not have made those changes to Americanisms myself, and if it helped the title to sell then all the better. I did not have an amanuensis and I very rarely went back over my work to check on syntax or spelling, so it was up to Watt to deal with any issues. I firmly believe that my easy-to-read mixture of 'real' and sometimes aspirational characters, drama and full-blooded adventure gave the me loyal reader following that I had. This was a difficult time for Britain and I provided an escape from the real world. My readers were buying an escape from me and I respected their loyalty.

While I wrote Ella volunteered as a VAD nurse during the Great War looking after injured officers, but this was not something that was ever discussed. If Ella had spoken about her experiences I am sure that I would never have made light of the fighting. I really did not understand the horrors of the conflict in France.

I have never travelled to India, Africa or Australia but reading Kipling, Diver, Flora Annie Steel, Croker, Alice Perrin and seeing the pictures in the newspapers and the *Illustrated London News* provided me with so much story character and environment. It was also very helpful being able to talk to my friend Alfred Mason.

My writing was from my imagination fuelled by my circumstances. I had my ideas but reading other writers and of course the Bible were a help in putting some 'flesh on the bones' of my texts. One of the ironies of my stories is that some of my earliest girlish stories leapfrogged my more mature ones as my agent saw fit to sell anything that I wrote once I had gained a following.

I write for enjoyment not just for myself but my readers, and of course my writing reflects my life and experiences, and my imagination. My writing was certainly that of a schoolgirl in the beginning, and at the end of my career especially when I knew that I was dying I can perhaps be allowed some introspection. The middle part of my career was really the most enjoyable where I felt able to escape from my family and have a freedom to just let my writing flow, even if there was a plethora of superlatives.

12 Ethel and The New Woman

'I've got to have room to grow, freedom of action and thought. Girls of my age – heaps of them – are out in the world, making their own living …'[1]

In Britain at this time 'the New Woman' was a very controversial idea because it challenged the social norms of the time and was perhaps, by and large, a cultural concept, but it fed into a groundswell of greater awareness of the need for female emancipation across all forms of the socio-political environment. This concept challenged the established norms of male dominance and by definition the objectification of women. D.H. Lawrence (1885–1930) perhaps helped stoke the flames of this social dissent.

Politically there was the Matrimonial Causes Act of 1856 which made divorce easier, but still easier for men than women, the Married Women's Property Act 1882, and the general rise of women's suffrage movements (the Primose League, Women's Liberal associations, and pressure groups nationwide). *Punch*, the satirical magazine, contributed to this febrile atmosphere with pointed cartoons and articles: A woman offering to carry a Mr. Smithereen's suitcase, a woman dressed in male clothing wearing a trilby hat riding a bicycle next to a precipice, and many more. There was at this time a groundswell of rational indignation exploring the possibilities of greater social freedom for women that was also fed by the literary world. Ménie Muriel Dowie (1867–1945), an adventurous woman whose first work *A Girl in the Karpathians* (1891), covering her journey to the Carpathian mountains in Poland dressed as a man carrying a revolver, was a great success. On the back of this acclaim she published her most notable work *Gallia* in 1895. *Gallia* was remarkable for Dowie's focus on eugenics as a guide for human relationships. The novel also stood out for its general explicitness regarding issues of gender equality and heterosexual relations. Gallia, the heroine, is very attractive, healthy, university educated but never behaves in an easy-going, flirtatious manner. Within the narrative those around her seem shocked by the topics, such as politics and sex, that she chooses for conversation. Dowie wrote:

> How can we wonder that only one person in ten is handsome and well made, when you reflect that they were most likely haps [a happening] of hazard, that they were unintended, the offspring of people quite unfitted to have children at all? There are people fitted, for instance, to be mothers, which every woman isn't; there are women fitted to bring up children, who may not be mothers. Think of this: a man may love a woman and marry her; they may be devoted to each other, and long for a child to bring up and to love; but the woman may be too delicate to run the risk. What are they to do? What would be the reasonable thing to do? Sacrifice the poor woman for the sake of a weakly baby? No, of course not, but get in a mother![2]

This was extreme copy and at the most radical end of the spectrum for a woman writer of the period and received significant publicity. Dowie's work is very much in the realms of a philosophical study. H.G. Wells (1866–1946), himself a serial and very public philanderer, published *Ann Veronica* in 1909. In this work Wells espouses eugenics in relation to birth control, hardly surprising and not in the same vein as Nietzsche, but also the concept of the independent and strong woman. Well's own affairs were with strong women, one of whom was believed to be a Russian spy. The heroine tries to forge a life for herself without the help of men but is forced to borrow funds from a Mr. Ramage (Wells has a sense of humour amidst the seriousness of the topic) who in return demands sexual favours, and this is the start of her realisation of really how women stood in society.

> the meagre realities of such freedom as permitted her, the almost unavoidable obligation to some individual man under which she must labour for even a foothold in the world. She had flung away from her father's support with the finest assumption of personal independence. And here she was – in a mess because it had been impossible for her to avoid leaning upon another man.[3]

Ann Veronica joins the Women's Movement and is arrested during a prescient raid on Houses of Parliament. Women's sexual and relational needs are highlighted when Ann Veronica confronts her male target and she tells him, 'I want you. I am clear I want you. You are different from all the world for me. You can think all round me. You are the one person I can understand and feel – feel right with'.[4] This was a debate about both feminism and femininity, but the young Rebecca West writing a review of Wells' novel *Marriage* (1912) said, 'Of course he is the old maid among novelists; even the sex obsession that lay clotted on Ann Veronica and The New Machiavelli like cold white sauce was merely an old maid's mania'.[5] Having slated Wells' work she then had a long and very public relationship with him and by 1922 was complimenting Ethel on her success writing romantic 'tosh'. Ironically T. Fisher Unwin picked up this work by other publishers after it had been rejected, in the same way as Ethel's *The Way of an Eagle*.

There is a cross-over period between writing related to the 'New Woman' and romantic and sexual fiction over the period of the fin de siècle. Sarah Grand (1854–1943), a feminist also writing during this period, shocked the public with her openness about sexual issues, in particular venereal disease as it might affect the middle classes.[6] There is therefore a duality of a background of emancipation and the parallel one of sexual openness and then the public debate on the subjects. Ethel's first title in the UK, *The Repentant Rogue*, published in 1898 when she was eighteen years old can be seen as being, despite the naiveté of the narrative, as having been influenced if even in a minor way by the 'New Woman' groundswell. This story incorporates romance, sexual fantasy (the couple pointedly do not sleep together), female independence, weaknesses, without understanding she admires the culture and ready flow of his talk, and his strengths. But then the heroine shoots her suitor's accomplice.

With the suffragette movement effectively starting in 1897 and Millicent Fawcett's founding of the National Union of Women's Suffrage, Ethel keeps her options open with a foot in both socio-political camps. The heroine is a rich but not very bright socialite with an independent mind. She rides a bicycle, plays billiards, hunts, indulges in boating, plays tennis, is 'no ignoramus' of the manly exploits of her suitor, one can see a potential proto-feminist character developing but then she reads not very earnest material but, more importantly, she refuses to vote. Ethel was perspicacious in this as women were not enfranchised in Australia, the setting for the narrative, until 1911, seven years earlier than Britain. It is notable that neither Ethel nor Ella participated in the 1911 census, the boycott of which was promoted by the Women's Freedom League ... no vote – no census.[7] This is then all turned on its head in *The Rocks of Valpré*, '... unless she's a suffragette, in which case she may be safely relied on to make a howling donkey of herself for all time'.[8] Apart from donkeys not howling, Ethel in fifteen years has lost her proto-feminist edge which she had seemed to have been developing in her late teens.

Ethel's *The Black Knight* has a young woman coming to grief through her independence and waywardness: 'That kind of girl never marries before she's tired out everybody with any sense of decency...', but provides a handhold for modernity and stability with, "'Ermine – dear! Your pyjamas!" was all the remonstrance that she managed to utter. "What's wrong with them?" said Ermine. "I'm sure that they're highly respectable and don't flap in the breeze like your antediluvian nightdress."'[9]

The young women characters in the latter part of her career were clearly kicking the traces of female social confinement and lack of independence. In both *Peggy by Request* and *Honeyball Farm* the heroine proposes marriage. In *The Gate Marked Private* she states, 'I've got to grow up, whether you try to hold me back or not. I've got to have room to grow, freedom of action and thought. Girls of my age – heaps of them – are out in the world, making their own living ... I'm going out into it (the world) to make my own living like the rest'.[10] Flying appeared latterly in Ethel's narratives but she demonstrated the ultimate symbol in female emancipation in *The Juice of the Pomegranate* where the heroine states that, 'What I really want to do is take out a pilot's licence'.[11]

Her men tend not to be handsome, and in some cases very ugly, but all have an inner strength, and the bad men in the narratives never succeed. Romance always wins the day, as do her heroines. The latter are by and large as Leavis pointed out Bohemian boyish heroines who say 'damn and "hell" shocking the company, the authoress and presumably the reader'.[12] Perhaps, but that was the limit of the excessive language and content, and this lack of specificity in erotic language allowed for her acceptance whereas Glyn's *Three Weeks* (1907) is 'the novel that overstepped the mark'.[13] Glyn's *It* (1927) is referred to by D. Maurer as a third rate writer's work, however, it created an environment of greater freedom of sexual expression where in America, 'The English Language in America was hardly equipped to meet this revolution, considering that two of the most heavily taboo words in the middle class, about whom we are speaking in the main, were pregnant and menstruation'.[14]

Ethel's Perspective

It was a truism during my life that generally wives were legally and financially dependent on their husbands except in my case where Gerald and my brother lived off me. However, there were very strong political and social moves to create female autonomy. We saw this with the suffragettes and increasing publicity surrounding the 1911 census with many women including Norah Savage refusing to be counted. Sexual autonomy was socially unacceptable, even immoral during the earlier part of my career, but it was seen as increasingly part of the enfranchisement of women's rights especially after the death of Queen Victoria. Perhaps the most influential book affecting my change in heroine focus was Ménie Dowie's travelogue through the Carpathians. Goodness what an amazing woman, and I did not enjoy being out of England. The early women's enfranchisement in Australia in 1911 helped me of course. From the start of the First World War there was a severe shortage of men in the UK and my writing tried to fill that void. However, I also had to keep the independent-minded woman happy. So you will see in my writing that although the women very often have traits and activities independent of men at the end they comply to socially acceptable norms.

13 The Humour

'But the honour of mounting Lady Carfax was not for Ralph'[1]

Ethel's first published story *A Repentant Rogue* (1899) features a gold mining company improbably and satirically named the Great Poobah Gold Company. This is clearly not a nomenclature that is at all likely and has of course been lifted straight from Gilbert and Sullivan's *The Mikado* (1885). In this comic opera the Grand Poobah, holds numerous exalted offices, including: first lord of the treasury, lord chief justice, commander-in-chief, lord high admiral, archbishop of titipu, lord mayor and lord high everything else. The value of the colonial stocks that the repentant rogue of the story has left to his daughter is an amount so large that it falls into the realms of satirical fantasy.

In *The Knave of Diamonds*, 'the honour of mounting Lady Carfax was not for Ralph ...' is a pun as what is intended is the mounting of Lady Carfax's horse. In *The Way of an Eagle* there is a very clever and sophisticated reversal of the expected reaction to the man's self-perception of lack of worth and the concept of uniqueness. '"Can you imagine any girl falling in love with me?" he asked. "Of course I can. You are not so unique as that. There isn't a man in the universe ..."'[2]

In 1909 Kipling published *In Flood Time,* a story of an Englishman whose journey is impeded by a flooded river. The Indian warden of the ford narrates the story and warns that jungle near the river is very full of snakes, little karaits that sleep on the sand ... Ethel seems to have picked up this information and in *Lamp in the Desert* (1919) she refers to 'the dear little karaits'.[3] This is either humour, or her ignorance, as the karait (sic. Krait) is a highly venomous nocturnal snake.

Poking fun at the French with Gallicised English has been a regular fallback for popular writing. Ethel does not shirk from this in *The Rocks of Valpré* with the character Bertie using Gallicised English as a caricature of an un-worldly Englishman where his word order is as if it is a literal translation from the French, with errors in conjugation and missed auxiliary verbs. We see this again in 1915 in *Bars of Iron* with '*Ah mais Monsieur Pierre*, how you are wet!'[4]

Can one really take seriously a literary reference to a man of great wealth being called Plutarch? This is humour or extreme naiveté. In *The Passer-By*, we read of a man of great wealth and considerable importance called Plutarch. Early in the narrative of this title the hero sings the song 'Passing-By' (arranged by Henry Purcell), but the song which was popular at the end of the nineteenth and early twentieth century, is not identified by its title. It is a humorous twist of the reader's intellect to make the connection. Only later in the story does the hero mention that he is a 'passer-by'. In this same work we see a wonderful demonstration of bitchy humour: 'you ought to be proud of your only talent'.[5] In other titles we see the comment 'borrow a gas oven and take a trip to Hades,' and the wonderful nomenclature for a doctor known as Spot.

"'My dear Mrs. Randal, you'd find points to admire in a wax candle," grunted the Major. "She always makes me think of one; pale and pure and saintly – I can't stand the type …"' This clever and again somewhat bitchy analogy with a candle appears in *The Knave of Diamonds*.[6]

There is humour and perhaps a latent revulsion in *The Lamp in the Desert* when the bridegroom-to-be kisses the bride-to-be with a lingering persistence: 'It made her think of an epicurean tasting some favourite dish and smacking his lips over it'.[7] Sex and relationships despite the generally serious nature of the narratives come in for humorous asides: 'she had survived a dozen London seasons without any symptoms of heart-trouble'. In reference to marriage and talking to a doctor: "'My good man, what of your theory of inoculation. I was inoculated long ago – and am now immune." "Oh!" said Vaughn. "But it sometimes takes more than one dose." "Not such a dose as I had!" said Sir Rodney. "Why, man, I was engaged – actually engaged once.'"[8]

But as Spain commented 'there are still some sad snobs who think her work is "tripe".' but Ethel was aware of this hence her self-denigrating comments in *The Juice of the Pomegranate*. Ethel read the following review of one of her books by St. John Ervine:

> The rise to popularity, for instance, of Miss Ethel M. Dell coincided with the period of the war. Two million people read her works and saw nothing ridiculous in them, because they had become accustomed to see equally ridiculous stuff in the cinemas. In England to-day we had a generation which when the war began were 14 or 15 years of age. It is now adult, but spiritually and mentally it is still in the condition that it was before the war.[9]

Spain (who must have been staying with Ethel) reported that having read this Ethel came down to breakfast laughing heartedly with her own mocking poem.

~

'What a pity for St. John Ervine,' she said,
'that he finds it all so un-nerving
That stuff written by Dell
Should sell and should sell
When his is so much more deserving.'[10]

~

Ethel cannot have failed to read that Ervine was standing next to Emily Davidson at the Derby in June 1913, when she was fatally injured by the king's horse as she seemed to try and attach a suffragette banner to the horse's bridle. Some of the politics and drama of the period just drifted by her. It must have disheartened Ethel to read in *The Times* of 25 June 1925 that Ervine's negativity was supported, as follows:

The rise and popularity, for instance of Miss Ethel M. Dell coincided with the period of the war. Two million people read her works and saw nothing ridiculous in them, because they had been accustomed to see equally ridiculous stuff in the cinemas. In England today we are a generation which when the war began were 14 or 15 years of age. It is now adult, but spiritually and mentally it was still in the condition that it was before the war.

Ethel's humour was often à point. Describing a man as 'there was nothing ready-made about him' clearly positions the subject of the comment as from the upper classes, and in the same work we see the use of a joke, if the reader understands it, when Francesco Tosti's 'Goodbye' (1908) is played as a cheerful song on Christmas Day.[11] The sea captain in *Charles Rex* is tired of his ship owner's social life and seeks a 'deeper draught' at sea, a simple pun.

There is an irony in that Wodehouse, who had a dig at Ethel, is himself satired in *The Good Turn* (1927). The hero of the story is a Wooster-like mimicked character, Shandy, who has money but little grounding in the realities of life, and is dominated by an aunt, as was Wodehouse's Wooster. Shandy sees his aunt in a shoe shop surrounded by a pile of shoes. '"Are you buying that lot, eh? Where in wonder are you going to put them all?" "As a matter of fact," said Aunt Olivia, returning to her grievance, "I'm not buying a single one." "But you don't buy them in singles, do you?" questioned Shandy'.[12] This short story is brimming with Ethel's humour. '"Why, that's exactly what I liked about you," he said. "You actually forgot to powder your nose before you came out. It's so rare nowadays to see a feminine nose in all its natural beauty, and yet, you know, it's heaps more appealing to the masculine sense than when it's all fogged over with paste and stuff.'"[13] Continuing the focus on noses, 'The customer sniffed. She had a thin arched nose that seemed specifically adapted for that kind of sniff'.[14] And then in *The Black Knight* there are biting comment on faces, 'And oh, my sister do shorten that beloved countenance by at least four inches before I see it again! The chin worn long does not become you. And it isn't fashionable either. Everything must be short and *chic* these days'.[15] Wodehouse, like Ethel's brother Reggie, was educated at Dulwich College. Did Ethel deliberately engage in a gentle literary war of humorous attrition? It is pleasing to think so.

With her work being lampooned by her peers it is ironical and extremely funny that she chooses one of her last works, *Honeyball Farm* to engage the reader in a grammatical lesson, '"what an extraordinary person! He'll have to completely rebuild it." "Must we split our infinitives?" remonstrated Sir Philip mildly .... "you must allow youth its split infinitives as well as it's jazzed oats. It isn't much to throw in. Pardon the intrusion of the preposition at the end of the sentence!"'[16]

In *The Serpent in the Garden* Ethel has a delightful play on words with: 'This little pig was rash ... that little pig was rasher ...I do not have much use for the rashers. They ought to know better'.[17] A humorous and candid revelation of her feelings is hidden in the same work:

'You think it funny do you?' said Voltano somberly. 'Would it seem funny to you if I were indeed ready to commit murder for your sake? Would you scream and run away you golden haired siren? Or would you laugh and revel in your power?' 'Not being Cleapatra or Boadicea or any other of those ancient harridans, I should probably do the first,' said Gabrielle, 'bar screaming. I don't like people who scream. It's so futile. But I'm not fond of murders, even in books. It's going too far.'[18]

Ethel's screenplays gave her entry to the world of stage directions. In *The Live Bait* (1928) some elderly bald men are being fleeced by a card sharp and are forced to leave the card room. As they leave the hero mutters to himself 'Exuent Romeos' (tongue in cheek for the handsome men now leave the stage.)

A play on words and perhaps a dig at her husband who seems to have contributed little to her life are the humorous dénouements to her writing. At the end of her life in her penultimate title she has a very unsubtle dig at the only man other than her brother with whom she has a relationship: 'Jim saw nothing of course, but then Jim's discernment – even for a man – was rather limited. It was rather foolish to attempt to interest him in the matter. He would never grasp anything but the obvious'.[19]

Ethel's Perspective

Inwardly I am really not a very happy person but every now and then I find myself having fun with my writing. Sometimes it is just silly fun as in *The Repentant Rogue* and the occasional double entendre in *The Knave of Diamonds*. But in *Lamp in the Desert* I deliberately identified the venomous krait snake as implicitly harmless as it meant more to the story to have it that way. I was really playing a joke with the reader … if only they knew how dangerous these snakes really are. Although it is a bit unfair I do play a joke on my reader in *The Unknown Quantity* where I have a family playing Tosti's 'Goodbye', which is really very sad and not a happy tune for Christmas Day. Would they see it as a joke? Perhaps not, as they probably would not know the piece. But, I enjoyed the humour of the social differences in the interface exacerbated by the wrong choice of music.

As a writer I of course have my critics, but none more so than St. John Ervine in the public press. As a novelist himself he no doubt was not too happy with my wide readership compared to his, so I was subjected to some very aggressive critiques from him. But at the end of the day he did me no harm and I enjoyed my parodies of him. Then of course I have had such fun with the French speaking English. So easy to create a smile that way.

P.G. Wodehouse used me as a humorous foil. I like to think that I did the same to him in *The Good Turn*. If I was a tennis player, which I'm sure Wodehouse was, it was certainly a 'love' game in 1927.

14 The Empire and Notions of Masculinity

'indomitable, unfailing, and always fulfilling his duties with machine-like regularity, stern, impenetrable, hard as granite'.[1]

'she {India} is a hard mistress'.[2]

'Like a throbbing undersong – the fiendish accompaniment to the devil's chorus – the gossip of the station as detailed by Tessa ran with glib mockery through her brain. Ah, they only suspected. But she knew – she knew!'[3]

Ethel wrote upon many themes but her work is particularly associated with ideas of empire. Her white interpretations of the contact zones in India, the United States, Australia and South Africa, and the related exotic ethnicities where there was white dominance was substance to the narrative. We see Australian bushmen and stock drivers, South African entrepreneurs, exotic American Indians and demonised Asian Indians.

The historian Edward John Thompson wrote in 1925 that, 'The tension existing in India has been bad for our race; and a conception of Indian life based on the writings of Ethel M. Dell or Maud Diver, or even Kipling has not helped'.[4] This was an undeserved compliment and in Ethel's defence, however, in her *The Way of an Eagle, Lamp in the Desert* and her *The Electric Torch* she only used India as a stage prop to the stories, but India and Indians are not engaged in the narrative in any meaningful way. The influence on Ethel' reader universe is unlikely to have been of significance to Thompson's tensions.

In novels such as *The Way of an Eagle, Lamp in the Desert* and *The Electric Torch*, Ethel uses India as an exotic veneer. Life in the empire of her stories is not an aspiration but a largely exotic and unpleasant experience and this unpleasantness was an important part of her orientalist narrative. These narratives are stories in India but not of India.

The *Lamp in the Desert* paints a socially correct environment for a single British woman in an army barracks town of this time in India, 'she was an interloper, and as such they united to treat [the implication in the narrative is mistreat] her' but of Indians there are but four characters and one a deformed Kashmiri beggar turns out to be British.[5] The others are a large turbaned Sikh improbably called Peter who behaves like 'a faithful watch-dog' and has 'dog-like fidelity', a 'furtive and avaricious' stall holder who turns out to be a police spy and his assistant who has an 'insincere and obsequious manner'. Even a Khansama (butler) does not escape this pervasive pejoration as he is again an 'obsequious' Indian. A nameless group of coolies 'huddled in the open space before her, like an assembly of monkeys holding a discussion' completes the canvass. India is an environment that strains the fibres of Britishness and one has to 'stick to it like a Briton'. 'India again! India the ruthless! India the bloodthirsty! India the vampire!'[6]

Ethel also used the pejorative 'dog-like fidelity' in *The Unknown Quantity* in a totally different context.[7] In *The Electric Torch* there is a mad Hindu wallah who on the same page is then described as a mad Pathan. Pathans are of course Muslim.

Ethel had access to Kipling's works, but the India of her stories is the product of her own ill-informed representations. In the main there is a correct use of Hindi terminology, but her readers were not to know that 'atcha' should be accha and that 'shikaree' is a sportsman whereas shikari is a shooting boat. There is here a degree of phonetic misunderstanding, indicating that Ethel had engaged in albeit limited discussion with someone who possessed Indian knowledge. *The Way of an Eagle*, her first major work, demonstrated her adherence to Kipling with her use of the term *Bandar-log*, Kipling's monkey people from *The Jungle Book* (1894), as a description for the European hero who is in need of a wash. The illustrations in *The Way of an Eagle* with the exception of two could be related to an aspirational, well-heeled country house environment in England. They were neither portraying the plains nor a hill station.

Ethel never travelled to India so she was under the influence of what she read or heard: from Kipling with whom she shared an accountant, Steel, Diver, Perrin and almost certainly Croker. Her vision of and ideals related to notions of empire were developed from these third-party authors, the general press and without doubt the *Illustrated London News*. Alan Greenberger's somewhat arbitrary division of his eighty years of imperialism into eras: 'Confidence' 1880–1910, 'Doubt' 1910–1935 and 'Melancholy' 1935–1960 provides a basis for contextualising Ethel's works.[8] Her Indian stories were, however, published in his 'Doubt' years (*The Way of an Eagle*, 1912; *Lamp in the Desert*, 1919; *The Electric Torch*, 1924). Although he does state that Ethel's works, which were reflected together with Steel and Croker, sat in his Confidence era he has allowed for some time slippage given Ethel's output after the close of this era.[9] A review of Edmund Candler's novel *Abdication* (1922 in the *Irish Quarterly Review*), during Greenberger's 'doubt' years makes the point that Candler's novel, which in reality is a story of Anglo-Indian politics, is the India of non-cooperation, an India seething with discontent caused by the action of men like General Dyer and the 1919 Amritsar Massacre, a realistic picture. As the hero Riley says, 'It must be beastly being run by foreigners.' This is not the India of Mrs. Croker, or of Miss Ethel M. Dell.[10]

In Croker's *Diana Barrington* the description of her husband as an ideal is not dissimilar to Ethel's male character profiles and also those as portrayed by Hull and Elinor Glyn:

> I should hate a man who took an hour over his tie, lolled on a
> sofa reading poetry, or sat hand in hand with me looking at the
> moon, and criticized my dress like a milliner. I like to know that

my husband is a man, and not an old woman. He shoots tigers, plays polo, and rides races, with my full approval.[11]

As Allen Greenberger has pointed out in his study of the typical British image of India in this period, 'its sheer pluck that counts, nothing else – the pluck to hang on and worry, worry, worry, till you get your heart's desire'.[12] In *The Way of an Eagle* Ethel concurs with this 'above all else, it was thought that the Englishman in India should not be a shirker'.[13] The ideal English hero of this period 'works like an ox' and is 'indomitable, unfailing, and always fulfilling his duties with machine-like regularity, stern, impenetrable, hard as granite'.[14] As Greenberger caustically adds, 'to a large extent he is only an overgrown public schoolboy'.[15]

Ethel's primeval male ideals appear in *The Hundredth Chance*. 'He looked her hard and straight in the face, and she was conscious of something fiery, something elementary, wholly uncivilised, behind his look. There was a suggestion of violence in him. She saw him as a man tracking his enemy through an endless wilderness, breasting mighty rivers, hewing his was through pathless forests, conquering every obstacle with fixed determination, mercilessly riding him down.' The importance of Britishness was emphasised in *A Question of Trust* with 'He was a man of fierce independence and passionate temperament, possessing withal a dogged tenacity that she always ascribed to the fact that he was borne of an English mother'.[16] Again this is emphasised in *Bars of Iron* where the hero has an Italian grandmother which accounts for, by implication, his not very British passion and mood swings. It is very hard especially today not to mutter 'tosh' when reading parts of *Bars of Iron* and *The Keeper of the Door*: '... held himself with the superb British assurance that has its root in the British public school and which, once planted, in certain soils is wholly ineradicable', and, seeing a man walk up a path '... I liked the business-like way you tackled it. It was British';[17] 'He swung along it, erect and British, caring nothing for dust and cold';[18] '... with the sublime audacity of the dominant race ...'[19]

A.E.W. Mason, the novelist whose works also formed part of the Stoll Picture Productions Eminent Authors series, was a further influence on Ethel's Indian adventures. Mason also had not lived abroad in the empire about which he wrote but he had travelled widely. His *The Four Feathers* (1902) – a story of apparent cowardice, heroism, duty and true Britishness – provided the gut and sinew for her men. In the novels of this genre it is the imagined imperial adventure that to some extent self-perpetuates itself. Ethel had presented Mason with a signed copy of her title *The Gate Marked Private* (1928). As critic Rosemary M. George explains: 'The "preview" that the book provided thus becomes identical to the reality inhabited and represented by writers. For the author to have visited India did not necessarily add or subtract from the quality or success of the novels she wrote – hence the phenomenal success of writers like Ethel M. Dell ...'[20] Splatter the text with her own Indianness and a story in India but not of India emerges.

It seems unlikely that Ethel had access to Hobson-Jobson (the Anglo-Indian dictionary), as a check on her uses of Hindi terminology would have revealed errors in these stories; she clearly had access to Kipling's works but the Indianness of the stories are her own ill-informed representation.[21] In the main there is a correct use of Hindi terminology, which shows an attention to detail. Particularly pleasing are her use of *Budmash* (bad people), and *Mem's*, (the colloquial use of memsahib)[22] and *Khit.* (the colloquial use of Kitmutgar) shows a depth of research.[23,24] However her assertion that '.....though not strictly a Plains station, could not claim to be a really cool spot at that time of year' damages the credibility of the story.[25] Given that the implication here is that any plains stations were cool is geographical nonsense. They were not and of course this polarity with the hill stations was a fundamental part of the expatriate European life in India. But, the reader universe were not to know better. Chuddah (Chuddar) is used to describe a man's clothing but it is in fact female attire.[26]

The Way of an Eagle, her first major work, demonstrated her adherence to Kipling with her use of the Bandar-log, Kipling's monkey people from the Jungle Books as a description for the European hero who is in need of a wash. *Chota-bursat*, the early rains, is straight from Kipling and does not even feature in Hobson Jobson. We also see Kipling's influence in *The Safety Curtain* (1917) with her splattering of Hindi terms. The Indian focus of her stories was always emphasised by the use of italics for any word that helped paint an Indianness for which she had little knowledge and for which there was in reality not a lot of need. This use of italics was a device used by Kipling. The delightful illustrations in *The Way of an Eagle* with the exception of two could be related to an aspirational well-incomed country house environment in England.

Mason must be seen to have had an influence on Ethel's Indian writing adventures. Mason's *The Four Feathers* published in 1902 and a first film version appearing in 1915 with the hero unjustly wronged proving his worth in a story of apparent cowardice, heroism, duty and true Britishness was the gut and sinew of her men. Mason's *Sapphire* (1932) allowed that a drop of English blood brings out qualities of leadership, even in a girl.[27] Alan Greenberger comments that, 'The only Indians in *The Way of an Eagle* are an ayah and a butler, neither of whom appear more than a couple of times. This was highly unlikely in an urban setting. The rural India that the British writers describe is an almost Indianless India' supports the view that Ethel did not write about India'.[28] Mason had also not lived in the empire about which he wrote. It is this creativity of the imagined imperial travelogue in the novel that to some extent self-perpetuated itself and thus the 'preview that the book provided thus becomes identical to the reality inhabited and represented by writers'.[29] The exception to this was of course Kipling. It is important to consider Kipling not in the twenty-first century understanding of him as an anti-Semite, misogynist, or of perhaps of ambivalent sexuality and a racist, but in the context of a shallow un-nuanced appreciation of his writing about India. Ethel's empire was mainly India but there was a foray into an exoticised Australia in *The Repentant Rogue*. As a generality her Indian canvases were well researched and portrayed. Historically her reference to (John) Nicholson, the hero of the retaking of Delhi during the Indian Mutiny of 1857, is apt and correct. Flying foxes, stripped squirrels, rhododendron and kutcha grass are correct for the environment, and in *The Lamp in the Desert* there are very accurate descriptions of the monsoon on the plains then the whole piece is destroyed by referring to the plains as the jungle! It is hot and humid and yet a rug is put around a frightened girl. A very perceptive analysis of the turmoil in India at that time is provided with: 'In the dark depths of that native stall she pictured him, a watcher, furtive and avaricious, a man who lent himself and his shrewd covetous brain to a government he probably despised as alien ... He was a serpent in the dark, an evil dream'.[30] in *The Keeper of the Door* we have '... long, narrow bazaar with its dim booths and crafty peering faces'.[31]

The whole edifice of 'empire' is, however, destroyed by the comment in *Rosa Mundi* that 'They lay down in the dread shadow of a mighty empire and slept secure in the very jaws of danger'.[32] Surely the danger is the 'dread' not the 'shadow of the empire' which is the comfort.

Ethel's Perspective

I of course have never been to India, Australia, Canada nor South Africa, but these places were the forefront of our empire of which I was very proud. We controlled the world as far as I was concerned. My empire was a product of my reading. Women writers of whom I could not get enough of were Steel with her magnificent *On The Face of the Waters*, Diver, Perrin and of course Croker. I knew so few men and the men I knew were not of a kind to be put on a pedestal, nor were they aspirational to lonely women, so Croker's writing gave me great inspiration. Kipling's descriptions of life in India, and I will freely admit that I borrowed some of his terminology, were also fundamental to my ability to describe life in India as I saw it. We were in the colonies to civilise the natives. I wrote about India but I have never even met an Indian person. But with such a huge country managed by so few of us there must have been serious undercurrents of dissatisfaction. Of course, the Amritsar Massacre in 1919 was perhaps a turning point in our relationship with India, and I saw the potential for resistance to our rule emerging. I often wrote about the obsequious Indian, but I saw this as a cover for something much deeper. A cynical reverence for imposed authority that was disliked. I was extremely surprised that Kipling went to the Press to express his satisfaction that the army had done their duty. I met Kipling briefly through the auspices of Watt and of course there was my friend Alfred Mason. Through these discussions I heard many Indian terms and phrases which I used as often as I could. My stories are about relationships between men and women and women and women and it helped me to portray these stories within our empire and this in itself helped my imagination.

15. Violence, Sexuality and Male and Female Roles

'... it was rather a brutal thrashing. Perhaps some women wouldn't have minded it much'[1]

'... why don't you take what you want? I -I should respect you then'.[2]

'I am only a woman. I am afraid that your experience of women has not taught you to respect them'.[3]

The conclusion of a heterosexual relationship is the denouement in most of Ethel's narratives, and it is the subject of a significant amount of narrative comment. The year that Ethel eventually married, her *Death's Head* was published. In it the heroine states, 'Never get married Big Bear! ... It is the most miserable state in Christendom'.[4] In *The Electric Torch* (1924) there is discourse on an unconsummated marriage (Ethel married in 1922), suggestions of single-sex relationships and significantly, a knowledge of drugs.

When one considers the objectification of women and male desires one is of course drawn to D.H. Lawrence. Ethel, however, alternately both fanned and doused the flames of this objectification. I am only a woman but respect me is a very mixed message, a polarity of subservience and female rights. In the evolution of her female character, we can see a drift from perhaps the adolescent ideals of emancipation to the commercial reality and opportunity of a more subservient role model and the complexity of her sexual musings. There is a polarity of views expressed from the extreme of subservient woman to dominant emancipation. In her first work *The Repentant Rogue* we see largely an independent woman and in the story she takes control and shoots the villain. In the *Lamp in the Desert* we see a suggestion of emancipation with a tolerance of male domination, where her surrender to his embrace was 'eloquent of mute endurance rather than glad surrender'.[5]

In *Her Compensation* we hear: 'but what of the woman whose life lies in just that one groove, who is set about with limitations and boundaries in every direction? It's not so easy then to break free, is it?'[6] A woman with no apparent understanding of love and affection is overwhelmed by the forcefulness of a man she did not understand before in *Where the Heart Is*. In *A Hundredth Chance* the man states 'I'm not disputing that most women need a burden of some sort',[7] and in *Storm Drift* the man still considered that feminine weakness had a call upon masculine strength: 'He did not find the modern woman very attractive ... the fetish of modern independence ...'[8] and '... even a dog has his rights' in *Bars of Iron*, is an extremely pejorative association.[9] And in the same work referring to a conversation between two men and the unlikelihood of that discussion being relayed further ... '"I'm not a woman!" said Tudor [a man] contemptuously. "That affair was between the two of us."'[10] There is a duality of submissiveness and control in an inversion of I will never resist you again, I am in control in *A Question of Trust* (1911): Having agreed to marry him the heroine states 'Pierre – my Pierre – you will never again – kiss me – against my will'.[11]

Ethel, it seems, was acutely aware of the status of women of the period but realised that whatever she might have thought from time to time was not commercial when she injected a stronger position for the role and the character of women she then softened it with commercial emollient, and thus a monetising of her narrative.

Ethel's works are brimming with sexuality and sexualised violence in a great many guises, and in all its manifested variations, and not just as the reaction to 'love'. It is quite a stretch to imagine how this reclusive author who married so late in life and with no known intimate male friends with whom she might have been sexually active before this, even if the marriage was intimate, having such a melodramatic and vivid imagination of sexual activity to which she appears not to have been privy. This would seem to have been confirmed by the sad comment in *Greatheart* that 'he would not make such ardent love to her once they were married'.[12]

The relationship plots move so fast that their intertextuality hides their exaggerated improbability. In *The Bars of Iron* the hero's violence is part of his strength, weakness and passion – it is written as part of this character's apparent appeal. It is all without any grounding in reality, but in this work the sexuality and violence is cloaked in quasi-religiosity to make it no doubt more palatable. Beauman quotes Lord Riddell advising Ruby M Ayres that '... writers of her type should take her heroines as far as the bedroom door and leave them there'.[13] Clearly Ethel was not a party to this advice.

The sexual 'carrot' in most of her works is the implicit sexual consummation of a male and female relationship. In her very first work, *The Repentant Rogue*, the hero and heroine pointedly do not sleep together, and this must be seen as a sexual fantasy. In *Storm Drift* we see an implied demand for male conjugal rights ... 'I was never more to you than – storm drift ...', and she begs him to leave her life as she is damaging his.[14] Norman has threated to kill Tiggie if Viola does not grant him his implied conjugal rights. In *The Electric Torch*, published after Ethel had been married for twelve years, the hero states, 'I married my wife for my own pleasure and not for anyone else's', but then there are five pages devoted to the subject of the marriage apparently not being consummated.[15,16] Female sexual needs are exposed by the statement by the heroine in *The Sacrifice* (1919) that 'by heaven I'll have my turn first' in reference to her yet unconsummated marriage.[17] The conclusions from this as a reflection on her personal life are no doubt obvious. Denial of sex in a marriage produces the astonishing suggestion of adultery as a cure: 'there's nothing for it nowadays for a married man but to sit in a corner and get tight – unless he gets off with somebody else's wife'.[18]

In *The Hundredth Chance* although married, the heroine implies the withholding of sexual favours: 'though I can't give him everything – he shall not repent his bargain. We are going to be – friends'.[19] The notion of a real marriage is consummation as in *The Hundredth Chance* where the hero and the heroine are married but separated. 'Maud, if we ever live alone together, it must be as man and wife'.[20] In *The Electric Torch* Pax and Claire come together in a 'real' marriage (inverted commas inserted by this author). Eight years before her marriage Ethel writes as if a committed spinster, 'I think marriage except for good people like Hilda – is a mistake. It's terribly cold-blooded – and irrevocable'.[21] And then again in the same year: 'Only those who have done it realise the bitterness of finding out too late that they have made a mistake'.[22] It is hard to reconcile Ethel's written views demonstrated here with her later personal life.

The Magic Circle is a simple and non-controversial tale about difficulties in marriage and faithfulness, however, in *Bars of Iron* after the marriage of the protagonists: 'He desired passion from her rather than love'.[23] Given her youth, was there perhaps something in her parent's relationship that gave rise to these reflections? In *The Experiment* Ethel's hero states, 'What puzzles me, he said, is how a girl with your natural independence and love of freedom can endure to remain unmarried'.[24] The notion here is that relationships in normal life are hedged around with conventions. There is displayed here a very confusing yet interesting polarity between single and fettered and married and unfettered. There is of course a significant contradiction here, especially so in the general context of all her narratives.

Ethel debates the separation between sexual activity and romance and sexual activity in marriage. In *Bars of Iron* she writes: 'do you think experience destroys romance?'[25] This is surely a comment on virginity? In *The Lamp in the Desert* she writes that the heroine Stella admitted to herself that she never loved her husband and was at times repulsed by him. But having been married she had come into womanhood, although what she had done she thought as a sin.[26]

Sexually, her men are straining at the leash to have their way with their dominated women. 'Love! Love! But what was Love? Was any man capable of it? Was it ever anything more than brutal passion or callous amusement? And hearts were broken and lives were ruined to bring men sport'.[27] 'Don't you realize – yet – that when a man of my stamp wants a woman – he takes her'?[28] Men must be sexually satisfied: 'a kiss cut short or brief might have left him unsatisfied'.[29]

In *The Hundredth Chance*, published when Ethel was nineteen, the heroine is given a lecture from an uncle about a man's needs and the impossibility of a platonic relationship especially within a marriage.

'I am eighty,' he said. 'I've seen a little of men in my time, and I've been a man myself. So let me tell you this! There's not a man on this earth who would be satisfied for long with this kind of farce [a platonic marriage]. You've got him on a leash now. He's tame and good. But there's a ravening wolf inside us all, my dear, and when we are thwarted, and the longer we're thwarted the more savage we get. You cannot bring up a wolf – not the tamest wolf in the world – on bread and butter. Sooner or later he will feel a bit empty and whine for the real thing. And if you still go on starving the brute till he's famished, he'll either break away and go elsewhere for food, or else he'll round on you one day and tear you to pieces. You'll suffer either way. It's nature I tell you, it's nature. You will have to give all or drive him away at the outset. There can't be half measures with a man who is a

man. If you offer them you must expect trouble. And remember
it's always the woman who pays in the end – always the woman
who pays.'[30]

The male's apparent insatiable sexual appetite is exposed in *Greatheart*:
'Did they make you without a heart, I wonder? Like a robin that mates a dozen
times in a season!'[31] Again, in *Greatheart* the heroine is hesitant about kissing
her fiancé, who states, 'If you treat me like a monster, I shall behave like one.
I'm made that way'.[32]

It takes little imagination to understand the import of what is intended but
not said in *The Safety Curtain* just prior to the marriage being consummated,
by implication, '"My, Billikins, how you've grown!" she said, admiringly.
"You always were-pretty big. But to-night you're just-titanic!"'[33] Did Ethel
understand the sexual implications of her heroine who had spread herself by
writing about confidences in *The Unknown Quantity*?[34] I think she might well
have done and created this very unsubtle double entendre.

In *The Rocks of Valpré* a subsidiary male character is marooned in a cave
all night with the pubescent heroine. Ethel's search for sexuality ranges far
as we see the incipient sexuality of a young girl: 'He saw the curve of her
body in the sunshine'.[35] There is the implication of pubescent sexuality here
as we have seen that she has a governess, and she is revealed as being only
seventeen years old. But by the end of the narrative she had 'the dainty pride
of budding womanhood', on seeing this pubescent innocent girl 'To the man
it meant the sudden, primal tumult of all the deepest forces of his nature; it
meant the awakening of his soul, the birth of his manhood'. Also, 'his "heart"
[inverted commas inserted by this author] throbbed all night long like the
beat of a drum that calls men to action'.[36] We see sexual innocence again in
The Tidal Wave and this is perhaps a reflection of her own situation as a young

woman. "'But the shyness had all gone now. The girlish immaturity was fast vanishing in soft curves and tender lines. And the beauty of her! – the beauty of her was as the gold of a summer morning breaking over a pearly sea", and "'I might be tempted to take too much – more than I have any right to take." "You have a right to all," she said. But he shook his head. "No – no! You are too young.'"[37] Ethel's narratives are littered with kissing. There is of course romantic and unpleasant kissing, kissing on the lips, on the cheeks, on the hand, perfunctory kissing. Obligatory socially required kissing, heterosexual kissing and same-sex kissing. And Ethel's kisses are always delivered with sexual intent. 'Gravely, he bent his face to hers and kissed her with the lips of a conqueror'.[38] In *Greatheart* there are thirty-three kissing instances but this has reduced to only eleven by her *Charles Rex*, and she establishes throughout her narratives that a kiss, especially on the lips, is a sign of great intimacy and even capitulation and sexual surrender. In *The Way of an Eagle* the hero Nick has given the heroine a ring which is admired by her friend Daisy, and after a chat the women briefly kiss on the lips. This is a clear indication of same-sex or ambivalent sexuality. Heterosexual women would not normally kiss other woman on the lips. Surprisingly, for British women at this time, lesbianism wasn't illegal, as long as it was discreet. Vita Sackville-West had many female lovers. As a teen, Sackville-West fell in love with Violet Trefusis, the daughter of Alice Keppel, who was King Edward VII's mistress.

In Ethel's narrative, before a marriage of one of them the two women friends discuss their friendship, having kissed: 'Before Yvonne married Guy we were completely happy – alone'.[39] The implication is clear that these two women were involved in a relationship. This is now a delicate area of debate filled with emotional socio-political potholes. Can one ascertain the sexual inclinations of Ethel's friends from material to hand, and why is this important? It is important in that this might give some clues to Ethel's creative inspirations.

From the author's perspective the photographs of Ethel's friends shown would tend to indicate this. Some of Ethel's female friends do indicate a degree of butchness. They are certainly not glamorous women. Violet Ebsworth, Ethel's secretary and close friend was reported to have a deep growly voice. In *The Way of an Eagle* we discover that Muriel also has a deep voice. An acknowledgement that Ethel's female friends were perhaps a bit butch appears in *Death's Property*: 'good looking women are not always the best sort'.[40]

Suggestions of homosexuality were not limited to women. In *Bars of Iron* the French valet '... trotted with a woman's nimbleness to the door'.[41] A very heavy handed and unveiled suggestion of homosexuality.

The nadir of Ethel's narrated sexual violence appears in *Bars of Iron* where there is clearly a description of a rape. 'You are not your own any longer – to give or to take away. You are mine'.[42] The heroine pleads but the man has no mercy. Significantly the man's actions are not castigated in the remaining narrative, and no other perspective for the reader is hinted at and Ethel even, it seems, justifies the man's actions. Earlier in this title, which is dominated by violent sex and sexualised violence, Ethel primes the reader's imagination. We read:

> Piers exclaimed also, and sprang forward. His arms were about her before she reached the ground. He lifted her bodily ere she could recover her balance; and suddenly she knew that with the touch of her the fire of his passion had burst into scorching flame – knew herself powerless – a woman in the hold of her captor. For he held her so fast that she gasped for breath, and with her head pressed back against his shoulder, he kissed her on the lips, fiercely, violently, hungrily – kissed her eyes, her hair, and again her lips, sealing them closely with his own, making protest impossible. Neither could she resist him, for he held her

gathered up against his heart, bearing her whole weight with a strength that mocked her weakness, compelling her to lie at his mercy while the wild storm of his passion swept on its way.

She was as one caught in the molten stream of a volcano, and carried by the fiery current that seethed all about her, consuming her with its heat.

Once when his lips left hers she tried to whisper his name, to call him back from his madness; but her voice was gone. She could only gasp and gasp till with an odd, half-savage laugh he silenced her again with those burning kisses that made her feel that he had stormed his way to the last and inner sanctuary of her soul, depriving her even of the right to dispute his overwhelming possession. ...

'I must have you or die.' Avery tells Piers, 'That – is not the way to make me love you'.[43] But, then they become engaged, so the violence paid off.

And, in *The Juice of the Pomegranate* at the end of her life Ethel's heroine is pregnant as a result of a rape. This is romance – but extremely violent sexualised romance. Was Ethel constrained because sexual activity could not, at that time, be overtly described, creating the sexual interface through violence? It seems that in a period when sex could not be described, sexual violence became a substitute, a vehicle for the imagination.

But not all of the sexual violence was potentially penetrative. The heroine in *The Hundredth Chance*, who is only wearing a nightdress with a shawl is savagely beaten, implicitly on her backside, with a carpet slipper by her father-in-law and her night dress is torn, again implicitly, revealing her bosom. The narrative continues with the comment that 'Perhaps some women wouldn't have minded it much'.[44] Was this not a very strange notion for women during the First World War? A time when many hundreds of thousands of women were enfranchised in the workplace, taking on male functions in factories across the country.

Whether ugly, handsome, kind or devious, men dominated her narratives. Whatever their strengths the woman is dominated sometimes by strange notions. In *The Way of an Eagle* the heroine has a ring but declines to marry the hero but she is to keep the ring on the promise that if she changes her mind she is to 'come like a brave woman and tell me'. His part of the bargain is: 'I swear to you – before God – that I will never marry you unless you ask me to'.[45] At any time, this concept is very hard to comprehend. As is the following: 'Yes, that … and because I care too much about you to – marry you against your will'.[46]

Sexual titillation is surely the backbone of the appeal of her narratives in whatever form this titillation appears. As the antecedent for Mills and Boon stories, Ethel has a narrative drive and a real and an appealing un-healthiness which the latter stories lack. In a like vein, Michael Arlen's *The Green Hat* (1924) was a huge bestseller and was quite scandalous at the time. Few books in that era featured an eighteen-year-old heroine who declared that she needed to have sex and would do so whether she married her true love or not.

But Arlen leant on Ethel and clearly positioned her reader universe as a low socio-economic one. Iris Storm, the femme fatale, is talking about her breasts on the telephone and the person on the other end of the line protests: 'Iris, you are shocking the girl at the exchange!' and Iris replies, 'No, no, Miss Dell has prepared her for anything'.[47] Ethel's titillation came in many real and superlative enhanced guises, and are very understandable, even out of context:

In *The Tidal Wave*[48]

- 'He kissed the throbbing whiteness of her throat, the loose clusters of her hair. He laid his hot face against her neck, and held it so, not breathing. Her arms stretched upwards, clasping him. She was panting – panting as one in deep waters'. Panting here is clearly an euphemism for orgasm.

- 'He held her closely, passionately. He kissed her face, her neck, her bosom, as if he would devour the sweetness of her in a few mad moments of utter abandonment'.

- 'Here for a second she stood, motionless it seemed. And then strangely, amazingly, she moved again. The brown garment slipped from her, and like a streak of light, she was gone, and the still pool received her with a rippling splash as of fairy laughter'. The heroine dives naked into the water.

In *Bars of Iron*[49]

- 'For he held her so fast that she gasped for breath, and with her head pressed back against her shoulder, he kissed her on the lips, fiercely, violently, hungrily kissed her eyes, her hair, and again her lips, sealing them closely with his own, making protest impossible. Neither could she resist him, for he held her gathered up against his heart, bearing her whole weight with a strength that mocked her weakness, compelling her to lie at his mercy while the wild storm of his passion swept on its way'. Clearly there has been sexual intercourse.

In *Greatheart*[50]

- '... this is Mr Studley, he saw you at the window without anything on'.

- Eustace promises to show Daphne the sort of things she missed when she ran away. As a result 'her whole body was tingling, her heart beat, wildly a-quiver'.

- '... I am all yours – all yours! But don't – don't take too much – at a time!'

- Counting the days until their marriage Eustace says, 'Need we wait – all that time?'

- "'Married people are different, aren't they? They are not always going off by themselves and kissing in corners." "Not as a rule," admitted Scott. "But I've been told that there is usually a good deal of that sort of thing done during the honeymoon."'

In *Tetherstones*[51]

- 'she did not resist him. Burningly, afterwards, she remembered her submission, remembered how, panting, her lips met his, and were held and crushed till blindly she fought for breath but not for freedom. It all came like a fevered dream. One moment she had been a woman of the world – a business woman – cold, collected, calm; the next she a girl again, living, palpitating, thrilling to the rapture which all her life she had missed, drinking the ecstasy of the moment as only those who have been parched with thirst can drink. She was as it were borne on a great wave of amazed exultation. That he should love her – that he should love her! Ah, the marvel of it – and the gladness that was like to pain!'

In *The Black Knight*[52]

We see here the most alarming invectives against marriage and men:

- 'His hands closed very gently upon her. "Ermine look up!" he said again. "You know me. You know what I say has to be. It has come to this. You are a woman and I am a man – your master ..."'

- 'I've so often watched you and wondered. Of course, Joyce always says that married life is ideal, but – God if any man treated me as you treat her, I believe that I would kill him; I do honestly! That perpetual baiting, being held up to ridicule, treated as a slave – worse – as a doormat! Always the scapegoat when things go wrong. Always the one to be tortured when you feel in the mood for bloodshed! And to bear it – to keep one's mouth shut – even to pretend one likes it! Oh, what is it that makes these things worthwhile? Nothing that men can give! That I know. Children overgrown in selfishness and cruelty; that's what most of you are. You take pleasure in hurting those you profess to love. You can't leave them alone and keep out of the way when the brute mood is on you. You needs drag them out, make them suffer, make them writhe – to propitiate your own vile tempers. And then when it's all over and you're feeling better, you let them crawl away to hide their wounds – wounds that may never heal! – in solitude'.

-   'Wait till you have been married as long as I have dear! It's a fearsome ordeal being compelled to spend every minute of one's existence in the sole company of one person ...'

In *Honeyball Farm*[53]

-   This is a threat to a woman of eighteen from her father. 'Oh yes ... I'll treat you as my daughter all right. I'll turn you over and spank you if you do not behave yourself'.

In *The Juice of the Pomegranate*[54]

-   The villain bites the heroine's finger repeatedly to leave marks so that she does not forget that she belongs to him when he is away.

Slipping off the edge of sexual titillation into both gratuitous violence, sex with violence or sexual violence and the implication of a deviant violent behaviour is a shocking aberration from the fun and games of a light read. Although, this could be seen as a natural progression from sexually related violent behaviour in a writer with a fervent imagination, it is still of speculative interest where the stimulus for this imagination was developed. In *The Lamp in the Desert* Ethel demonstrates this imagination or even experience well: Captain Ermsted slaps his daughter with 'thoroughness'.

His wife comments, "'I'm not a sentimental mother," she observed, "You won't punish me in that way. I object to a commotion, that's all."'[55] The point here is that beating of a child and his wife is not an issue to his wife. However, later on in the narrative the wife comments to her husband that it does not pay to bully a woman. She can always get her own back one way or another. Remember that! This repost provokes her husband into a rage. Also, in the same title the daughter is tied tightly to a pillar with a belt for irritating her aggressor but she is freed by the Indian servant who is duly admonished.[56] Sexual tensions and perhaps frustrations come to the fore as even a game of billiards is subject to sexual interpretation. After winning a game the hero 'stood up again, moving with that free swing of his as of one born to conquer'.[57] Despite or even because of her own marriage Ethel had a very cynical view of married heterosexual union.

e Unknown Quantity[58]
- 'I should hate to be bothered with a husband if I did not like him'.

In The House of Happiness
- The theme of this title is that there is real loneliness in a marriage without love.

In Quits[59]
- 'But marriage nowadays does not place a girl within baulk. It increases rather than restricts their freedom'.
- 'I used to think that it [marriage] was such an exciting thing – the acme of everything. But it isn't. It has just turned everything dull, that's all'.

In *Pageant of Youth*[60]

- 'But you are so old fashioned. I believe it's because you never married. Married men have to go with the times – whether they like it or not'.

In *Charles Rex*[61]

- '… I mean, marriage is such a speculation, isn't it?'

In *Misunderstanding*[62]

- 'He [the cat] reminds me of my husband – so satisfied – so sensible – so selfish'.

In *The Black Knight*[63]

- 'If I had my way, said Sam, lighting a cigarette, you would lose everything you have straight away and start over again'.
- 'she threw him a swift glance. Haven't you had your way? … What more do you want'?
- '… I believe that I could take a beating from you without hating you. I believe that it might even do me good'.

In *Honeyball Farm*[64]

'… if I even bolt, dear Papa, it will not be in the direction of matrimony. I think that I may safely promise you that my progress to the altar will be a very slow march indeed'.

- 'sybil spoke with sudden feeling. And yet if you were married, I'll bet you'd never be satisfied till you'd made your unlucky wife bear you children!'
- With reference to marriage: 'I suppose it's all right for a man … He can always get away. But it might mean prison for life for a woman'.

In *The Juice of the Pomegranate*[65]

- "'Married!" Diana laughed in a scoffing note. "Can you picture me – I can't – living the sort of life you do, and knuckling under all the time? I should never survive it. There'd be murder done – suicide – or both.'"
- 'You married people all know the various ingredients that go to make up the matrimonial mixture, and yet you always try and serve it up as if it were sheer treacle and nothing else'.

Naomi Wolf writes that: 'Wharton [Edith] was drawn away from American discourses of sexuality in fiction which were generally moralistic in this period, regardless of the gender of the writer, and towards British and European aestheticism and sexual liberation'.[66] A counter to this comment on American attitudes to sex and sexuality is Ethel's significant success in the United States from her very first publication. Wolf's discourses on romantic fiction do not relate to Ethel's mass market universe. Wharton created literary fiction, but Ethel created mass appeal sexual titillation and outsold her.

Ethel's Perspective

My experience of intimate relationships with men was very limited, and certainly there never was a passionate one. My marriage was a social convenience and I am very fond of my husband but there was no passion. We slept separately and our marriage was never consummated. My stories are how I imagine relationships to be played-out, but I never witnessed a happy married relationship, as the only ones that I knew of were that of my parents and my brother. I was never involved in the politics of heterosexual marriage or even unmarried sexuality. I also never understood how a married couple can have intimate sexuality when there is prior experience. Surely the experience destroys the romance of marriage. My intimate relationships prior to my marriage were exclusively with women.

Do men really have an insatiable sexual appetite? I like to think so but it certainly was not the case in my marriage. A forced sexual encounter is perhaps a natural progression from male sexual dominance and appetite and I have written about that although such aggression was only in my purview with my father.

16 Religion and Moral Musings

'He does not command us to make bricks without straw'.[1]

In examining Ethel's influence on Barbara Cartland, Robert Jensen-Rix suggests that her stories were underpinned by a religious sensibility. This may be in evidence with regards to the epigraphs, but the suggestion that the heroines and heroes of her narratives sought or were blessed with a spiritual endgame seems to be beyond the imagination or intent of the author. Anderson, Florence Barclay's great great niece, writing from the Barclay perspective has suggested that Ethel combined the spiritual and quasi-religious themes from Barclay and the full-blooded heroes from Ouida. This questionably suggests a lack of originality in Ethel's works. In *The Bars of Iron*, Ethel demonstrates a deep knowledge of the Bible but as a balance has her protagonist, an Anglican vicar, write a sermon that is neither 'mythical nor allegorical'.[2] Religiousness was a vehicle for the narrative born out of her personal knowledge and not for theo-philosophical convictions. The extent of the religious or semi religious narratives in Ethel's works would, however, seem to create an aura and an underpinning of religiosity. This is understandable from a cursory and unthinking read, but perhaps misleading as her use of religion is a vehicle for creativity and character dialogue, and she does not shy from using phrases from religious texts either as a whole without acknowledgement or adjusted texts seemingly as a misquote. It is all too easy to pigeon hole Ethel into writing with a religious sensibility. Her scattering of religious but irrelevant religious texts and associations and her use of sex and violence would seem to contradict this.

Ethel is evidently well versed in religious tracts and practices covering a wide spectrum of beliefs. Within the Dell family there was religious polarity, her father was a Catholic and her mother a fervent Protestant, but this seems to have sparked a curiosity for other forms of worship. We can see evidence of Anglican, Catholic, Methodist, Hinduism, Buddhism, Sufiism Judaism and even Japanese Shinto in her narratives.[3]

In *The Swindler's Handicap* the hero declines to renew the acquaintance of the heroine as he likens himself to the proverb of touching pitch. 'He that touches pitch shall be defiled herewith'.[4] This reference by Ethel is of considerable significance as the reference comes from Ecclesiasticus 13.1 in the Apocrypha section, Book of Wisdom in the Jerusalem Bible. This is the Bible version used by Catholics. The Anglican King James Bible does not include Ecclesiasticus. In *The Keeper of the Door Keeper* there is also a curious reference, almost out of context, to the Pope needing to be asked permission for two marriages.[5] In *The House of Happiness* there is a non-relevant reference to the Agony in the Garden (Luke 22: 22–39 & 43–44) which is represented as the first Catholic Stations of the Cross.[6] Clearly there is Catholicism in her mind-set and Ethel seems to grasp at suitable phrases and terminology as both narrative links and narrative enhancements and occasionally for releasing her own views.

The Anglican Book of Common Prayer with which Ethel is clearly very familiar is subject to a pejorative comment in *The Rocks of Valpré* 'You're as simple as the Book of Common Prayer', yet, the book is a key part of the narrative in *The Way of an Eagle* when the heroine's father underlines the service for the dead.[78] 'In the midst of life we are in death' from the Book of Common Prayer is used by a man servant in *The Altar of Honour* to announce a pending death. The Book of Common Prayer is again quoted in *Tetherstones*, 'From all devil and mischief, from sin, from the crafts and assaults of the devil, good Lord deliver us'.[9] And, in *The Keeper of the Door* the injured hero quotes the Third Collect, 'for Aid against all Perils' from the Book of Common Prayer.[10] The Anglican Advent hymn 'He comes, the prisoners to release' is quoted in

The Bars of Iron.[11]

The Bible is the most frequently used third-party narrative and is not at any time acknowledged as being used or quoted. We can see this in Ethel's use of other literary works in the body of her narratives all, also, without acknowledgement. Some of the 'quotes' have, however, been adjusted and changed, but their origins are very obvious, and in order to contextualise these 'quotes', and to try and understand why Ethel used some of these references the meaning of each, as theorised by biblical scholars, is indicated below, with a suggested intertextual interpretation where possible:

The Way of an Eagle: '... and I quite agree with Solomon, childhood and youth are vanity'.[12]
Ecclesiastes 11.10: 'Therefore remove sorrow from thy heart, and put away evil from thy flesh: for childhood and youth are vanity'.
Biblical interpretation: This is what Solomon wished for youth in general.
Intertextuality: I have matured.

Greatheart: The heroine is ill and goes down 'the valley of the shadow'.[13]
Psalm 23.4: 'Yea, though I walk through the valley of the shadow of death, I will fear no evil: for thou art with me; thy rod and thy staff they comfort me.'
Biblical interpretation: Comfort and protection.
Intertextuality: A dramatic vehicle for describing the proximity of death.

Greatheart: 'Eustace spoke, a species of half-veiled insolence in his tone. "Like the psalmist she went forth weeping and has returned bearing her sheaf with her – in the form of a fairly substantial fiancé."'[14]
Psalm 126:6: 'He that goeth forth and weepeth, bearing precious seed, shall doubtless come again with rejoicing, bringing his sheaves with him'.

Biblical interpretation: Suffering and trouble can change into joy because of opening hearts to God.

Intertextuality: There is no link between the biblical meaning and Ethel's narrative except that for the reader it might at a stretch be seen to have a bearing on the situation.

The Lamp in the Desert: '... camped beside a rushing stream that filled the air with its crystal music day and night ... And this is Heaven ... but it is the Heaven of the Orient, and I am not sure that I have any part or lot in it. I believe I shall feel myself an interloper for all time. I dread to turn each corner lest I should meet the Angel with the Flaming Sword and be driven forth into the desert'.[15]

Genesis 3.24 'After he sent the man out, God placed angels and a flaming sword that turned in all directions east of the Garden of Eden. He placed them there to guard the way ...'

Biblical interpretation: ... swords to lead the way to paradise.

Intertextuality: Ethel has inverted this parable. She is in a good place and does not want to leave it. The use of this biblical narrational crutch is without meaning or relevance.

The Lamp in the Desert: 'Perhaps – David – said the same thing about Uriah the Hittite'.[16]

Samuel 2:11–12: 'David sees Bathsheba Uriah's wife and sleeps with her. She becomes pregnant. Uriah is placed in battle by David where he was killed. Bathsheba mourns her husband's death and marries David. God is displeased'.

Biblical interpretation: David was a dishonest adulterer.

Intertextuality: Was Monck lying about the death of Ralph Dacre as King David must have done over Uriah? This analogy works well.

The Keeper of the Door: 'love is the fulfilling of the law'.[17]

Romans 13:10: 'Love worketh no ill to his neighbour: therefore love is the fulfilling of the law'.

Biblical interpretation: Do not hold back on just taxes and honour, but love others. We may take this to mean not to owe money when it is due.

Intertextuality: There seems to be no rationale for Ethel's reference to the Bible and in this part of the narrative it seems to be totally out of context and without substance.

Bars of Iron: 'If I go down to hell- Thou art there also ...'[18]

Psalm 139:8: 'If I ascend into heaven thou art there: If I make my bed in hell, behold, thou art there'.

Biblical interpretation: God is wherever you are, therefore everywhere.

Intertextuality: The analogy here is clear but there is an elision between the hero being with the dying heroine for ever and the concept of God always being there. Ethel has used this biblical device as a narrational vehicle without any substantive meaning.

Bars of Iron: '... and, I often think as he's like to bring the old master's hairs with sorrow to the grave'.[19]

Genesis 44.29: 'then shall ye bring down my grey hairs with sorrow to the grave'.

Biblical interpretation: To weary someone to death.

Intertextuality: Wear him out.

Bars of Iron: 'I saw Heaven opened, and behold a white horse; and He that sat upon him was called Faithful and True ... His Eyes were as a flame of fire and on His Head were many crowns ... And He was clothed with a vesture dipped in blood ... And the armies which were in Heaven followed Him upon white horses, clothed in fine linen, white and clean ... And He treadeth the wine-press ... He treadeth the wine-press ...'[20] [The character Piers sings this psalm.] Revelation 19:11 'And I saw heaven opened, and behold a white horse; and he that sat upon him was called Faithful and True, and in righteousness he doth judge and make war'.

Biblical interpretation: The exposition of the majesty of Christ.

Intertextuality: The aura of the music and the psalm create an environment for the lovers, they are washed over with the sentimentality of it but of the words themselves there seems of no relevance.

Storm Drift: '....the scales fell from his eyes'.[21]

Acts of the Apostles 9.18: 'And immediately there fell from his eyes as it had been scales and he received sight forthwith and was baptised'.

Biblical interpretation: He understood the truth

Intertextuality: He understands the truth

The Keeper of the Door: '... charm she never so wisely'.[22]

Psalm 58.5: 'Which will not hearken to the voice of charmers, charming never so wisely'.

Biblical interpretation: Be careful that you are not influenced by the charmer.

Intertextuality: Be careful not to be too influenced.

The Rocks of Valpré 'He does not command us to make bricks without straw'.[23]

Exodus 5:8: 'Ye shall no more give the people straw to make brick, as heretofore: let them go and gather straw for themselves'.

Biblical interpretation: Do it yourself.

Intertextuality: We are not being told to do something impossible.

The Unknown Quantity: Ethel displays a complexity of knowledge and a challenge to the Bible where she questions the notion that 'God will provide'. Then in the middle of the title she tries to engage her reader in what can only be described as a rambling religious diatribe with no apparent meaning or focus, for example: 'What many of us call reform is very often another form of corruption. The aspiration may be good, but the conception is wrong ... only another form of death. What the world, social and political, concrete and mental really needs is not new things, but the old things made new – God's gifts as they were in the beginning, freed from the petrification of antiquity and the rust of disuse, restored to all their former beauty, sanctified afresh by His unchanging love'. This lack of narrative cohesion could perhaps be indicative of the effects of substance abuse.[24]

Those Who Wait: The biblical woman Damaris is mentioned in the context of a love affair that his paramour had had some fifteen years previously. Damaris is mentioned in a single verse in the Acts of the Apostles (17:34) as one of those present when Paul of Tarsus preached in Athens. Damaris embraced the Christian faith following Paul's speech. Apart from a demonstration of an in-depth knowledge of the Acts this reference seems to have been thrown into the narrative without any consideration of the contextuality within the narrative, as a filler.

The Knave of Diamonds: 'Through her mind flashed a single sentence that had often and often set her wondering: From him that hath not shall be taken away even that which he seemeth to have. She knew its meaning now. It scorched her inmost soul. Such a one was she. No effort had she ever made to possess her husband's love. No love had she ever offered to him; duty and submission indeed, but love-never'.[25]

RIDING THE TOSH HORSE

Matthew 25:29: 'For unto every one that hath shall be given, and he shall have abundance: but from him that hath not shall be taken away even that which he hath'. Biblical interpretation: The notion that more will be given to those that already have.

Intertextuality: She had not given her love to her husband but this is not related in any way to the parable in the Bible which is the Mathew principle of giving to those who have.

Ethel's apparently open mind also allowed her to question Anglican practices. In *The Bars of Iron* the Rev. Lorimer prepares his advent homily on a theme of eternal punishment. The Four Last Things – Death, Judgement, Heaven and Hell – have been traditional themes for Advent meditation, but as she states this priest wants his congregation to tremble, and he does not love his flock. And, later in the same work she describes Anglican Christianity delivered almost by rote without compassion or feeling. Perhaps most significantly she seems to believe in the power of prayer in a dilemma and the hero agrees to pray for six months to see what happens, and she also questions a God that can allow a hell.[26] Ethel engages her reader in a long discourse on the nature of God's love in *The Hundredth Chance*, and on the Resurrection in *Greatheart*.[27][28] But, there can be little doubt that she had a deep Christian faith. In *The Rocks of Valpré* she states, 'they are no more than the tools with which the good God shapes us to His destiny'. There is significance in the upper-case H in 'His'.[29] But the use of religion in her narratives seldom has any great relevance to the textual environment in which they appear.

Robert Southey's colossal poetical work the *Curse of Kehama* was a Hindu fantasy, part of which was slightly misquoted in the epigraph to *The Rocks of Valpré*.[30] In the preface to *The Curse of Kehama* (1812), Southey wrote: 'In the religion of the Hindoos, which of all false religions is the most monstrous in its fables, and the most fatal in its effects, there is one remarkable peculiarity. Prayers, penances, and sacrifices, are supposed to possess an inherent and actual value, in no degree depending upon the disposition or motive of the person who performs them'.[31] To a novelist who led a cloistered life this statement alone would have fired Ethel's imagination of an India almost beyond comprehension. Did reading Southey fire-up Ethel's interest in non-Christian religions? In Storm Drift the hero has a sudden reawakening: 'And the – very suddenly it happened – that third turn of the wheel that was to alter the whole course of his existence'.[32] As it is not within the context of Storm Drift narrative this, it seems is a reference to the Buddhist Third Wheel of Dharma derived from a group of sutras in the systematisation of the Mind Only school, the wheel itself symbolising the endless cycle of birth and re-birth.

In 1908 Florence Petz in the United States registered a design patent for a good luck charm, and it became fashionable to buy to bring good luck. In 1912 the god/image of Billiken arrived in Japan, where it was enshrined in Osaka's Luna Park as 'The God of Things as They Ought to Be'. In 1923, however, the park was closed and the Billiken statue vanished. In 1979 it was re-discovered and it returned to popularity. In The Safety Curtain (1917) the hero, Merryon, is nicknamed Billikens, no doubt as he is the 'ideal/godlike' man. The god of things as they ought to be is totally appropriate for the excesses and the flow of the story, and thus it seems that Ethel had access to this specific knowledge from somewhere. The Illustrated London News, a global source of stories with visuals for the period, has no coverage of this god. From where did she source her knowledge or awareness of Billikens? It is just possible that in her research for American material she came across the United States Saint Louis Billikens men's basketball team.

Ethel's deep knowledge of the Bible and her apparent curiosity concerning non-Christian religions served her well in the construction of her narratives, but do not present in her character portrayals a moralistic or even theo-religious endgame, a trap that the academic text 'skimmer' could fall into.

Ethel's Perspective

I was brought up in a family environment where my abusive father was a Catholic and my mother an Anglican. My sister was very Anglican, even being a linesman in her local church, but despite my father I was more inclined towards Catholicism, but I never attended any religious services. Not from the viewpoint of having ambivalent or unclear beliefs but I did not want to appear in public. I know that the Press would hound me on a Sunday if I left home, but no Catholic priest ever visited me. Initially I do not think that Elizabeth would have allowed it.

I was of course very familiar with the Bible and used my father's copy extensively as a reference, but it was really just a tool for delivering my stories, nothing more than that. It is too easy and perhaps a compliment to think otherwise. The words of the Bible were very useful to make a point, I thought, but not really in the context of their deeper meaning.

My circle of friends was very small and I did not write many letters to express my views, so my writing became my personal medium for these expressions. I would never think of myself as a writer of essays but perhaps some of my views could have been developed as such, but for me encasing them in a story worked very well.

17 Ethel's Hidden Philosophies

'It is up to the swimmers to keep the sinkers afloat '.[1]

Despite the dominance of sex and violence throughout her narratives and the misuse of biblical quotations and themes, Ethel used her narratives to put forward her own personal moral, social and philosophical concerns and views, views that are profound, understandable and challenging. Her own loneliness and an apparent traumatised childhood, and a possibly ambivalent sexuality, would have been triggers for a very lively and intelligent mind subsumed by her extreme writing style. It is easy to dismiss these as just pithy sayings but combined now with our knowledge of her life and the content of her narratives they have a depth and a meaning even outside what we know of her life.

Happiness and the Challenge of Finding Happiness

- 'the way to happiness does not lie in pleasing oneself. The self-seekers never get there ...'[2]
- 'tolerance is the key to happiness' and later '... or is it kindness!'[3]
- 'The world is very cruel, monsieur. It has no place for losers. And it ridicules those whom fate has tortured'.[4]
- 'In comforting others – one comforts oneself'.[5]
- 'I think even the dullest life can be made beautiful ... Even the desert sand is gold when the sun shines on it. The trouble is ... to get the sun to shine'.[6]
- '"Life isn't what it was. It is an infernal fraud, most of it," said Saltash. "Always promising and seldom fulfilling."'[7]
- '... that the best things in life are the things that we never see and only dimly understand'.[8]

Selfishness

- 'Were half the world suffering because of the selfishness of the other half?'[9]
- '"I realize," she said, "that no great good can ever be attained without sacrifice: but it is not always easy to know how far one ought to go ... the good to be attained should be at least equal to the sacrifice."'[10]

Male Sexuality

- After an attempted sexual assault the man says 'don't you understand that when this kind of thing gets hold of you, there's no getting away from it'.[11]

Self-control

- 'But it's a pity ever to lose one's temper. It involves a waste of power'.[12]

Male and Female Relationships

Ethel engages the reader in a philosophical discourse on male–female relationships:

- 'You are not afraid?' She met his look, a certain wistfulness in her grey eyes. 'Oh, no, not afraid – only sceptical.' 'Only sceptical!' he echoed. 'That is a worldwide complaint. But anyone with imagination can always pretend. You are not good at pretending?' 'Not particularly'. His eyes challenged hers. 'Perhaps you have never needed an anaesthetic?' he said coolly. She looked slightly startled. 'What do you mean? He leaned deliberately forward across the table. 'You know what an anaesthetic does, don't you? It cheats the senses of pain. And a little humbug does the same for the mind. Of course you don't believe anything. I don't myself. But you can't stand for ever and contemplate an abyss of utter ignorance. You must weave a little romance about it for the sake of your self-respect'. She looked straight into the challenging eyes. The wistfulness was still in her own [this appears to be an incomplete sentence]. 'Then you are offering to weave a little romance for me?' she said, with a faint involuntary sigh. He made her a brief bow. 'If you will permit me to do so. To relieve your boredom?' she suggested with a smile. 'And yours,' he smiled back, taking up the cards.'[13]

- 'Has any man ever understood a woman?'[14]
- 'There are two kinds of love ... there the big unselfish kind – the real thing; and there's the other kind – that demands everything, and even then perhaps, is never satisfied'.[15]

Sex

- '"love – true love – is a sacred thing – not to be turned into sin. Sin," he said, "What is sin? Is it a sin to fulfil the very purpose for which we were created?"'[16]

Intolerance and Wickedness

- '... but isn't it rather a pity to let oneself get intolerant? It does spoil life so'.[17]
- 'Perhaps few men have realized the utter waste of wickedness as Charles Rex realized it that night'.[18]

The Lives of Children

- '... it's the children I want to help. I hate to think of fresh, clean lives being thrown on the dust heap. It's so futile – such a crying waste'.[19]

The Challenge of Finding the Best Course in Life

- 'The Philosopher is not always a wise man ... A philosopher may recognize what is best, but it is seldom within his reach ...'[20]

Unhappiness and Pain

- '... how sometimes when you're unhappy music makes you feel worse ... It's the jolliness that does it...'[21]
- 'But I don't think pain is a thing to cry for, do you? It isn't like grief.'[22]

The Nature of Goodness

Ethel engages the reader in a philosophical discourse in the nature of goodness:
- 'Bertie, you once said – that there was no goodness without Love. Then why – why is Love – wrong?' 'Love is not wrong, *chérie*.' Instant and reassuring came his answer. 'Let us be true to Love, and we are true to God. For Love is God, and in every heart. He is to be found; sometimes in much, sometimes in very, very little, but He is always there.' 'I don't understand,' said Chris. 'If that were so – why mustn't we love each other? Why is it wrong?' 'It is not wrong.' Again with absolute assurance Bertrand spoke. 'so long as it is pure, it is also holy. There is no sin in Love. We shall love each other always, dear, always. With me it will be more – and ever more. Though I shall not be with you, though I shall not see your face or touch your hand, you will know that I am loving you still. It will be as an Altar Flame that burns for ever. But I will be faithful. My love shall never hurt you again. That is where I sinned. I was selfish enough to show you the earthly part of my love – the part that dies, just as our bodies die, setting our spirits free. For see, *chérie*, it is not the material part that endures. All things material must pass, but the spiritual lives on for ever. That is why Love is immortal. That is why Love can never die.' She listened to him in silence, scarcely comprehending at the moment words that later were to become the only light to guide her stumbling feet. 'Would you say that you love the dead no more because you see them not?' he questioned gently. 'The sight – the touch – what is it? Only the earthly medium of Love; Love Itself is a higher thing, capable of the last sacrifice, greater than evil, stronger than death. Oh, believe me, Christine, Death is a very small thing compared with Love. If our love were of the spirit only, Death would be less than nothing; for it is only the body that can

ever die.' 'But why can't we be happy before we die?' whispered Chris. 'Other people are.' He shook his head. 'I doubt it, *chérie*. With death in the world there can be no perfection. All passes – all passes – except only the Love that is our Life.'[23]

- 'I think goodness is comparative at the best of times'.[24]

The Anaesthetic Nature of Pleasure

"'Who wants pleasure?" demanded Nap fiercely. "That's only the anaesthetic when things get unbearable. You use duty in the same way. But what we both want, what we both hanker for, starve for, is just life! Who cares if there is pain with it? I don't, nor do you. And yet we keep on stunting and stultifying ourselves with these old-fashioned remedies for a disease we only half understand, when we might have all the world and then some. Oh, we're fools – we're fools!" His voice rang wildly passionate. He flung out his arms as if he wrestled with something. "We've been cheated for centuries of our birthright, and we still put up with it, still bring our human sacrifices to an empty shrine!"'[25]

The Nature of Cynicism

- "'I can't bear cynicism," she told him frankly. He shrugged his shoulders. "Cynics – real cynics – never can." "But I am not a cynic." "Are you sure of that?" "Yes, quite sure." "And yet you tell me that you never take the trouble to flatter the inferior male. That's conflicting evidence, you know. Are you a man-hater, by the way?"'[26]

The Nature of Success

- 'Lucas shook his head. "What's success anyway? I guess the Creator finds the failures just as useful to Him in the long run."'[27]

Ambition

- 'What I can't understand … is how anyone can barter their happiness, their self-respect, and all that is worth having, for this world's goods, this world's ambitions, and expect to come out of it anything but losers. Oh I know it's done every day. People fight and scramble – yes, and grovel in the mud – for what they think is gold; and when they've got it, it's only the basest alloy. Some of them never find it out. Others do – and break their hearts'.[28]
- 'some of the stepping stones are sure to be filthy but one can always change one's shoes when one gets there'.[29]

Feminism

- 'You can't hammer a girl into submission like a boy'. [Toby, a girl, the subject of this aside was an accomplished 'boy' and dressed like one.][30]
- 'If a woman hasn't the spunk to defend herself, she's better dead'.[31]

The Implications of Individuality

- 'I suppose we are all slaves … of one kind or another. But only the rebels know it'.[32]

Being Virtuous

- 'There is no virtue in being virtuous if there has never been any temptation to be anything else'.[33]

Social Awareness

- In order to create a differentiation between different levels of British social class Ethel's heroine asks a male suitor if his tea is in fact 'tea' or 'ham and eggs'.[34] For a recluse this was a very perceptive comment and one has to wonder where Ethel gained this insight to class differences in British eating habits.

Commercial Morality

- There is no evidence that Ethel made any comment to or even about Elinor Glyn and her use of the 'IT' concept that Ethel had created as was discussed at the start of this work, but the plagiarism must have rankled.

What is significant is that Ethel's narratives were used to communicate her own philosophies and moral views albeit submerged in a Karma Sutra-like complexity and variation in sexual relationships. Perhaps the most surprising of the views expressed, a directly pertinent one, was that concerning the welfare of children in *The Bars of Iron,* published in 1919, the year after Penelope was adopted by her maiden sister Ella.

Ethel's Perspective

Writing is a very lonely profession which occupied me in the early hours every day. That creative quiet time not only allowed my stories to develop but also fuelled my loneliness and frustration that I had so much in terms of wealth but so little calmness in my life. I will freely admit that I never felt really secure in my own skin. The early hours are a very peaceful and quiet time but they can also exacerbate personal issues. The walls would sometimes crowd in on me and I felt pressured to think about my situation.

I enjoyed the company of women and certainly held some infatuations but until Gerald was introduced to me the only men that I had really known were my abusive father and my wastrel brother Reggie. Gerald was a lynchpin onto which I could cling for some kind of a normal life. Normal to outsiders but did I really love him? I certainly cared for him but it was very much a platonic relationship. He looked after our houses and spent my money on his toys. My sister Ella lived a very nouveau and expensive lifestyle only through the monies that I gave her. She inherited nothing except from me and never earnt a living through her own hard work. Her tutoring was short-term and only for the Bowra brothers.

Am I bitter, yes I suppose I am, but it is this bitterness that has given me the edge to be able philosophise from a point of strength. I have never really cared too much about critical press reviews as they never did any harm as my readers, given their social status would have been unlikely to have seen them anyway. It was almost 'so what' as my readers in their millions around the world read and bought my stories

My family was my given 'lot' and I coped with them in the fairest way possible, but it deep down I was truly exercised by Glyn's purloining of the concept of IT that I had created. But she developed the concept further and made a lot of money from the idea.

18 The Reading Public and Reading Environment

'you're making yourself conspicuous with that three volume novel baronet'.[1]

The social periphery to reading matter provides a fascinating insight into the profile that Ethel had developed. An examination of Edwardian parlour games provides some of this social insight and a window into Ethel's literary associations that her reader universe saw as her literary equals.

The game of **Un Authorised Editions** asks the players to match the title of twenty-four books with their authors. Of the twenty-four books three are Ethel's. Among the other authors on offer are: Compton Mackenzie, Conan Doyle, Hall Caine, Sheridan, George Bernard Shaw, Rudyard Kipling, John Buchan, Galsworthy, Charles Dickens, J.M. Barrie, Ouida, Hugh Walpole, and W.J. Locke. Excellent company indeed for Ethel's 'tosh'.

~

The game **Novel Whist** features Ethel's Knave of Diamonds as diamonds trumps for four hands.

~

Party Games Celebrities Past & Present provides riddles of 'well-known persons'. The clue for Ethel is: 'Give the name for a valley where green mosses grow, and you name too, an authoress, whom you all know'. Francis Bacon is, 'state a dish often see on the breakfast table, and you mention an essayist, witty and able'.

Henry Longfellow, 'Here's a riddle to solve. Let those guess it who can. What great poet's name would suggest a tall man?'

~

It would seem from this that the games themselves were perhaps aimed at different socio-economic markets and like *The Friend Who Stood By* appearing in totally different socially stratified media from the majority of the magazine published titles. The editor of *Weldon's Ladies Journal* indicated concern that *The Friend Who Stood By* had appeared in a cheap magazine like *Sunday Circle*.[2]

Libraries were of course key levers for Ethel's success. Orwell noted in 1936 that 'It is in a Lending Library you see people's real tastes, not their pretended ones: people buy books for mixed motives of pretension or display but they then borrow the books that they really went to read'.[3] The distributive development and increased accessibility of reading material in British libraries during the first half of the twentieth century was of great importance to the success of Ethel's work. The UK Public Libraries Act of 1919 gave library powers to the counties and it also made possible a complimentary provision in rural areas. 'Public Libraries Act 1919 … by giving library powers to the counties it also made possible a complimentary provision in rural areas'.[4] In 1913/14 there were 54.5 million issues and in 1934/35 165.8 million issues. Between 1913/14 and 1934/35 there was a very significant change in the availability of public library material with an 83% increase in library populated areas and a concurrent 65% increase in library issues per head of the library population. This resulted in total library book issues increasing by 204% over the period; in 1913/14 there were 54.5M book issues and in 1934/35 165.8M.[5] There is no evidence that Watt targeted the UK or the US library markets with Ethel's works but there can be no doubt that the distributive development in UK libraries were to his and her advantage. Between 1913/14 and 1934/35 we can see a very significant change in the availability of library material with an 83% increase in library populated areas and a 65% increase in library issues per head of library population, resulting in a 204% increase over the period in library book issues – in 1913/14 there were 54.5 million issues and in 1934/35 165.8 million issues.

	Great Britain		
	1913/14	1934/35	Change
Total Population, Ms.	40,979	45,598	+11.3%
Population in library areas	24,444	44,939	+83%
Library volumes per head of library population	0.47	0.59	+25.5%
Library issues per head of library population	2.23	3.69	+65%

In 1917 Marie Corelli and Ethel along with Rider Haggard were among the most popular authors in the North of Scotland. The effect of advertising weighting is clearly evident, and it is not too far-fetched to assume that the same applied in urban areas in Britain.[6] By 1938 the Boots Booklover's Library were exchanging thirty-five million books per annum, the borrowers of which were 90% women.[7] Again, it can be assumed therefore that a significant proportion of public library borrowers in Britain in this period were women. A study conducted in 1936 in the United States indicated that 66% of library users were women and their library use accounted for four-fifths of their reading.[8] An extrapolation of this data, with many caveats, and the assumption that say 10% of women readers were borrowing an Ethel work could indicate that in the 1934/5 period, a boom time for her writing, some eight million issues of her works were made through libraries.[9] The library was without doubt a vital part of the marketing mix. In the same study which listed 254 different authors Ethel was ranked no. 31 in terms of numbers of readers with an average of four titles read by these readers. Warwick Deeping, however, listed at no. 24, had a significantly greater apparent loyalty than Ethel with 6.9 titles per reader. This perhaps indicates that by 1936, Ethel's appeal was waning.

The expansion of the British rail network and the concurrent increase in station platform traffic will have had a dramatic effect on magazine sales with the increased importance of platform news kiosks. The W.H. Smith house magazine *Newsbasket* which surveyed 'their monthly trade in its principal railway bookstalls and urban bookshops' noted that Ethel's work, among many others 'stood out in the popular fiction and new edition categories'.[10]

Theatre and radio were not mainstream marketing activities, with the former receiving almost without exception negative reviews on their short runs in London, but generally more positive reviews in the counties. This does of course confirm Ethel's reader profile as not being those who would frequent theatres in London's West End. Between 1920 and 1929 Ethel's work was staged in ten cities outside London. Orwell's misogynistic observation that 'Dell's novels, of course, are read solely by women, but by women of all kinds and ages and not, as one might expect, merely by wistful spinsters and the fat wives of tobacconists', would, however, seem to be correct.[11] Whether in magazines, book editions or films and theatres her titles were actively marketed in the national and the regional Press on an ongoing basis. Advertising support for Ethel's works outside the national papers was dominated by support in Scotland's Tayside at 34.9%, followed by the south west of England at 25.2% and east Midlands at 17%, and the influence of this weighting can be seen in the regionally weighted readership.[12]

Ethel's national reviews were, however, seldom very good, but it did not matter. Those that read the reviews were not the target audience.

Her establishment in popular culture and the popularity of her work in twopenny libraries also firmly anchored her to a lowbrow reading public. In Ronald Batty's treatise on the management of a twopenny library he clearly defines the socio-economic status of its patrons: 'it is far easier to get matey over the last book that Mae West has written than two ounces of almond jelly'. Confirming the importance of this environment for Ethel, Batty notes that she appeared in a list of the most popular authors.[13]

Seven stories were published in four different magazines before Ethel's seminal success in Britain with *The Way of an Eagle*. Three of these early publications were in the United States. *The Way of an Eagle* was itself released by two different publishing houses in the United States and serialised in the *Red Magazine* in Britain before 1912. These early successes must have had some influence on Watt's views of Ethel's commercial potential, and it was he that signed up Ethel with T. Fisher Unwin for the release of *The Way of an Eagle* in hardback in June 1912, although he had not been involved in the release of the material either in the United States nor to *The Red Magazine*. Mary Ann Gillies' comment that 'Watt's business model had little room for championing new writers ...' would seem to be only partially correct.[14] T. Fisher Unwin who accepted the work in their First Novel Library series also clearly saw her potential. *The Way of an Eagle* and the early titles were to all intents and purposes subjected to test markets.

T. Fisher Unwin's multiple attempts to sharpen *The Way of an Eagle* by reducing the original manuscript from 300,000 words to 90,000 shows considerable patience, no doubt brought about by a realisation of the commercial opportunity demonstrated by volume sales through *The Red Magazine*, and her success in the United States.[15] The sale of rights to magazines created a focus which was a pivotal part of Watt's strategy during her lifetime (after her death, Watt was still pushing for magazine sales in Australia in

1953). It is in this context that we see the importance of the marketing mix, with serial publication in magazines exposing her work to a wide franchise of potential story buyers and book borrowers. Ethel's stories appeared in an eclectic selection of mainly female-oriented publications (ranging from *Love Stories*, a tuppenny weekly, to the more substantial story magazine *Strand* which sold at one shilling). Parallel or similar magazine content to her stories did not seem to be a prerequisite for securing publication as long as there was female readership. This approach and the increasing role and functionality of both the lending libraries and the local twopenny provided a wide distributive platform to provide for the greatest exposure of her works.

Mudie's Circulating Library, which had been such a force in the latter half of the nineteenth century had ceased trading by the start of the Second World War. 'What it boiled down to was that Mudie's was a "select" library and it was the librarian who selected ... the supplies of high class work!'[16] It is not known but it is highly likely that Mudie's would not have carried Ethel's work. The new and popular medium of film was also fundamental to her marketing and played an important part in increasing her reader franchise.

With the exception of *Weldon's Weekly* and *Strand Magazine*, the reader profile in the UK was at the lower end of the social economic scale. However, her readership was not necessarily all at the lower end of the socio-economic scale. In 1921 The *Western Mail* newspaper reported the death of a Mrs Catherin Howard, the wife of a deceased JP and that she was to be buried in the Jewish cemetery in London's Golder's Green with an armlet that she wore in memory of her husband, and that there was a bequest of her 'cat's eye pendant surrounded with diamonds and platinum chain, to "Miss Ethel M. Dell, authoress, in appreciation of the pleasure that she derived from reading her books, especially *The Knave of Diamonds*".[17] We had here we can assume a well-educated widow being enthralled by: a swarthy male, a disabled man, frequent uses of French, cynicism, sanity/mental asylum, American and a mixed-race American Indian, wealth, drunkenness, callousness, theft, violence (marital, spiteful, sexual), morphine, marriage (duty and sanctity of), adoption, murder and eventually love. In 1928 Dorothy Sayers in her novel *The Unpleasantness at the Bellona Club* (1828) mentions Ethel as an example of escapist literature '... And passionate spinsters read Ethel M Dell'.[18] Clearly Mrs. Howard was one of those lonely escapists.

All of this ignored the important American library and sales market, which was the start of Ethel's global literary presence. The literary and academic environment in which she operated in the United States was not too dissimilar to the environment in the UK. B.H. Lehman, professor of English, University of California, at Berkeley defined Ethel's readership profile in very clear terms as being of the less educated 'lower' class:

That is an illusion, the kind of illusion that is called 'hokum' by the lower classes. Not all readers can become good readers of good books. It depends upon certain later training no doubt, but it depends also and fundamentally on whether that given person began life with the reality or with the fantasy sense. Those people who, when they were babies, imagined that because the bottle appeared when they cried, therefore, they created the bottle by crying for it, never make good readers of good books, for after a while they discover that they didn't create the bottle by crying for it and they do what the psychologists call 'take flight'; they live in a world of fantasy. Such people become in the end the devoted readers of Harold Bell Wright and Ethel M. Dell.[19]

The papers and proceedings of the American Library Association also help identify Ethel's American environment and her success. A minute from 1927 defines not just Ethel's literary position but also the power of the library to guide the borrower to better material and reads:

> When fiction readers confess to experiencing thrills through the daring exploits of Zane Grey's cowboys, and more thrills from the romantic settings of Ethel M. Dell, they only exhibit additional evidence of their humanity, and of the normal functioning of their desires. These books offer an undeniable appeal in the nature of an emotional outlet, which is certainly legitimate enough. It is now up to the adviser to analyze the basic quality of these books and to discover through this analysis the best means of satisfying that want through a better grade of fiction.[20]

The American Library Association clearly also saw themselves as a guardian of the reading habits of American youth: 'attention of school librarians is called to the very misleading 1933 catalog of the Follett Book Company, Chicago, entitled A Guide to Good Reading? Titles Approved by the National Council of Teachers of English?' The first list is called Approved Fiction for High Schools and Libraries. In an introductory statement we learn that 'this entire list has been approved by our own Library Department and is suitable for grades 8–12. Any book will be found to be of real literary and informative value, and appealing to all tastes'.[21] There follows practically the whole output of E. R. Burroughs, with a generous sampling of Ethel's titles.

Dora Smith, professor of the teaching of English at the University of Minnesota (also a past president of the National Council of Teachers of English), wrote: 'In the first place, we must provide teachers who know books first hand and recognize their place in the lives of boys and girls. It is fair

RIDING THE TOSH HORSE

neither to young people nor to their teachers to send out from our colleges and universities men and women trained alone in Chaucer and Milton and Browning to compete with Zane Grey, Robert W. Chambers, and Ethel M. Dell'.[22] This theme was endorsed by American teachers who acknowledged the importance of accepting what is read and building upon that. Ethel was not seen in the same context as that shown by the Library Association. One viewpoint was financial and the other well being.

It's time we about faced and looked at literature for our students from their viewpoint. They are reading; most of them read a great deal. I need not recount what they read – Ethel M. Dell, Temple Bailey, Vina Delmar, Edgar Guest, True Romances, True Confessions – but it isn't Shakespeare. They have turned as far away from that vibrant personality as they can get to indulge in present-day literature-milk and water, harmless, harmful, pernicious – it matters not. It is the timeliness of the content, the realism of characters battling in a present-day world of which the students are an integral part, that captures them. We need to take a cue from what they read and meet them where they are and build on that toward an appreciation of the masters.[23]

In 1932, the American Library Association's locations in Baltimore (Maryland) and St. Louis (Missouri) undertook research to understand their library reader profiles. Although not statistically significant the indications are the first attempt that I have seen for establishing a sort of qualitative fix on who reads what in this period, and is not too dissimilar to what one might have expected. The research was undertaken in all branches of all their circulating library departments, although regrettably the number of locations was not disclosed. On a fixed day starting at 16.30 the first twenty readers' borrowings were logged. A total of 414 titles were borrowed in this time frame of which 58% were fiction. The arbitrary fiction genre was divided as follows and some of the profiles of the readers noted:

- Good modern 24% of titles: e.g.

    S. Maugham – motorman

    Barrie – housemaid

    Kipling – housemaid, painter

    J. London – waitress

    C.R. Morley – bookkeeper

- Western and adventure 21% of titles: e.g. Grey ...

    Bus girl, painters, carpenters, clerks, salesmen, attorney's wife.

- Nice sweet stories 17% of titles: e.g. Dell, J. Porter, and D. Lutz.

    Wife of a lawyer

    Wife of insurance agent

    A worker in a pretzel factory reading Ethel was noted specifically

    A vamper (specialised in shaping and sewing the top part of the shoe) reading D. Lutz.

- Mystery 16% titles e.g.: E. Wallace, E.D. Biggers, Doyle, M.R. Rinehart, J.S. Fletcher, S.S. van Dyne ...

    Clerk, printer, lawyer's wife, high school teacher ...

- Standards 9% of titles: e.g. Victor Hugo, Jonathan Swift, E.A. Poe, George Eliot, N. Hawthorne ...

    Eliot – wife of a bookkeeper, wife of an unemployed

    Poe – chiropractor, unemployed widow

    Swift – salesman and lawyer

Hawthorne – clerk

- Humorous 3% of titles

In this very small and not professional piece of research Ethel is represented amongst the major novelists of the time. However, it is clear the librarians had not read Ethel's works. Patently Nice Sweet Stories they are not.[24]

Between 1933 and 1934 the Graduate Library School of the University of Chicago undertook a survey of the material that was read within the greater Chicago environment. This study, which was an amalgam of quantification of raw data and the quantification of qualitative analysis, would today be unacceptable as a benchmark study of any validity. However, an examination of the quantified data on readers of fictional material, ignoring the quantification of quality of the material read, covering some 11,000 readers can give an indication of reader choice in America at this time. Within the many categories of fiction Ethel, along with Bronte, Deeping, Barclay and others, accounts for the fourth largest number of readers, Ferber (*Show Boat*, *Cimarron*) was the largest at 17.6%, and Bronte 3% near the bottom of the list. Of significance is that the Ethel's readers read the second highest number of titles of any author within this category.[25] In 1920 Ethel was listed in top bestsellers in the United States, but by 1940 Ethel was off the list completely.[26]

It was clear that Ethel's titles were widely borrowed throughout the United States. In 1921 when in answer to a question as to whether Ethel sold in New Jersey, a minute of the Library Association read 'Is Ethel M. Dell known in New Jersey? It was admitted that Miss Dell had no geographical limitations'.[27] This can be understood to mean that she was widely borrowed throughout the United States. Confirming this, the library chain owner Nelson R. McNaughton recalled that in the 1920s his own library in Altoona (rural Pennsylvania) in the 1920s. 'We had on our shelves about 15% detective stories, 15% westerns, 35% light fiction, and about 30% more serious fiction and non-fiction. It was no uncommon thing for us to put in the library fifty copies of a Grace Livingston Hill title, twenty of Ethel Dell, and up to thirty or so of Zane Grey.'[28]

In 1919 and 1920 Ethel appeared in the top twelve bestsellers in America: 'Five of the twelve ranking best-sellers in 1919 were of foreign origin; the rest were created by Zane Grey, Harold Bell Wright, Gene Stratton Porter, Temple Bailey, and Ethel M. Dell, with Mary Roberts Rinehart to bring up the intellectual level of the lot. Another classic year for romance was 1920; Zane Grey, Peter B. Kyne, James Oliver Curwood, Ethel M. Dell …'[29]

What is fascinating is that Ethel is clearly a dominant author in the United States and seemed so embedded with the American reading public and no doubt to a great extent result of the editing of her texts that she was thought to be an American author.

19 Poetry

'And to my judges make this one protest – A poor performance but I did my best!'[1]

A great many middlebrow writers have dabbled in the creation of poetry, but few if any lowbrow writers in this period have attempted this form of narrative. Poetry can perhaps be considered outside of this literary focus as it can portray an intimacy of feeling that can be masked in published fiction. It is not necessarily telling a story. A literary style for a novelist is their published fiction, but can one separate the fictional narrative from the poetry? Surely, however, these two forms of writing reflect a style relating to the writer's creative output as a totality. Evelyn Waugh reflected on this total and inseparability of style between the two writing forms in his essay *Literary Style in England and America*.[2] Poetry is a specialised literary style, but that does not preclude a bifurcated ability in each domain. Kipling's poetry earnings were apparently nearly as great as his earnings from fiction.[3]

Ethel wrote poetry which, although published, was clearly not destined for her mass readership universe, unless it appeared in her published fiction, as it only appeared as a stand-alone work in a small green suede and in a red cloth bound volume with gold printed title pages in the UK, and in a red and gold edition in the United States.[4] All the thirteen poems in this volume are accompanied by illuminated first letters of each poem making the volume an important keepsake. Ethel's thirteen published poems as a stand-alone volume are accompanied by four others that she created as epigraphs to some of her novels. No other Ethel poems have been located. Ethel's located output can be divided into the following categories:

Love and Relationships
- Dedication, *Verses* 1923.
- Beyond 1920, *Verses* 1923.
- The Queen's Jester 1921, *Verses* 1923.

Friendship
- Strong and Faithful (M.N.G.S.). *Verses* 1923.

Solitude
- The Stones, *Verses* 1923, and *Tetherstones*, 1923.

Self-denigration
- The Race, *The Obstacle Race*, and 1921, *Verses,* 1923.

Grief and Mourning
- To the beloved memory of my mother 1919, *Verses,* 1923.
- Grief, *Verses,* 1923.

Pietistic
- The Lamp in the Desert 1919, *Verses,* 1923.
- The Top of the World 1920, *Verses,* 1923.
- The Gods 1922, *Charles Rex* 1922 and *Verses,* 1923.
- The Wilderness, *Verses,* 1923.
- When the World was New, *The Unknown Quantity*, 1923.
- Servant of all – No higher, *A Man under Authority*, 1925.

Romantic Domesticity
- Home 1923, *Verses,* 1923.

Romantic Fiction
- The Crusader, *The Black Knight*, 1926.

Non-specific Rhyming
- A pound of blame for a faithful friend, *The Prison Wall*, 1923.

The most striking conclusion is that despite being a writer of sexually explicit and sometimes violent romantic fiction, Ethel's poetry displayed a much wider encompassment of genres, a creative ingenuity and an outstanding sensitivity. It is hard to imagine that the same writer was responsible for the two different styles of narrative, that of the fiction and the poetry. Perhaps Ethel's most accomplished poem is the epigraph to *Tetherstones* titled Stones:

The lonely circle on the hill

Where mist-wreaths float and rise

Hither and thither, lingering still,

Like smoke of sacrifice –

Forgotten fires, forgotten rites,

Forgotten agonies.

The heaven-blue flowers bloom below

About the grim stone's foot,

The sweet hare-bells that always grow

Where nought else e'er takes root.

Of all that stony wilderness,

The only fruit.

A presence in the moonlit night
Unseen doth ever brood,
As though it kept in silent sight
The stones rough-hewn and rude;
The shrine of which it was the god, –
The moorland solitude.

And never shall that vigil tire,
And never the great spell pass,
Where the Druids built their altar-fire
Over the dew-drenched grass,
Till the last loud trump shall shatter
The gates of brass.

And then forgotten priests shall wake
And forgotten victims rise,
And the old grey stones of the circle shake
In the place of sacrifice. ...
But the heaven-blue flowers will bloom for aye
As flowers of Paradise.

Despite this she displayed her lack of confidence in, for example, 'The Race'
and linked her poem to the Bible, a device she used often.[5]

The Race
'So run, that ye may obtain' (1 Cor.ix 24)
Give me the ready brain and steadfast ace
To dare the hazard and run the race,

The high heart that no scathing word can stay,

O'erleaping obstacles that bar the way,

The sportsman's soul that, failing at the end,

Can smile upon the victory of a friend,

And to my judges make this one protest –

A poor performance but I did my best!

1921

The device to hang her work onto an established text or creativity can be seen in her epigraph to *Charles Rex* (1922) which has as its title an adapted last line from Ralph Waldo Emerson's poem *Give All to Love,* 'When half-gods go, The gods arrive'[6]

So they derided the strangers –

Those gods whom the old folk call

Courage and Honour and Faithfulness

And Love which is greater than all.

But when the night is over

And the new day pierced within

The half-gods were gone from the temple,

And the gods had entered in.

The device of quality or acceptability by association is again a demonstration of her lack of confidence in her own abilities, despite her huge earnings. Ethel's very tangible emotions in all her 'personal' poems are perhaps an indication of a very lonely and isolated person. Her reader universe was her emotional shoulder when perhaps there was none at home. There is little if any contemporary context against which to align Ethel's work but it is interesting to examine Barbara Cartland's poetry of the time. In comparison to Ethel's work this is kitsch and puerile verse. For example:

Enchantment[7]
(about young men and cars)
Your headlamps like two golden moons
Shine on the silver way,
The wind is singing you faery tunes,
Drive on till you find the day ...

An analogous kitschiness from Ethel might be her motorcar narrative when the heroine 'listens to the thundering wheels of destiny'.[8] But Cartland was surely in her own league in respect of kitschiness.

Yearning[9]
I want- I stretch out hungry hands
To dreams which always evade my touch.
And treasures of wisdom from ancient lands
Are lost because I ask too much ...

Cartland's book of forty poems were published as a free addition to the fourth volume, her work *Lost Enchantment* (1972) which was included as part of the set of Cartland's 'Eternal Collection'.

Ethel's Perspective
In my writing I managed to squeeze in my views on issues that affected me or on which I had an opinion, but with my poetry I felt more empowered to an intimacy with my reader. I was really expressing myself. Kipling's prolific

poetry was melodic and topical, mine was just me. Even though most of my poems appeared in the epigraphs to my published fiction, they were so special that Hutchinson's arranged that I should have a unique binding for them. Here in England, they were published with a beautiful suede cover with illuminated text. What were my inspirations? Clearly my own life in its various guises. I used the Bible to explain my lack of confidence, but the balance of the works were straight from my imagination. Throughout my stories I have included my personal feelings and comments on the issues that I faced. It was in poetry, however, that I wrote unencumbered by the story's narrative. My publication *Verses* did not sell in any great volume but then no one thought that they would. The publication was for my benefit and as a keepsake for dedicated readers.

I admired other poet's work, especially Emerson, Southey, Tennyson and Kipling and I borrowed some of their work. I also borrowed from Robert Burns but an acknowledgement was not regrettably included. For my use of Emerson's 'Give all to Love' I did change the title a bit to fit in with my story, but the body of the poem stayed the same.

20 Literary Influences

'And I used to pretend I was Persephone. I did so wish Pluto would appear some day with his chariot and his black horses and take me underground. ...he never did'.[1]

There is no evidence to suggest that Ethel received any formal education beyond the age of sixteen, but we know that she was moderately well read. Her literary influences and the domestic and contemporary literary environment in which she worked were very important in providing raw creativity, flesh on the bones of an idea and sometimes disguised plagiarism. Apart from where there is empirical evidence there can only be conjecture about her literary crutches. This empirical evidence is established from where she has quoted or in some cases perhaps deliberately misquoted other authors, lifted names and characters but seldom acknowledging that she had done so. Ethel, like her sister, had literary knowledge. There is the visible empirical evidence, but what is not revealed and can only be surmised is the influence of writers already discussed such as Steel, Diver, Perrin and Croker. Ethel it seems developed her ideas, created an environment from the latter novelists and recorders of empire life and then added bolstering material from other sources.

The male character in Ethel's *The Sea Urchin and the Prince* was named as Prince von Steinwald. She has clearly borrowed the character of the same name from George Macdonald's *Phantastes: A Faerie Romance for Men and Women* (1858).[2] Steinwald is too unusual a name for this to have this been otherwise. George Macdonald (1824–1905) was a Scottish clergyman novelist and writer of juvenile literature, and fantastical verse. Writing in the introduction to *George MacDonald An Anthology* in 1947 C.S. Lewis wrote, 'I dare not say that he is never in error; but to speak plainly I know hardly any other writer who seems to be closer, or more continually close, to the Spirit of Christ Himself'. W.H. Auden and J.R.R. Tolkien also admired his efforts, and Macdonald was known to be a mentor to Lewis Carol. Not a mentor, but a resource for Ethel.

Ethel's *Lamp in the Desert* describes a character's mother's infatuation with a young rajah after her father is killed as 'the slithy tove'.[3] This is plagiarism. Victorian children in 'educated' households would have been exposed to Lewis Carol's child fiction, and so was Ethel. In Lewis Carol's *Through the Looking-Glass and What Alice Found There* (1871), included the very memorable poem of the Jabberwocky:

> 'Twas brillig, and the slithy toves. Did gyre and gimble in the wabe: All mimsy were the borogoves, And the mome raths outgrabe. 'Beware the Jabberwock, my son! The jaws that bite, the claws that catch! Beware the Jubjub bird, and shun. The frumious Bandersnatch!'

Ethel did not hesitate to 'borrow'. Ralph Waldo Emerson's (1803–1882) poem of love and grief *Give All to Love* (1858), was published after his death in 1899.[4] Ethel quoted the last line of this poem 'When half-gods go, The gods arrive' as the title to her poem which was the epigraph to *Charles Rex*. It is hard to countenance that Ethel did anything other than read all his poetry and came across 'her' epigraph title. This was clearly more than an example of just being 'well read' but a demonstration of a studied interest in religions different from her conflicted religiosity at home. Emerson was an American intellectual and literary giant who explored Asian and Middle Eastern religions and writing and raised questions regarding the importance of the non-Western world. The most readily available source of intellectual input for this part of the world at this time was the writings emanating out of the British Empire, especially India. In 1831 he resigned his post as the rector at the Protestant Second Church Boston, stating that he no longer believed in the divinity of Jesus when his first wife Ellen died. As a result of the 1844 publication of Emerson's *Essays: Second Series*, which had a strong Asiatic overtone, he became a transatlantic literary celebrity. His poems are not an easy read and must be considered somewhat esoteric when examined in the light of Ethel's non-poetic output, but she had read them.

Robert Southey's (1774–1843) poem the *Curse of Kehama* was a Hindu fantasy, part of which was slightly misquoted in the epigraph to *The Rocks of Valpré*.[5] In the preface to *The Curse of Kehama* (1812), Southey wrote: 'In the religion of the Hindoos, which of all false religions is the most monstrous in its fables, and the most fatal in its effects, there is one remarkable peculiarity. Prayers, penances, and sacrifices, are supposed to possess an inherent and actual value, in no degree depending upon the disposition or motive of the person who performs them'.[6] To a novelist who led a cloistered life this statement alone would have fired Ethel's imagination of an India almost beyond comprehension. Did reading Southey, like her reading of Emerson, fire-up her interest in non-Christian religions? In *Storm Drift* the hero has a sudden reawakening: 'And the – very suddenly it happened – that third turn of the wheel [Buddhist Third Wheel of Dharma] that was to alter the whole course of his existence.'[7]

As we have seen earlier Ethel had clearly read Kipling's works relating to India. This can be seen in her use of Hindi, all lifted from Kipling's texts or even possibly through conversation with him: In *The Way of an Eagle*, the lovers go for a ride near Jakko. This would without doubt have been influenced by Kipling's love poem set in Simla, *A Ballad of Jakko's Hill* (1886). Jakko Hill exists in Simla but one has to doubt if Ethel knew this geographical fact.[8]

Ethel quotes one line from Geoffrey Chaucer's (1343–1400) *The Pilgrim's Progress* in the epigraph to *Greatheart*: 'Now Mr. Greatheart was a strong man'.

One has to wonder which came first, the idea generated by Chaucer or the narrative of the title. She also quotes from Shakespeare's *As you Like It*, 'Who ever loved that loved not at first sight' in *The Eleventh Hour*.[9]

Lord Robert Lytton (1831–1891), viceroy of India 1876–80 a man of letters and obviously of considerable Indian experience, published poetry under his nom de plume of Owen Meredith. Ethel, however, chose one of his quotations which was cited: 'That man is great, and he alone', in the double epigraph to *Greatheart*. This would seem to be an attempt to add gravitas to the title.

A full poem from Robert Burns, without attribution, appears in *The Keeper of the Door:*

> O, wert thou in the cauld blast,
> On yonder lea, on yonder lea,
> My plaidie to the angry airt,
> I'd shelter thee, I'd shelter thee.
> Or did misfortune's bitter storms
> Around thee blaw, around thee blaw,
> Thy bield should be my bosom,
> To share it a', to share it a' [10]

A poem from Thomas Moore, *The High Borne Ladye* (1841) is also quoted without attribution;

> In vain all the knights of the Underworld woo'd her,
> Though brightest of maidens,
> the proudest was she;
> Brave chieftains they sought,
> and young minstrels they sued her,
> But worthy were none of the high-born Ladye[11]

Homer's *Iliad* and *Odyssey* would have been a source for comments about Persephone and Pluto in the *Rocks of Valpré*.[12] Greek mythology also appears in *The Way of an Eagle* where Triton, the demigod of the sea is used with the polarity to minnows to describe a clumsy man, and in *Tetherstones* where the heroine is nicknamed Circe (the goddess), nymph, enchantress and sorceress.[13]. Ethel uses Circe again in *Peggy By Request,* and also in *Honeyball Farm.*

The Juice of the Pomegranate, her penultimate work, delves deep into Greek, Hindu Persian and Chinese culture. Persephone features again in this narrative, as the fecund heroine is raped and becomes pregnant. Ethel understood the legend. Persephone had eaten six pomegranate seeds, and she had to remain in the underworld for six months of each year. Hades agreed to release her to the world above for the other six months of the year. This is how the ancient Greeks explained the cycle of the seasons: when Persephone was away from Hades, the earth flourished and the crops grew; when she returned to Hades, the earth was infertile. As a consequence, pomegranates were often offered in prayer for fertile land. In the Koran there is mention that pomegranates grow in the gardens of Paradise, and in Hindu, Persian and in Chinese culture, the pomegranate is also considered a symbol of fertility.

In *The Keeper of the Door* Ethel uses the Latin phrase 'Dum spiro spero' meaning, 'while I breathe, I hope', a paraphrase of ideas that survive in two Greek Roman authors, Theocritus and Cicero. But she does explain it later in the narrative: '"Oh, that's a pity," he said. "Pray let me enlighten your ignorance. It means, 'While I breathe I hope' – a very proper sentiment which does the young man infinite credit."'[14] Also in *The Hundredth Chance* we have the Latin legal term 'cui bono' for 'who is to benefit?'[15] Surely only used for reasons of gravitas as the average lowbrow reader would not be able to translate or understand this phrase.

There is a rare case of Ethel citing a source in *The Keeper of the Door*: 'It's a case of the wicked uncle and the lost babes over again … It also smacks of The Pilgrim's Progress. Old Bunyan would have made some good copy out of this. He'd have dubbed you Mistress Timorous and me Master Overbold'.[16] Bunyan's 'slough of Despond' from his *Pilgrim's Progress* is also used in this narrative. And *Pilgrim's Progress* also appears as a humorous aside in *Peggy by Request* (1928).[17] Curiously upper case S and D are used, indicating perhaps that this is being acknowledged as not her creativity.[18]

Sir Walter Scott was reading material for *The Hundredth Chance*: 'Perhaps it wouldn't have taken place at all if you had … You know the legend of Young Lochinvar. … I presume you know my reputation'.[19]

Throughout Ethel's works there seems to be a curious detachment from reality but then the reader is suddenly exposed to a comment about current affairs. In *The Keeper of the Door* she comments about the massacre of 1.5 million Armenians in Turkey between 1915 and 1917: 'Absolutely revolting massacres of Armenians by the Turks. This is the beastliest thing I've ever read. You shall have it when I've finished. It's all about the Turkish massacres in Armenia – revolting –absolutely revolting'. [20]

Lord Tennyson is quoted but not cited in *The Hundredth Chance*: 'The song came to an end. Her fingers began to wander idly over the keys. She played a dreamy air with an old-world waltz refrain, too lost in her trance of delight to realize what she played, and again half-unconsciously she was singing, as she had sung long ago before the gates of youth.

> There has fall'n a splendid tear,
> From the passion flower at the gate,
> She is coming, my dove, my dear;
> She is coming, my life, my fate.
> The red rose cries, 'she is near, she is near';

And the white rose weeps, 'she is late';

The larkspur listens, 'I hear, I hear';

And the lily whispers, 'I wait.'[21]

Tennyson is quoted again in *The Altar of Honour* with a reference to King Cophetua and the Beggar Maid.[22] This simile is interesting as it incapsulates the heroine's lack of social self-confidence, and her own self-image. 'There has fallen a splendid tear' again from Lord Tennyson is repeated in *Charles Rex*. What is significant about this repeated and uncited use of Tennyson's work is that not just that the verse is very apt for the setting of the narrative but that Tennyson's poem is from his work *Maud* (1855) which is also the name of the heroine of Ethel's work.[23]

'Are you going, alma mater? Don't let me drive you away!' In this context the hero is referring to his mother. Alma mater is of course a previous seat of learning that has been attended. With this narrative in *Knave of Diamonds* is Ethel demonstrating a misunderstanding of the meaning of alma mater or is she in fact using the American Indian Baptist Minister Samson Occum's (1792–1792) the play on words? 'I am very Jealous that instead of your Semenary becoming alma Mater, she will be too alba mater to Suckle the Tawnees'. in reverse. (Alba mater meaning white mother.)[24] Within the same title the hero made a grimace. 'Where is your native shrewdness? And I never admired her skating anyway. It's about on a par with Mrs. Damer's dancing. In the name of charity, don't ask that woman to come and help us dance again. I'm not equal to her. It's yoking an elephant to a zebra'. This text would seem to have been heavily influenced by John Keats' sonnet *Endymion 11*, and a peculiarly out of context reference.[25] Perhaps it was just inserted as a convenient narrative vehicle?

There is a surprising and esoteric reference to Persian mythology in

Death's Property when there is comment that: 'I guess we are just a couple of Peris shut outside'. The Peri is a mythical superhuman being, originally represented as evil but subsequently as a good or graceful genie or fairy.[26] But unless the reader was familiar with Robert Southey's *Thalaba the Destroyer* this was a meaningless descriptive. Why did she use it? There is here, almost a demonstration of literary schizophrenia; I am very well read but I will use phrases that the 'hoi polloi' will not understand but from whom perhaps there could be admiration for such erudition.

John Milton's *Paradise Lost* as a tough task is used in *Bars of Iron*. 'It is my intention to impose a holiday-task of sufficient magnitude to keep you all out of mischief during the rest of the holidays. You will therefore commit to memory various different portions of Milton's *Paradise Lost* which I shall select ...'[27]

In *The Passer-By* one of the characters, is an artist and this is a segue into the discussion of the painting of 'The Little Seamstress' being sold to America instead of the National Gallery. It is apparent that this is a painting reminiscent of Charles Dickens' *A Tale of Two Cities*, where the little seamstress holds Carton's hand as they ride together in the tumbril to the guillotine.

In 1914 Ethel is joined by some dominant contemporary 'easy reading' authors, including, Conrad, Buchan, Barrie, Caine, Doyle, Jerome, Diver, Galsworthy in contributing to *The Queen Mary's Gift Book* which was sold in aid of limbless soldiers and sailors at Queen Mary's convalescence and auxiliary hospitals at Roehampton. Not only that, but her contribution was illustrated by Russell Flint and E.H. Shepherd of *Winnie the Pooh* (1926) fame. Clearly Ethel was seen as acceptable reading material for war veterans. She gave the rights to Hodder and Stoughton for this publication but retained the overall copyright, but the work was not published again.[28]

As a novelist who wrote from his 'own experience' Ernest Hemingway's *A*

Farewell to Arms (1929) became a public domain literary benchmark for the 1917 Italian Caporetto disaster. He had been there and wrote about it, fiction overlaid on reality, a factoid. But was this honest creativity, and was it true he had been there? He had not. His visualisation of the battle was lifted from the historian G.M. Trevelyan (*Scene's from Italy's War,* 1919) and Hugh Dalton, later chancellor of the exchequer under Attlee (*With British Guns in Italy,* 1919), both of whom were there and wrote extensively about this conflict. His ability to write and his name allowed him to use the environments created by Trevelyan and Dalton to make his fortune. He was forced to own up eventually to misleading his public about his real experiences. The dishonesty was misleading his readership that he had been there and not acknowledging his use of Trevelyan and Dalton's experiences. He skirted around plagiarism as did Ethel.

Cartland stated that Ethel was the greatest influence on her career as a romantic novelist. Under the headline 'Why Ethel is my romantic heroine' she wrote, 'When I first borrowed an Ethel M. Dell it was not only a revelation, but it set out for me clearly the principles which I have tried to follow all my life'.[29] But there can be little doubt Cartland's high profile life and her name also helped her work to endure and continue to be published.

Cartland was influenced and so was Heyer. In Jennifer Kloester's biography of Heyer (2011) she states that Heyer was a fan of Ethel's hugely popular angst-ridden novels and their breathless heroines and cruel heroes.

Perhaps that influence verged on plagiarism. In Heyer's *These Old Shades* (1926) one can see a disturbing similarity in this story to Dell's *Charles Rex* (1923) published earlier. A slight plot and period change but we have the like in *Charles Rex* a boy who is in fact a young woman who is rescued from an abuser. Charles Rex calls his charge mignone, as does Heyer's hero. There are 'at least half-a-dozen points of similarity'. She was influenced but also 'infuriated' by the advertisement for her novel *Roxhythe* (1922) included at the end of Dell's *Charles Rex*, this amongst some ninety other selling write-ups, which explained the plot and gave away the ending.[30]

It is not even remotely possible that Ethel went down to her local pub and ordered a shandy gaff (beer and ginger beer or ginger ale). In Well's comic novel *The History of Mr. Polly* (1910), he refers to a shandygaff as 'two bottles of beer mixed with ginger beer in a round-bellied jug'. Her hero in *The Good Turn* is known to his friends as Shandygaff.

Plays from the German poet, philosopher and playwright Friedrich Schiller, friend of Goethe, considered by many Germans as their greatest classical playwright, are used as a punishment in *The Gate Marked Private*. Money and power, personal freedoms, anarchy, the hypocrisies of class and religion, the economic inequities of society and the nature of evil are the foci of his works. It is both interesting that these plays are mentioned as being in German, not translations but also perhaps their influence on Ethel and her own philosophies.

Ethel's Perspective

Ella and I were very lucky in that our mother collected books for us to read and for us to be read to from a very early age. Like many Victorian households we were exposed to Lewis Carol and George Macdonald and all of Kipling's works. These were fun and exciting romances and my earliest stories were no doubt were influenced by these tales.

We could, I suppose, be considered well read. Our homes were filled with the Greek and Roman classics, English classics and a wide ranging amount of literature and poetry of all sorts. Like many of our age group our formal education finished when we left our secondary school at the Streatham College for Girls. However, at our school we had a curriculum that encompassed Latin.

RIDING THE TOSH HORSE

The first year was compulsory, and Greek as well as the classics, and a reading of the literary greats.[31] This grounding allowed for Ella to be a tutor to the Bowra brothers.[32] It also provided me with a basic academic background from which I was able to quote. Ella's focus were the Greek and Roman classics and mine dreams of empire and romance. It was my mother who collected material for us sisters, not our father who concentrated on his senior role in The Equitable.

I think that our mother was very advanced in acquiring both Emerson and Southey's poetry for us. These two poets had a significant influence on me and created a lasting interest in both the East and in non-Christian religions. Combining this interest with the atmosphere of Kipling's empire gave me so much inspiration. In my mind I transported myself from Winchester to India. Although I was writing for an unsophisticated readership whom I respected I could not now and then avoid a demonstration of my knowledge of the classics and literature generally.

There was no opportunity for me to express political views except in my writing and I only did this once and that was a result of the massacre of the Armenians by the Turkish government. What an atrocity. Although I rarely left home except to visit Watt I read the newspapers every day and this situation incensed me, as did the General Dyer's massacre in Amritsar. But I did not publicly comment on the latter as that would have run counter to my themes of empire.

21 Marketing and Selling

'it is far easier to get matey over the last book that Mae West has written than two ounces of almond jelly'.[1]

It is very simplistic in a literary environment to consider the literary merits of a publication as the lever for 'success'. From a monetising perspective perhaps more important is how the publication is exposed to the potential reader universe, and how they are encouraged to read and buy. Michael Joseph's view of a good book was one that sold well, and a good review of a bad book in this context was meaningless if the public would not buy. Ethel, however, rarely had good reviews but her reader universe liked what she wrote.

There is no evidence to suggest that there was any strategic creative planning of content to Ethel's stories. She sold escapism and romance however far-fetched it seemed. Watt was instrumental in creating demand, and unlike Charles Boon (Mills and Boon) he did not set down any ground rules. Ethel's writing sold with his help. Boon set the rules for his authors, but the creative content under Watt's management was entirely Ethel's choice, with stories sold in advance of a title or even a synopsis. The key influences on her style which could produce such a cocktail of creativity would seem to have been her own dysfunctional and financially demanding family and of course her reading. The literary formula was so successful both in the UK and the United States that although appearing to self-denigrate it seems clear that Ethel took trouble to write for consumption by the lower socio-economic parts of society with her lowbrow content, and as such was marketing what at first sight seems to be a lack of self-esteem.

Following the sale of the copyrights to her earlier titles to *The Red*

Magazine and to *Pearsons*, which were all then re-acquired, as expected one sees a dominance of 'First Published' appearing in magazine format. In the UK 55% of titles were first published in magazines, and Watt continued with this strategy in the United States where twenty-two titles were first exposed to the potential reader universe in magazines. Watt saw the commercial potential and benefits of a multi-media approach and aggressively sold Ethel's works into magazines. Parallel or similar magazine content to Ethel's stories was not necessarily a prerequisite for securing publication as long as there was female readership. At least eighteen magazine stories were published before *The Way of an Eagle* and at least three of these early publications appeared in the United States.[2] *The Way of an Eagle* was itself released by two different publishing houses in the United States and serialised in *The Red Magazine* in Britain before 1912. Watt had not been involved in the distribution of this title either in the United States or to *The Red Magazine* to whom Ethel had not sold the copyright.

It is in this context that we see the importance of the marketing mix, with serial publication in magazines exposing Ethel's work to a mass reading audience and a wide franchise of potential story buyers and book-borrowers. Ethel's stories appeared in an eclectic selection of mainly female-oriented publications ranging from *Love Stories*, a twopenny weekly, through *Eve's Own Stories* and *Peg's Companion*, *Weldon's Ladies Journal* and *Women's Weekly*, to the more substantial story magazine *Strand* which sold at one shilling. With the exception of the American *McCall's* and *Strand* magazine, the reader profile was at the lower end of the social scale where fiction magazines constituted important reading material.[3] Of Ethel's total output of ninety-eight titles published, 73% were supported by magazine exposure, 78% titles appeared in hard-copy book form, 23% in film, 4% in theatre and one on the radio.

The expansion of the film industry in the 1920s was fundamental to her marketing and played an important part in increasing her reader franchise. In 1926, Iris Barry stated that the 'one thing never to be lost sight of in considering the cinema is that it exists for the purpose of pleasing women. Three out of every four cinema audiences are women'.[4] However, a study undertaken of cinema-goers in the 1930s indicates a fairly even balance of male/female attendance, which is more likely.[5] Within this study, a higher percentage of women than men (89.4%/76.1%) indicated reading as another leisure activity. In Britain, the Stoll Picture Company produced eighteen interpretations of Ethel's titles from 1919 to 1922 as part of the Stoll Eminent British Author series that also included Doyle, Mason and Wallace. Eminent in this context was not an Orwellian literary highbrow but eminently bankable authors and stories. Stoll understood the importance and commercial value of the demographic imbalance created by the First World War, and saw the potential of targeting the female viewer. Dennis Gifford reported that Maurice Elvey (Stoll film producer) recalled that Ethel was more interested in creative control than commercial considerations.[6] This might well have been the impression given but a study of her commercial correspondence suggests that Ethel was also astute financially. She saw the financial potential of this new market and even acquired shares in the Stoll Picture Company, despite her 10% commission on box office takings.[7] Five of the film titles were produced in the US, and, as in Britain, they supported the magazine and book sales. Theatre and radio were not mainstream marketing activities. The theatrical productions of her works received almost wholly negative reviews on their short runs in London, but generally more positive reviews in the counties. This does of course confirm Ethel's reader universe as largely not being those who would frequent theatres in London's West End.

Developments in distribution and increased public library provision in rural areas after the 1919 Public Libraries Act gave more readers access to her work in book form.[8] Her establishment in film and popular culture contributed to the popularity of her work in the twopenny libraries which sprang up in newsagents and tobacconists throughout the 1930s to cater for a working-class readership, further anchoring Ethel's name to a lowbrow reading public. In Ronald F. Batty's treatise on the management of a twopenny library he clearly defines the socio-economic status of its patrons: 'it is far easier to get matey over the last book that Mae West has written than two ounces of almond jelly.'[9] Confirming the importance of this informal shop-space environment for Ethel, Batty includes her in his 'short check list of the most popular twopenny library authors'.[10]

Her provincial audience was important and targeted advertising was used in regional newspapers. During Ethel's writing career only four areas in Britain (the east Midlands, south west England, Yorkshire and Humber, and Tayside) accounted for nearly 90% of the advertising volume supporting her work, a total of 1,051 advertisements. In comparison, in the serious national press *The Times* carried only ninety advertisements. This bias would also indicate targeting for a lowbrow readership.

The bundling of titles into 'collections' to re-energise Ethel's cash flow also was a feature of Watt's monetising activities. In most cases the gap between 'first published' and the bundled 'collection' was at least two years thus obviating the possibility of being seen as a repeat. In effect these bundles or 'collections' became new titles and refreshed her brand without the requirement of effort from Ethel. Additionally, these 'collections' were also used to launch nine new titles in the UK. This methodology became a standard marketing feature towards the end of Ethel's literary career with established titles being used as the buyer's bait.

1914, The Swindler: And Other Stories
- 1908, *Her Freedom*, first published in *Grand Magazine*
- 1909, *The Consolation Prize*, first published in *The Strand Magazine*
- 1910, *Where the Heart is*, first published in *The Red Magazine*
- 1910, *Her Hero*, first published in *The Red Magazine*
- 1910, *The Right Man*, first published in *The Red Magazine*
- 1910, *Her Own Free Will*, first published in *The Red Magazine*
- 1910, *The Swindler*, first published in *The Red Magazine*
- 1910, *The Swindler's Handicap*, first published in *The Red Magazine*
- 1912, *The Knight Errant*, first published in *The Red Magazine*
- 1912, *The Nonentity*, first published in *The Red Magazine*
- 1912, *A Question of Trust*, first published in *The Red Magazine*

1917, The Safety Curtain: And Other Stories
- 1909, *The Place of Honour*, first published in *The Novel Magazine*
- 1909, *The Friend Who Stood By*, first published in *The Red Magazine*
- 1911, *Those Who Wait*, first published in *The Red Magazine*
- 1912, *The Experiment*, first published in *The Novel Magazine*
- 1914, *The Eleventh Hour*, first published in *The Story-Teller Magazine*
- 1916, *The Safety Curtain*, first published in *The Strand Magazine*

1919, The Tidal Wave: And Other Stories
- 1908, *Her Place of Honour*, first published in *Story-Teller Magazine*
- 1912, *The Return Game*, first published in *The Red Magazine*
- 1912, *The Woman of his Dream*, first published in *The Red Magazine*
- 1912, *The Tidal Wave*, first published in *The Red Magazine*
- 1914, *The Desire of his Life*, first published with *Her Compensation*

1921, Rosa Mundi: And Other Stories
- 1906, *The Secret Service Man*, first published in *The Novel Magazine*
- 1907, *The Deliverer*, first published in *The Novel Magazine*
- 1909, *A Debt of Honour*, first published in *The Red Magazine*
- 1912, *The Prey of the Dragon*, first published in *The Red Magazine*
- 1913, *The Penalty*, first published in *The Red Magazine*
- 1918, *Rosa Mundi*, first published in *Lloyds Magazine*

1922, The Odds: And Other Stories
- 1919, *The Odds*, first published in *Hutchinson's Magazine*
- 1919, *The Sacrifice*, first published in *Hutchinson's Magazine*
- 1920, *Without Prejudice*, first published in *The Strand Magazine*
- 1922, *Death's Property*, first published in any medium

1925, The Passer-By and Other Stories
- 1919, *The Lucky Number*, first published in *Cassell's Magazine*
- 1920, *The Tenth Point*, first published in *Hutchinson's Magazine*
- 1924, *The Passer-By*, first published in *Hutchinson's Magazine*
- 1923, *Tommy Rot*, first published in *Home Magazine*
- 1925, *The Money Monster*, first published in any medium

1927, The House of Happiness and Other Stories
- 1926, *The Good Turn*, first published in *Hutchinson's Magazine*
- 1927, *The Real Thing*, first published in any medium
- 1927, *The House of Happiness*, first published in any medium

1932, Live Bait: And Other Stories

- 1908, *Her Compensation,* first published in *Story-Teller Magazine*
- 1928, *Live Bait,* first published in *Cassell's Magazine*
- 1932, *Quest,* first published in any medium
- 1932, *The Losers,* first published in any medium
- 1932, *The Chatelaine,* first published in any medium
- 1932, *Pageant of Youth,* first published in any medium
- 1932, *Misunderstanding,* first published in any medium

Without an agent, the publication of *The Repentant Rogue* in the United States (*Everybody's Magazine*, March 1900) was a significant achievement, but the narrative was subject to considerable editing for the American market, as were all the other titles sold there. Ethel and Watt in this respect were classic global marketers where they adjusted their product or it was adjusted for them to suit the market into which it was to be sold. As a result, in 1920 Ethel was in the list of the top ten best-selling novelists in the United States.[11] The pattern of printing and distribution in the United States did not replicate that of the UK. *The Desire of his Life* for example appeared as a novelette in *Tidal Wave and Other Stories* in the UK but was sold as a stand-alone publication in the United States and a full story only in the United States.

On publication selected titles were also translated into Swedish, German, Dutch, Spanish, Portuguese and Italian, some as late as 2008 with *Charles Rex* into French.

Ethel's Perspective

I was so lucky in my new literary agent as I did not think that my commercial viability would survive the sale of my initial title copyrights, but Alexander

Watt my replacement literary agent engineered their retrieval and we never looked back. Watt – and I never, despite my closeness and reliance in him, ever used his Christian name – was my commercial guide although he never executed any arrangement without my approval, and he never provided any suggestion or guidance on what I should write. The formula worked so he let me run with it, often selling a story before it had even been written.

I will, however, claim first blood in my eventual success as without any help from an agent I started selling my titles not just in the UK but also in the United States. It was this initial exposure that created the start of my growing number of readers. Although my first major work *The Way of an Eagle* was published first in magazine form in the United States it was Fisher Unwin who saw the potential of the story and worked with me to reduce the volume from 300,000 words to just 90,000. They were very patient with me as any author knows an author does not like their work being so drastically attacked. But it worked and *Eagle* became a bestseller. I am not sure that it was technically correct to include me in their First Novel Library series, but again it worked.

The prospect of my novels appearing in film was very exciting and Oswald Stoll the eminent film producer suggested that I join with Arthur Conan Doyle, Arthur Mason and Edgar Wallace in a series of films under a suggested banner of Eminent British Authors. I was honoured and of course accepted. My relationship with Stoll was close and having asked me to reduce my fees, which I agreed to, he asked me to lobby on his behalf with the other authors. I saw the huge potential of the new film industry and invested directly in Stoll's business without the intervention of Watt. The transition from print to celluloid is a very difficult one and I insisted that I approve all film scripts.

Theatre representation of my work was really an ancillary activity and

Watt did not devote too much time to this, but it did have one significant side benefit for me in that it allowed me to develop a close friendship with the actress Violet Vanburgh.

Watt's efforts to maximise our joint incomes were ceaseless and one of his very clever initiatives was to take the titles that had been exposed in magazines and to then bundle them together in collections or omnibus editions as if they were new books. This was very successful.

22 The Marketing Mix and Magazines

'It must be a condition that a prominent acknowledgment of the "Red" is given. They also wish to see and pass the story before publication'.[1]

Ethel's relatively high profile in the United States does not correlate to the related exposure that she received within magazines compared to the exposure that she received in the UK. It is not, however, correct to consider this medium in isolation of the whole marketing mix and exposure plan. In various degrees her titles were supported by magazine, book and film versions: 61 titles were sold in the United States but only nine were supported by both Magazine and hard copy; 25 titles were only sold into magazines. To this one can add five book titles that were also produced in film and one title which had film-only exposure in the United States. Given the profiles of the magazines selected and their related circulations this strategy has significant commercial logic. The American reader universe was made aware of her work in magazines and then the larger margin book sales followed suit. As is detailed later this was not the case in the UK where magazine and book exposure overlapped and titles were sold multiple times in different and the same medium. The choice of magazines in the USA demonstrates, by and large, a careful media selection:

Everybody's Magazine: Initially, the magazine published a combination of non-fiction articles and new fiction stories.

People's Home Journal: The magazine specialising in domestic and agricultural subjects and cheap fiction reprints. Ethel only used this medium once, probably wisely.

Gunter's Magazine: A monthly magazine published both in the UK and the United States and sold extensively on transatlantic crossings. Contributors included Rider Haggard among many other well-known authors.

Pictorial Review: Specifically focused on women readers featuring dressmaking patterns. By the late 1920s it was one of the largest of the women's magazines.[2] In June, 1931 Pictorial Review enjoyed a circulation of 2,540,000.[3]

Metropolitan Magazine: A monthly periodical with articles on politics and literature. Contributors included: Conan Doyle, F. Scott Fitzgerald and Theodore Roosevelt.

McCall's Magazine: A major player in the home and family oriented magazines market that were competing for readership of the more affluent and educated modern woman. The magazine was divided into three sections: fiction and news, home making, style and beauty, and maintained a strong authorship profile with the publication of full-length novels. Contributors included Eleanor Roosevelt, the Duchess of Windsor, Alfred Kinsey the American sexologist. The latter is of course an interesting editor's association with Ethel.

Love Story Magazine: A bi-monthly romantic fiction pulp magazine, with a circulation of 100,000 in 1922, which had climbed to 600,000 by 1932.[4] This publication was also extensively used by Ruby Ayres.

All-Story: A weekly pulp magazine printed a range of fiction, including tales emphasising mystery, suspense, romance and western or exotic settings.[5]

Chicago Tribune: A dominant newspaper in Illinois with a circulation by the Second World War of approximately 440,000.

Physical Culture: a magazine focused on bodybuilding, health and fitness. Ethel's works were seen as 'healthy' in the United States.

Liberty: A weekly general-interest magazine. At one time it was said to be the second greatest magazine in America, ranking behind The Saturday Evening Post in circulation. The contents provided a unique look into popular culture, politics and world events. Contributors included: F. Scott Fitzgerald, Wodehouse, Dashiell Hammett, G. Bernard Shaw, Agatha Christie, Robert Benchley, Paul Gallico, John Galsworthy and H.G. Wells.[6]

Watt used targeted publications that provided high circulations and that laid the groundwork for her book publications, and that with few overlaps can only have assisted her published book efforts. In the UK, however, it is hard to discern any distinct strategy as freedom of strategic choice was initially dominated and restricted by the sale of titles to The Red Magazine and the Pearson Group (The Novel and Grand Magazines) and the subsequent re-purchase of these assets. Of the ninety-eight titles published in the UK, thirty-seven were published in magazines before the first hard copy/novel appeared in 1913. Ethel had had therefore enormous exposure before her seminal work The Way of an Eagle was accepted by T. Fisher Unwin. Even before T. Fisher Unwin accepted the modified manuscript for their publication it has already appeared in The Red Magazine. Of these thirty-seven magazine titles twenty-five were initially published in The Red Magazine. The monetising significance of rescuing and re-acquiring the copyrights is demonstrated here. Over 30% of future 'title' earnings were initially therefore tied-up and inaccessible.

In total thirty different magazines were employed. Unlike the USA a small proportion, just twenty-two titles were sold only in magazines, twenty-six titles just in book form. Other than the control exercised by *The Red Magazine* it appears that any magazine that would take a story was accepted. Despite the lowbrow dominance of the majority of the magazine media used she did, however, share exposure with many literary luminaries including Doyle, translations of Guy de Maupassant and Pushkin, Hall Caine, Arnold Bennett, H.G. Wells, Lawrence, Aldous Huxley, Baroness Orczy and Agatha Christie.

Perhaps the most surprising of the magazine choices made by Watt and Ethel in the UK was *Cassell's Family Magazine* in 1920. Regrettably it has not been possible to locate the text of the title *Heart of a Tyrant* published by Cassell. But of significance, however, 'is that the rigidity of his [Cassell's] social and literary values is suggested by his magazine formulae. In fiction Cassell's tastes were austere and moralistic, supportive of the Protestant work ethic and reflective of the social complacency of many a "self-made", self-educated religious man: he appreciated tales "ennobling and pure, in the place of that which is corrupting and false", tales "illustrative of the triumph of religion, temperance, morality, industry, energy and self-control over idleness, apathy, intemperance and habitual self-indulgence".'[7] Ethel's pietistic frontispieces were not alone in fighting the possible degenerative influences of the fin de siècle, and her poacher-turned-gamekeeper style would seem to reflect this. In summary, in the United States magazines accounted for 41% of solus exposure and the UK 22%, whereas in the USA book solus exposure accounted for 41% and the UK 26%. The UK is subjected to title and medium proliferation whereas in the United States the objective clearly was to create an exposure for the author and then her money-making titles.

Ethel's Perspective

It seemed to me that Watt would sell my work into any magazine that would accept it, and if course as I became more and more well-known there was very rarely any instances of a refusal. So my writing appeared in a hugely wide spectrum of publications from women and the home, fitness and general culture. Magazines like *Pictorial Review* with a huge mass circulation did not carry many well-known authors but generally this was not the case. It is interesting that there were not many women writers of romantic fiction who shared the same magazines as myself. I found myself aligned with the likes of Conan Doyle, Scott Fitzgerald and Rider Haggard. I suspect that Wodehouse used me as a role model for a character in some of his works. I of course did not mind as this all added exposure.

The most peculiar support that I had was Cassell, whose mainstream publishing house became a mainstream publisher of mine. But Cassell through his magazine espoused austerity and a pretty severe moral tone. Maybe his feelings were subsumed by his need for added circulation through the addition of my work.

Throughout my writing I have always tried to keep a balance between what some saw as the excesses of my prose style and a perhaps higher tone. I think that I managed this by my inclusion of religious thoughts both in the body of the works and in the frontispieces. These thoughts were very rarely of relevance to the stories themselves.

23 Films

'one thing never to be lost sight of in considering the cinema is that it exists for the purpose of pleasing women'.[1]

The expansion of the film industry in the 1920s was fundamental to the marketing plan and played an important part in increasing the reader franchise. In 1926, Iris Barry stated that the 'one thing never to be lost sight of in considering the cinema is that it exists for the purpose of pleasing women. Three out of every four cinema audiences are women'.[2] A later study, undertaken of cinema goers in the 1930s, indicates a fairly even balance of male/female attendance, but within this found that a higher percentage of women than men (89.4 to 76.1%) indicated reading as another leisure activity.[3] The first film adaption was for *The Way of an Eagle* produced by G.B. Samuelson in 1918, followed by an American version of *The Safety Curtain* (also 1918), starring and produced by Norma Talmadge. In Britain, the Stoll Picture Company produced seventeen interpretations of Ethel's titles from 1919 to 1922 as part of the Stoll Eminent British Author series that also included Doyle, Mason and Wallace. The first of Stoll's Ethel adaptions was *The Rocks of Valpré* (1919), directed by Elvey, and a further seventeen films were made in the UK by 1922.

As stated earlier keys to this strategy were of course eminently bankable authors and stories. Stoll clearly understood the importance and commercial value of the demographic imbalance created by the First World War, and saw the potential of targeting the female viewer.

Unlike her contemporary Glyn, who as Alexis Weedon comments, 'mastered the business of writing for different media to an unusual, and perhaps unique extent for the time', Ethel did not write the screenplays of her work but sought creative control of the end product.[4] This control did not, however, result in good results on every occasion. *The Times* reported that '*The Hundredth Chance* is not nearly so successful [comparing John Buchan's Prester John as the high water mark] but then Miss Dell does not write as though she were working for the screen ... The plot of the book might have been mistaken for a film were it not so wrapped around with verbiage and unconnected incidents'.[5] Ethel's twenty-four films were the result of screenplay adaptions by no less than twelve identifiable writers and ten different directors. No writer lasted more than three films and the suspicion is therefore that Ethel's creative approval process and demands wore thin with the writers. Of these twelve script writers only two were women: *The Swindler* (1919), scripted by Kate Gurney, and *Greatheart* (1921), by a Mrs Sidney Groome. Mrs. Groome was also a joint writer of *The Knight Errant* adaption in 1922.

In 1921 Ethel withdrew the US distribution rights for the film version of *The Top of the World* that had been given to Stoll and gave them to Jesse Lasky (Famous Players-Lasky Corporation). The latter released the film in 1925. The previous year Elinor Glyn had signed an initial contract with Lasky and within two years had moved to Metro-Goldwyn-Mayer. Both these two organisations also produced Ethel's films. It is hard to imagine that Glyn, who was employed with a significant salary, was neither involved not had any influence on the decisions of these two production houses in their selection of Ethel's work for the screen despite her contract stipulating that she write the screen play for her own *Three Weeks*. The author whose career had stalled in the UK as 'the later 1920s saw a shift in attitudes towards class, love, romance, and sex, and Glyn's signature combination of upper-class settings, old romanticism, and risqué eroticism fell out of favour, with a concomitant fall in the profitability of her films',[6] now saw herself confronted by Ethel's risqué works albeit aimed at a different socio-economic target. She was without doubt also subject to

Ethel's influence as was discussed earlier with the concept of *IT*.

Dennis Gifford reported that Maurice Elvey (Stoll film producer) recalled that Ethel, unlike Glyn was more interested in creative control than in commercial considerations.[7] This might well have been the impression given, but a study of her commercial correspondence suggests that Ethel was also astute financially. She saw the financial potential of this new market and even acquired shares in the Stoll Picture Company, despite her 10% commission on box office takings.[8] Five of the film titles were produced in the US, and, as in Britain, they supported the magazine and book sales.

The large run of successful film tie-ins of Ethel's works in the early interwar period helped to boost her renown in the lending libraries. Developments in distribution and increased public library provision in rural areas after the 1919 Public Libraries Act gave more readers access to Ethel's work in book form.[9] Her establishment in film and popular culture contributed to the popularity of her work in the twopenny libraries which sprang up in newsagents and tobacconists throughout the 1930s to cater for a working-class readership, further anchoring Ethel's name to a lowbrow reading public.

Stoll secured the rights to eighteen titles for the UK and thirteen for the USA, of which only one was exercised. Production within the USA other than the one Stoll film were undertaken by five different corporations including Metro-Goldwyn Meyer, Famous Players-Lasky and Columbia. As we saw earlier director Maurice Elvey recalled that Ethel was more concerned with holding some authority over the script than with the money she was going to make out of it.[10] Scenarios and film scripts were submitted to the reclusive author for approval. Understandably screenplays seldom mirrored the published narratives given the film limitations of silent and black and white. It would appear that Ethel and Stoll corresponded on content without passing matters through Watt, her agent. However, twelve different screenplay authors have been identified for the twenty-four films. The longest surviving screenwriter, Leslie Gordon, wrote five different adaptions of Ethel's works for film. However, Watt did act as a conduit for Ethel in her guidance to Eastern Productions in their adaption of *Her Own Free Will* confirming instructions to reduce the final kissing scene and that the thrashing scene should be cut to a minimum.[11] The relationship with Stoll seems initially to have been a comfortable one but dealing with the US side of the business through an agent in London, the impresario Louis Netherole and the US agent of the Eastern Productions for example, seems to have been a strain with telegrams being issued from Watt reading 'pay over the money' in one instance.[12] This related to an outstanding payment of $4,500 ($64,000 in today's values). In 1925 Field Roscoe, Ethel's lawyers send Stoll a notice of contract determination and a specific instruction from Ethel to destroy all negatives of their last joint activity the film of *The Eleventh Hour* (1922) and the earlier film of *The Place of Honour* (1921). Could these instructions have come about as, despite their long relationship, there was no longer a contractual binding of the parties and Ethel no longer trusted Stoll not to use the material? This was perhaps an indication of an ownership paranoia.

Film activity was intense between 1918 and 1922 with one film in each of 1924 and 1925, 1931 and finally three in the years 1936 and 1937 in the USA.

Ethel's Perspective

After my experiences with G.B. Samuelson and Norma Talmadge, and although I wanted Stoll to engineer the production of my stories into film I insisted that I have full control of and final sign-off for the film script. As a result of what screen writers might have perceived as interference Stoll and I went through a huge number of screen writers and directors. No creative person likes to have their work 'adjusted', but it was my creativity after all.

When it came to film making for the American market I realised that Stoll did not have the connections nor the distribution ability that he had in the UK. But dealing with Eastern Productions through Stoll we ended up with a significant bad debt. As such I contracted with Lasky and Metro-Goldywn-Mayer direct and severed my obligations with Stoll for America. Elinor Glyn, who became famous for 'IT' but whose sales in the UK were falling, was employed by MGM while my work was under production. However, she never made any contact or comment that I am aware of. Perhaps because my risqué material was selling and hers was not she kept out of the way, and also perhaps she had seen the potential of my suggestion for the 'IT' concept, and wanted as a result to keep her distance from me. And myself likewise. Glyn had a very high social profile and any action by me would have resulted in unwanted publicity.

I will freely admit that I suffered a degree of paranoia with regards to the use of my material. With celluloid it seemed to me that as it could be used again and again without any recourse to the copyright holder so it was better to destroy the material after the end of a contract. As such I issued legal instructions for material to be destroyed.

24 The Theatre

'Your dear Noel is acting up to his lights'.[1]

Theatre and radio meanwhile were not mainstream marketing activities. The theatrical productions of her works received almost wholly negative reviews on their short runs in London, but generally more positive reviews in the counties. This does of course suggest that Ethel's primary following was not those who would frequent theatres in London's West End.

In November 1918 G.B. Samuelson produced and directed the first theatrical staging of one of Ethel's novels, *The Way of an Eagle*, the same year as he released the silent film version of this title in the UK. This title did not appear on the stage again until 1922 where it appeared at the Aldwich Adelphi in London and in Manchester at the Princes Theatre and the Opera House. The latter in 1925. Of the 1923 performances in Manchester the art critic in the Manchester Guardian was less than complimentary of both the written work and the stage play:

> In any one of its metamorphoses whether as a novel, film, or drama *The Way of an Eagle* preserves its magnificent distance from art or life. The main falsity which the critics have attacked in the book at any rate, is that it reposes upon psychological error: the delusion that women are always ready sacrifices to the masterfully cruel male and the complimentary assumption that there are in real life such embodiment of ruthless will as Captain Nick Ratcliffe ... Some people have feared the consequences to public morals of the trashy psychology of the novel, but we will

go bail that the most impressionable husband in the audience
at the Prince's Theatre will not go home and thrash his wife ...[2]

Having created this manifestation of negativity relating to the source
material the critic then complained that the lead actor was not evil enough
in fact a bit of a 'wet blanket'. In London the lead was played by Godfrey
Tearle (1884–1953), later knighted and famous for his film role in *The 39
Steps* (1935) and *One of Our Aircraft is Missing* (1942). Tearle's performance
in *The Way of an Eagle* is reported by the *Illustrated London News* as being
'gallant rough mannered and consistently jocular'. The subject matter is
however acknowledged as a non-literary force: 'Whereas G.B.S [sic. George
Bernard Shaw] is fond of urging that the female of the species is its devastating
effect the less sophisticated Ethel M. Dell would seem to have won her tens of
thousands of readers by pictures of an all conquering ruthless male swooping
down on timid women as his quarry. That is her formula ...'[3]

Only three titles were ever performed on the stage: *The Way of an Eagle*,
The Odds and *The Knave of Diamonds*. *The Odds* received widest exposure in the
spring of 1920 playing in six different theatres in London and Manchester. By
this means Watt was generating the greatest short-term exposure for the title.

The Knave of Diamonds seems to have been a vehicle for the actress Violet
Vanburgh (1867–1942) playing in both London and Manchester but not in
the regional production in Ramsgate. The theatre critic in *The Observer* wrote
of this production: 'This adaption of one of Miss Ethel M. Dell's novels is
one of those immensely in-decorous pieces in which strong, garrulous men
behave like cads for two acts and then reveal their better nature in the third ...
I understand that the great city of Manchester went mad over the play. It
would!'[4]

There can be little doubt that Ethel would have relished these critiques as all they did was to enhance and emphasise the strength of her niche writing and demonstrate its appeal, as stated before, not to theatre-goers. Theatre was a fringe part of the marketing mix that helped her brand awareness.

Ethel's Perspective

G.B. Samuelson, who produced the first film version of *The Way of an Eagle,* persuaded me to allow its stage production. I do think that theatre representation of my titles worked well even when there were well-known names as the lead actors. The theatre critics, without fail, produced negative reports, and after seventeen showings of four titles we stopped the exercise. On reflection I do not think theatre-goers were my mainstream readers so cessation of theatre activity was no loss to either my reputation or my pocket.

25 An Invisible yet Successful Catharsis

'All extremes of feeling are allied with madness'.[1]

I have been tempted to use the academic student focus of contrast and compare, and this I have tried to do but it does not help us understand Ethel's character. A picture emerges of a lonely shy spinster writing as one would expect by herself, but in anti-social hours so that the duality of her existence could be maintained; part of a family unit and still a writer. Two totally different lives. Lives that can perhaps, except in reality, be paralleled with a split personality disorder. A circumscribed and isolated life that can only have exacerbated any latent instability as she delved deeper into her imagination. This isolation demonstrated by her lack of many friends and any extensive personal correspondence to ease her personal emotional pressure could have been fuelled by depression and suicidal thoughts as they appeared in her writing. An emotional and very personal pressure cooker of emotions. Writing is by definition a lonely and self-focused profession but fuelled by a positive non-imagined life, the life as a whole can be balanced. It is perhaps where there is insufficient balance that creativity can become dangerous.

Virginia Woolf (1882–1941), who it is suspected suffered from a bi-polar disorder and suffered bouts of depression before ultimately committing suicide, wrote in *The Lighthouse* (1927) that 'For now she need not think of anybody. She could be herself, by herself. And that was what now she often felt the need of – to think; well not even to think. To be silent; to be alone'[2] and in *The Waves* (1931), 'Better is silence … Let me sit with bare things, this coffee cup, this knife, this fork, things in themselves, myself being myself'.[3]

Woolf was of course influenced in her creativity by her own insecurities but if she wrote about them they were skilfully hidden in her narratives. In *The Waves* Woolf writes a portrait of six lives and how they change and develop. Six lives with distinct personalities: a loquacious linguist, an obsessive need for orderliness and beauty, security and ambition, physicality, an intense attraction to nature, and a dreamlike distance from everyday life. These are the foci of the narrative. Their personalities, not hers. Woolf's *Orlando*, which did not fit into any established academic categories, was in reality fiction disguised as a biography, as stated earlier, a stream of consciousness where one is guided to understand the thoughts and emotions of the characters in the narrative. Ethel wrote her tosh about predictable characters and predictable plots lines because it sold and used it as a vehicle to communicate her own demons.

Zelda Fitzgerald's *Save me the Waltz*, masqueraded as a novel but was in reality a discourse by a schizophrenic on her marriage to Scott Fitzgerald. A depressive, she had tried to commit suicide and was writing about her demons but with great skill and at times humour. *Anne of Green Gables'* Montgomery suffered from extreme depression, and apparently committed suicide, but was not able it seems to use her published writing as a way to ease her mental pressures.

Ethel's expression of emotion in her writing could both relieve and exacerbate emotional turmoil. However, her shyness, paranoia and perhaps ambivalent sexuality appear not to have been relieved by her public expression of them. Her reclusive, un-travelled and apparently sheltered life revealed, however, a trove of stimuli for a creative writer.

Within her immediate purview Ethel had access to foci of a manifest variety: being well read herself , bankruptcy, likely abuse from a dominant male, child sickness, child death, stillbirth, a dominant financially dependent sister, a brother who was in essence a wastrel, a spinster's child adoption, cancer, death, drug taking, glimpses of high society through the theatre, intimate female friendships, a gold digger, intra-familial religious differences, possibly an unconsummated marriage, permanent financial demands from her family, a Canadian connection, Indian army connections and the related romantic associations, no male relationships until her marriage late in life a connection with Kipling and an association with the winner of a gallantry medal.

There can be no doubt that this dysfunctional family environment affected her creative oeuvre. Patrick Hamilton (1904–1962) wrote about what came to be known as gaslighting, his stage play of the same name was first performed in 1938. 'Gaslighting' has become the term used for the psychological and sometimes physical dominance over a person. This would seem to have been evident in the relationship that Ethel had with her father Vincent, whose mores were certainly of the household dominant Victorian male. It is only possible to broadly surmise why Ethel adopted self-denigration and self-deprecation in her writing but one can posit that her self-confidence and self-belief were permanently damaged by that relationship with her father. Her inclusion of pietistic epigraphs, some written by herself, were unlikely to have been a moralistic counter to her narrative content and cannot have been aligned to the marketing mix but were probably a result of her searching for the only stable thing that she had in her difficult life and that was religion. Ethel was well versed in religious matters and frequently used the Bible as a prop but it was seldom relevant to the passage and flow of the narrative. She married late in life in what appears to have been a set-up. Four years after her marriage in her *The House of Happiness* there is a constant theme in the narrative of real loneliness that exists in a marriage without love.

Ethel published between 1898 and 1939, a period of significant social and political change and changes in security of empire, but it seems that apart from gently leaning on occasions to feminism she did not move with the changes but seemed to hang onto old and sometimes outdated social mores. She was of course a dedicated recluse and thus somewhat removed from normal social interfaces.

The polarity which Ethel faced was literary fiction produced by 'real' authors or commercial success of which many authors were perhaps envious. There is the reality of Ethel's success financially and her influence on her contemporary and future generations of lowbrow authors. Glyn, Heyer and Cartland were cases in point. Heyer and Cartland acknowledged this but Glyn pointedly did not. Ethel clearly fulfilled a need for such material both during and after the First World War. She understood the human condition and produced her 'tosh'. Tosh that readers in their millions wanted.

There can be little doubt that the 1919 Public Libraries Act and the broad marketing mix of hard copy, film combined with an almost feral attention to creating the maximum exposure in magazines even with a parallel hard copy release of a title was a significant contributor to her success. And as Orwell noted, it is in Public Libraries that one sees the true pretentions of the reader, and for many years Ethel was a dominant author within the lending libraries. Her establishment in film and popular culture also contributed to the popularity of her work in the twopenny libraries which sprang up in newsagents and tobacconists throughout the 1930s to cater for a working-class readership, further anchoring Ethel's name to a lowbrow reading public. Hammond commented that 'These statistics and fragments of clues seem to indicate that the higher the class or the more aspirational the clientele the less fiction it borrows'.[4] Ethel's marketing spend was driven towards both a regional and a lower socio-economic universe.

Was her writing superficial as in insignificant? Of course not, as she exposed her ideas to millions of eager readers. Specious maybe. Was she a serious literary force? The purists might think not. But books are of course part of a commercial trade in desires and Ethel filled that need, and as Simon Frost so eloquently states: 'When used in addition to a discourse of literary aesthetics, the language of consumption changes the discursive context and thus our understanding of what books are, namely objects that enable a trade in desires'.[5] Flannery O'Connor stated: 'There's many a best-seller that could have been prevented by a good teacher. The idea of being a writer attracts a good many shiftless people, those who are merely burdened with poetic feelings or afflicted with sensibility'.[6] This acerbic comment both endorses the literary value of aestheticism and also the value of writing that sells, Ethel's writing per se was a mass market product. Thus, it is the influence on society and not academic literary perfection that has the lasting resilience and success. A beautiful sign in a supermarket might be pleasing to the eye but it is the garish one that communicates the message clearly and moves product off the shelves. So it is with literature. Is *Fifty Shades of Grey* (2011) a 'literary, good' book? No, but it has been stupendously successful for the author and the publisher

Montgomery, following the publication of her work *Anne of Green Gables* (1908) was largely ignored by literary academia and was subject to negative comment from male critics who sought to construct a 'canon of high modernism for Canadian literature and literary criticism'.[7] Here again commercially successful creativity was ignored.

One can of course argue that literary aesthetic quality is inversely proportional to commercial interest. Ethel proved this point. She was successful and she was influential, but her fiction was neither 'literary' nor 'aesthetic'. Her narratives just gave her huge reader universe a lot of pleasure and made a lot of people very wealthy. In 1939 Leavis outlined the high and lowbrow stratification of reader profiles of this period in her comment that, 'It is not surprising that in a society of forty-three million so decisively stratified in taste that each stratum is catered for by its own novelists and journalists'.[8] Today it seems very obvious that the notion to write for a specific reader universe is to maximise commercial opportunity. Anderson refers to Ethel writing a pot boiler when she dedicated *By Request* to her readers, and included characters from *The Keeper of the Door*. There were indeed a number of characters that appeared again and again in her works. Technically and pejoratively a pot boiler but in essence she was writing very successfully what was wanted by a significant reader universe.[9]

Ethel's self-denigration and self-deprecation themes seen in many of her works has a certain poignancy as her penultimate title, *The Juice of the Pomegranate,* published the year before her death devotes a significant amount of narrative time to character assassination of the heroine who is seen to read her works and then hiding them from general view, the implication being that she is ashamed to let it be known that she is an Ethel reader. Ethel is very unwell and must understand by now that she has a terminal illness, yet she writes as if she is ashamed of her creativity, a terrible epitaph.

Can there be an underlying 'intellectual' foundation and drive for any of her works? Anderson posits in her writing about Ethel that 'For as interest in orthodox Christianity gradually waned, it was replaced in popular romantic fiction by new and less defined spiritual quest'.[10] No, there is no intellectual underpinning of the narratives. As a parallel thought, Emily Maitlis the BBC correspondent asked Judith Kerr the children's writer if the tiger in her work *The Tiger came to Tea* symbolised the 1960s sexual revolution, where normal mores and suburban life became upended by this wild and exotic creature. 'She told me no, it was about a tiger coming to tea'.[11] Ethel was telling stories heightened by her extraordinary imagination within her inward looking and reclusive environment. Ethel was, like Kerr, without literary ambitions, and just a very good storyteller in an environment that needed what Leavis referred to as her sheer luxuriant vitality. 'Bad writing, false sentiment, sheer silliness, and a preposterous narrative are all carried along by the magnificent vitality of the author, as they are in *Jane Eyre* (1847)'.[12] To seek a deeper meaning for

Ethel's creativity is an intellectual irrelevancy.

The publisher's frontispiece to the very violent *Honeyball Farm*, which featured a violent and abusive father figure stated:

> Honeyball Farm was not the outcome of pure imagination, but its sinister atmosphere may have been suggested by the grimness of the sea perpetually roaring at its doors. The evil deeds which took place within it were such as might have been enacted in any habitation where love is not at home.

The editors at Cassell were perhaps not that far off the mark with this observation about Ethel's imagination. Can one perhaps surmise that she opened up to the editors about her home life? I like to think so.

Ethel was a very perceptive analyser and documenter of the human condition, all wrapped up in her 'tosh'. She had a lot to say and had the intellect and the erudition to document these views. The positing of meaningful philosophical views within a fictional narrative is a rare talent, and not one seen in other female romantic novelists of the time. This erudition was of course subsumed in her style. She wrote full, lively, colourful, dramatic and often humorous stories bursting with throbbing and seething. She wrote without any pretentions and clearly enjoyed a creative process that dominated her life and provided an outlet for her thoughts and demons when there was nowhere else to turn. Her unhappy personal circumstances, her drug use and the suggestion of suicidal thoughts were demonstrated in *The Black Knight*: 'she had only to yield to that intense fatigue and sink down there on that bleak hillside in the driving snow, and Nature would have an easy victory. And how welcome would that long rest be!'[13] A comparison with Fitzgerald is apposite in that she was also a very troubled person but she chose to air the issues in her relationship with Scott Fitzgerald in her thinly disguised autobiographical novel *Save me the Waltz* (1932). Ethel's writing from the beginning seems to have been an almost invisible cathartic de-demonising tool, that made her, her family and her publishers very wealthy, and left her readers happy. Ethel was a religious person, and in her penultimate work, no doubt with the knowledge of her own terminal situation, refers to the power of prayer to overcome illness.

In summary, Ethel, who at no stage seemed to demonstrate any serious vacuity, used literary borrowings and insight from her life and we are left wondering whether this was deadly satire or a plea for help.

26 Ethel's Creative Catalysts

Ethel was a recluse and her limited view of the world was populated by stimuli that will have been her creative catalysts and one can see their influence in all of her narratives. When analysed outside of her narratives Ethel's connections created a significant cocktail of almost unbelievable extremes.

Religion
- John Caldicote Dell, paternal grandfather, Catholic.
- Mary Davis, paternal grandmother, Catholic.
- Sister Alphonsine OSB, Catholic, Ethel's aunt.
- Dame Joan McLaughlin O.S.B., Catholic, Ethel's second cousin.

Abuse and alcohol
- Vincent Dell, wealthy, abusive father, Catholic, but married under Anglican rites.
- Patricia Dell Reggie's wife, an alcoholic and a reported child abuser.

Society failures
- William Dell, uncle, insolvent low-level businessman.
- Reginald/Reggie Dell, brother, a wastrel who achieved little and lived off Ethel's earnings.

Society connections:
- Sir Maurice and Edward Bowra. Oxford educated with parents who served in China.
- Violet (Vi) Johnston the daughter of the barrister's daughter, close friend to Ella, who bought the house that had belonged to Lord Roberts of Indian army fame.

Adoption outside of marriage

- Poppy Dell, Ella's adopted daughter who showed early signs of an inclination towards Catholicism.

Nouveau riche

- Ella Dell Ethel's sister, Anglican, larger than life nouveau rich high flyer who lived off Ethel's earnings. A well-read musician.

Illness and death

- Her own breast cancer.
- Dorrington Dell, Reggie's son who died at birth.
- Jock Dell, Reggie's son who was mentally challenged and institutionalised.
- Patricia Dell, Reggie's daughter with learning difficulties who required special schooling which was apparently funded by Ethel's sister, her aunt.

Drug use

- Ethel's personal experience.

Gold digger

- Nora Savage. Gold digger who sought out Ethel, sister to Gerald Savage Ethel's husband.

Respectability:

- Irene Dell (Parrot), Ethel's mother, Anglican from a respectable family.
- The Parrot family, who were lawyers and upstanding members of local society.

Marriage that was probably a failure

- Major Gerald Savage (masquerading as a colonel). Ethel's eventual husband who used her funds to build model boats and trains, but provided no commercial or literary guidance. He managed her homes.

Female relationships:

- Patsy Philips, Ella's friend who eventually married.
- Madge Philips, an unmarried friend.
- Mary ('half-sister') Bastard, an unmarried friend who left England for Kenya in 1934.
- Violet Ebsworth, unmarried secretary who lived with Ethel.
- Violet Vanburgh, an actress on whom Ethel appeared to have a crush.
- Edith de Wolf, a seemingly butch unmarried friend.

Sharp business practice

- James B. Pinker Ethel's first literary agent who gave the young Ethel questionable advice and created in her a level of distrust in others. Pinker could possibly have been a contributory factor in her reclusiveness.

Successful commercial relationship:

- A.P. Watt her long-term literary agent. A sound commercial shoulder on which to lean, and probably the only person she really trusted.

27. The Foci of Ethel's Lampooned Style

Foci	In Titles
Sickness / disability / euthanasia / mental health	39%
British Empire (Australia, India, Africa, Canada)	36%
New (Strong) Women/Feminism	34%
Cruelty / female / abuse /violence /sadomasochism	33%
Dominant / strong / steady / driven man	31%
Death / stillbirth / miscarriage	29%
Dysfunctional marriage and divorce	27%
Ugly / unattractive / lecherous men	16%
Weak / shallow / naïve women	15%
Female bitchiness / manipulation	13%
Suicide	12%
Military as a story vehicle	12%
Drugs use / abuse	10%
Disguise	10%
Alcohol abuse	9%
Same-sex relationships / ambivalent sexuality	8%
Coquettish flirt / vamp	7%
Lost virginity	7%
Murder	7%
Male focus on sex / female sexual obligations / forced sexual relations	6%
Unattractive / callous women	4%
Child outside wedlock	4%
Women with a 'past'	3%
Adolescent sexuality	3%
Blackmail	3%
Rape	2%
Sex slaves / trafficking	2%
Adoption	2%

This qualitative analysis is used as an indication of Ethel's creative foci.

28. The Dell Family Tree

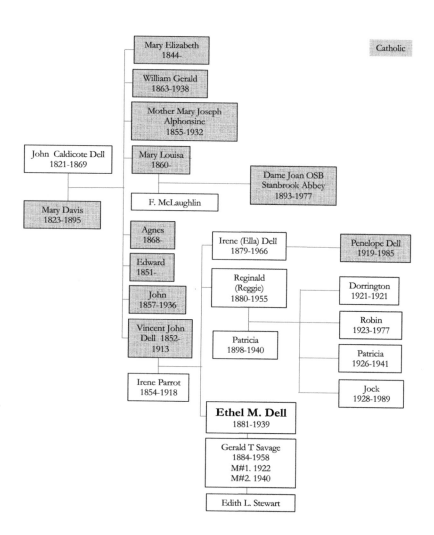

Mary Elizabeth
1844-

Catholic

William Gerald
1863-1938

Mother Mary Joseph
Alphonsine
1855-1932

John Caldicote Dell
1821-1869

Mary Louisa
1860-

Dame Joan OSB
Stanbrook Abbey
1893-1977

F. McLaughlin

Mary Davis
1823-1895

Agnes
1868-

Irene (Ella) Dell
1879-1966

Penelope Dell
1919-1985

Edward
1851-

Reginald
(Reggie)
1880-1955

Dorrington
1921-1921

John
1857-1936

Robin
1923-1977

Vincent John
Dell 1852-
1913

Patricia
1898-1940

Patricia
1926-1941

Irene Parrot
1854-1918

Jock
1928-1989

Ethel M. Dell
1881-1939

Gerald T Savage
1884-1958
M#1. 1922
M#2. 1940

Edith L. Stewart

29. Ethel's Forty-one Year Output

The titles are shown as when they were first published in any geopolitical location and by first time in any individual branded medium including films.

1898
A Repentant Rogue,   The Royal Magazine (UK)

1899
In Her Majesty's Service,   The Ludgate Magazine (UK)

1900
A Repentant Rogue,   Everybody's Magazine (US)

1905
His Heart's Desire,   The Novel Magazine (UK)

1906
The Honourable Burford,   The Novel Magazine (UK)
The Secret Service Man,   The Novel Magazine (UK)

1907
The Deliverer,   The Novel Magazine (UK)
The Looker-On,   The Novel Magazine (UK)

1908
Her Place of Honour,   Story-Teller Magazine (UK)
The Second Fiddle,   The Novel Magazine (UK)
Her Freedom,   Grand Magazine (UK)
Her Compensation,   Story-Teller Magazine (UK)

1909
The Place of Honour,   The Novel Magazine (UK)
The Consolation Prize,   The Strand Magazine (UK)
                                      The Strand Magazine (US)

The Sea Urchin and the Prince,   The Red Magazine (UK)

The Friend Who Stood By,	The Red Magazine (UK)
	People's Home Journal (US)
The Virtue of Prudence,	The Red Magazine (UK)
A Debt of Honour,	The Red Magazine (UK)
	Gunter's Magazine (US)

1910

The Right Man,	The Red Magazine (UK)
The Magic Circle,	The Red Magazine (UK)
Her Hero,	The Red Magazine (UK)
Where the Heart is,	The Red Magazine (UK)
The Example,	The Red Magazine (UK)
Her Weapon of Defence,	The Red Magazine (UK)
Her Own Free Will/The Chain,	The Red Magazine (UK)
The Swindler,	The Red Magazine (UK)
The Swindler's Handicap,	The Red Magazine (UK)
The Way of an Eagle,	Novel A.L. Burt (US)
The Heart of a Tyrant,	The Family Reader (UK)

1911

The Way of an Eagle,	The Red Magazine (UK)
Those Who Wait,	The Red Magazine (UK)
The Knave of Diamonds,	Novel A.L. Burt (US)

1912

The Woman of his Dream,	The Red Magazine (UK)
The Knight Errant,	The Red Magazine (UK)
The Prey of the Dragon,	The Red Magazine (UK)
The Nonentity,	The Red Magazine (UK)
The Return Game,	The Red Magazine (UK)
A Question of Trust,	The Red Magazine (UK)
The Tidal Wave,	The Red Magazine (UK)
	Novelette Grosset/Dunlap (US)
The Experiment,	The Novel Magazine (UK)
The Way of an Eagle,	Novel T Fisher Unwin (UK)
	Ernest Benn in paperback (UK)

RIDING THE TOSH HORSE

1913

The Knave of Diamonds,	Novel T. Fisher Unwin (UK)
The Way of an Eagle,	Novel Copp Clark (Canada)
The Magic City, The Magic Circle,	Novelette in Queen Mary's Gift Book Hodder (UK)
The Penalty,	The Red Magazine (UK)

1914

The Eleventh Hour,	The Story-Teller Magazine (UK)
The Keeper of the Door,	The Red Magazine (UK)
The Englishman from Heidelberg,	The Piccadilly Magazine (UK)
The Rocks of Valpré,	The Red Magazine (UK)
	Novel T. Fisher Unwin (UK)
The Desire of his Life,	Novelette Hardingham (UK)
Her Compensation,	Novelette Hardingham (UK)
Her Place of Honour,	Novelette Hardingham (UK)
A Question of Trust,	Novelette T. Fisher Unwin (UK)
The Nonentity,	Novelette T. Fisher Unwin (UK)
Where the Heart is,	Novelette T. Fisher Unwin (UK)
Her Hero,	Novelette T. Fisher Unwin (UK)
The Right Man,	Novelette T. Fisher Unwin (UK)
The Swindler,	Novelette T. Fisher Unwin (UK)
The Swindler's Handicap,	Novelette T. Fisher Unwin (UK)
The Knight Errant,	Novelette T. Fisher Unwin (UK)
A Question of Trust,	Novelette T. Fisher Unwin (UK)
The Nonentity,	Novelette T. Fisher Unwin (UK)

1915

Bars of Iron,	The Red Magazine (UK)
The Keeper of the Door,	Novel Hutchinson's (UK)

1916

Bars of Iron,	Novel Putnam (US)
The Hundredth Chance,	The Red Magazine (UK)
The Safety Curtain,	The Strand Magazine (UK)

1917

The Place of Hono(u)r,	Novelette T Fisher Unwin (UK)
	Novelette Putnam/Grosset/ Dunlap (US)
	Novelette Copp Clark (Canada)
The Hundredth Chance,	Novel Putnam (US)
	Novel T. Fisher Unwin (UK)
The Eleventh Hour,	Novel T. Fisher Unwin (UK)
	Novel Copp Clark (Canada)
	Novel Putnam/Grosset/Dunlap (US)
Those Who Wait,	Novelette Putnam/Grosset/ Dunlap (US)
	Novelette Copp Clark (Canada)
	Novelette T Fisher Unwin (UK)
The Experiment,	Novelette Putnam/Grosset/ Dunlap (US)
	Novelette T Fisher Unwin (UK)
The Rose of Dawn,	The Strand Magazine (UK)
The Englishman from Heidelberg,	Cassell's Penny Magazine (UK)
The Safety Curtain,	Novelette T Fisher Unwin (UK)

1918

The Knave of Diamonds,	Novel Copp Clark (Canada)
	Serial Boon (Netherlands) date assumed
Greatheart,	Novel T Fisher Unwin (UK)
	Novel Putnam/Grosset/ Dunlap (US)
Rosa Mundi,	Lloyds Magazine (UK)
The Way of an Eagle,	Film, G.B. Samuelson (UK)
The Safety Curtain,	Film, Norma Talmadge (US)

1919

The Lucky Number,	Cassell's Magazine (UK)
Rosa Mundi,	Pictorial Review (US)
The Lamp in the Desert,	Novel Hutchinson (UK)
The Odds,	Hutchinson's Magazine (UK)
	The Strand Magazine (US)
The Sacrifice,	Hutchinson's Magazine (UK)
Her Hero,	Weekly News (UK)

The Tidal Wave,	Story-Teller (UK)
	Novelette Cassell (UK)
The Experiment,	The Novel Magazine (UK)
	Weekly News (UK)
The Woman of his Dream,	Novelette from Cassell (UK)
The Keeper of the Door,	Film, Stoll (UK)
The Rocks of Valpré,	Film, Stoll (UK)
The Swindler,	Film, Stoll (UK)

1920

The Desire of his Life,	Novel A.L. Burt (US)
Where Three Roads Meet,	Novel Putnam (US)
The Tenth Point,	Hutchinson's Magazine (UK)
The Princess's Game,	Novel Hardingham (UK)
The Top of the World,	Novel Putnam/Grosset/ Dunlap (US)
	Novel from Cassell (UK)
Verses,	Hutchinson (UK)
Without Prejudice,	The Strand Magazine (UK)
The Prey of the Dragon,	Cassell's Magazine (UK)
A Question of Trust,	Film, Stoll (UK)
The Tidal Wave,	Film, Stoll (UK)
Bars of Iron,	Film, Stoll (UK)

1921

Rosa Mundi/Sunlit Sands,	Novelette Cassell (UK)
A Debt of Honour,	Novelette Cassell (UK)
The Prey of the Dragon,	Novelette Cassell (UK)
Her Place of Honour,	Novelette Cassell (UK)
The Deliverer,	Novel Magazine (UK)
The Nonentity,	Novelette T. Fisher Unwin (UK)
The Sacrifice,	Collier's Magazine (US)
The Tidal Wave,	Novel in Spanish and French Cassell
The Tenth Point,	Metropolitan Magazine (US)
	Sovereign Magazine (UK)
The Obstacle Race,	The New Magazine (UK)

	Serial Boon (Netherlands) date assumed
	Novel Cassell (UK)
	Novel Putnam (US)
	Novel McClelland & Stewart (Canada)
Greatheart,	Film, Stoll (UK)
The Place of Honour,	Film, Stoll (UK)
The Knave of Diamonds,	Film, Stoll (UK)
The Woman of his Dream,	Film, Stoll (UK)
The Prey of the Dragon,	Film, Stoll (UK)
The Lamp in the Desert,	Film, Stoll (UK)
	Film, Columbia (US)

1922

Her Freedom,	Novelette Putnam (US)
	Novelette Cassell (UK)
The Honorable Burford,	McCall's Magazine (US)
The Sacrifice,	Novel Putnam (US)
	Novelette from Cassell (UK)
Without Prejudice,	Collier's Magazine (US)
	Novel from Putnam (US)
Death's Property,	Novelette Cassell (UK)
	Novelette Putnam (US)
The Odds,	The Strand Magazine (US)
	Novelette Cassell (UK)
Charles Rex,	The Red Magazine (UK)
	Novel from Hutchinson (UK)
	McCall's Magazine (US)
	Novel Putnam/Grosset/Dunlap (US)
	Novel Ryerson (Canada)
Without Prejudice,	Novelette Cassell (UK)
Heart of a Tyrant,	Story-Teller Magazine (UK)
Her Own Free Will/The Chain,	Novelette Cassell (UK)
The Consolation Prize,	Novelette Cassell (UK)
	Novelette Putnam (US)

The Experiment,	Film, Stoll (UK)
The Nonentity,	Film, Stoll (UK)
A Debt of Honour,	Film, Stoll (UK)
The Knight Errant,	Film, Stoll (UK)
The Eleventh Hour,	Film, Stoll (UK)

1923

The Passer-By,	McCall's Magazine (US)
	Hutchinson's Magazine (UK)
Verses,	Putnam (US)
The Unknown Quantity,	Novel Hutchinson (UK)
	Novel Putnam/ A.L. Burt (US)
Tetherstones,	The Strand Magazine (UK)
	Novel Hutchinson (UK)
	McCall's Magazine (US)
Tommy Rot,	Home Magazine (UK)
	McCall's Magazine (US)
The Deliverer,	Peg's Companion (UK)

1924

Prey of the Dragon,	Serial in Norwegian and Danish from Berlingake
The Penalty,	Serial in Norwegian and Danish from Berlingake
Debt of Honour,	Serial in Norwegian and Danish from Berlingake
Rosa Mundi,	Serial in Norwegian and Danish from Berlingake
The Money Monster,	McCall's Magazine (US)
The Unknown Quantity,	The New Magazine (UK)
Her Own Free Will,	Film, Stoll (US)

1925

The Tenth Point,	Bonnier Serial in Scandinavia
	Novelette Hutchinson (UK)

The Lucky Number,	Bonnier Serial in Scandinavia
The Money Monster,	Novelette Hutchinson (UK)
	Serial in Scandinavia from Bonnier
A Man under Authority,	McCall's Magazine (US)
	The Royal Magazine (UK)
	Novel Cassell (UK)
The Master Key,	McCall's Magazine (US)
Full Measure,	Hutchinson's Magazine (UK)
	Our home Magazine (UK)
	McCall's Magazine (US)
The Passer-By	Serial in Scandinavia from Bonnier
Tommy Rot,	Serial rights in Scandinavia from Bonnier
	Novelette Hutchinson (UK)
(The) Quest,	McCall's Magazine (US)
The Top of the World,	Film, Famous Players-Lasky(US)

1926
The Real Thing,	McCall's Magazine (US)
The Black Knight,	Novel Cassell (UK)
	Novel Grosset/Dunlap (US)
The House of Happiness,	Novel Knickerbocker/A.L. Burt (US)
The Good Turn,	Hutchinson's Magazine (UK)
	McCall's Magazine (US)

1927
The Real Thing,	Novelette Cassell (UK)
Her Place of Honor,	Love Story Magazine (US)
His Heart's Desire.	Love Story Magazine (US)
Quits,	McCall's magazine (US)
	Hutchinson's Magazine (UK)
The Second Fiddle,	Love Story Magazine (US)
	Sunday Circle (UK)
The House of Happiness,	Novel from Cassell (UK)
By Request,	The Red Magazine (UK)
	Novel Hutchinson/T. Fisher Unwin (UK)

The Consolation Prize,   The Red Magazine (UK)
The Friend Who Stood By,   Sunday Circle (UK)

1928
By Request/Peggy by Request,   Novel Putnam / A.L. Burt (US)
                                          Novel Ryerson (Canada)
The Gate Marked Private,   Novel Cassell (UK)
                                          Novel Grosset/Dunlap (US)
Live Bait,   McCall's magazine (US)
                                          Cassell's Magazine (UK)
Picnics,   The Weekly Despatch (UK)
The Real Thing,   Eve's Own Stories (UK)
The Good Turn,   Eve's Own Stories (UK)

1929
The Altar of Honour,   Novel Hutchinson (UK)
The Love Master,   All-Story Magazine (US)
The Altar of Honor,   McCall's Magazine (US)
The Silver Bride,   Novel A.L. Burt (US)
Storm Drift,   Novel Hutchinson (UK)
The Hairpin Bend,   The Chicago Tribune (US)
The Way of an Eagle,   The Girl's Mirror magazine (UK)

1930
Quits,   Woman's Weekly Magazine (UK)

1931
Storm Drift,   Physical Culture Magazine (US)
Silver Wedding,   Novel Hutchinson (UK)
The Silver Bride,   Liberty Magazine (US)
The Right Man,   Illustrated Dressmaker (UK)
Sunlit Sands (Rosa Mundi),   Weldon Ladies Home Journal (UK)

1932
The Silver Bride,   Novel Hutchinson (UK)
The Hairpin Bend,   Novelette Ernest Benn (UK)

The Prison Wall,	Novel Cassell (UK)
	Novel Ryerson (Canada)
The Halting Place,	Help Yourself Annual (UK)
The Losers,	Novelette Ernest Benn (UK)
The Chatelaine,	Novelette Ernest Benn (UK)
The Pageant of Youth,	Novelette Ernest Benn (UK)
Misunderstanding,	Novelette Ernest Benn (UK)
The Quest,	Novelette Ernest Benn (UK)
The Serpent in the Garden,	Novel Hutchinson (UK)
The Friend Who Stood By,	Weldon Ladies Home Journal (UK)
The Sacrifice,	Weldon Ladies Home Journal (UK)

1933

The Prison Wall,	Novel Putnam/Grosset/ Dunlap (US)
Dona Celestis,	Novel Ernest Benn (UK)
	Novel Putnam's /A.L. Burt (US)

1934

The Electric Torch,	Novel Cassell (UK)
	Good Needlework Magazine (UK)
	Novel Putnam / Blue Ribbon Books (US)
	Novel Ryerson (Canada)

1935

Where Three Roads Meet,	Novel Cassell (UK)
	Novel Ryerson (Canada)
The Rocks of Valpré,	Film, Real Art (UK)

1936

The Way of an Eagle,	Film, Columbia (US)

1937

Honeyball Farm,	Novel Putnam/Grosset/ Dunlap (US)
	Novel Ryerson (Canada)
The Electric Torch,	Good Needlework Magazine (UK)
The Rocks of Valpré,	Film, Real Art (UK)

1938

Honeyball Farm,	Novel Hutchinson (UK)
The Serpent in the Garden,	Novel Doubleday Doran (US)
The Juice of the Pomegranate,	All-Story Magazine (US)
	Novel Doubleday Doran (US)
	Novel Ryerson (Canada)

1939

Sown among Thorns,	Woman's Weekly Magazine (UK)
	Novel Cassell (UK)

Ethel produced ninety-eight published titles over a published writing career spanning forty-one years. Of the ninety-eight titles published, at least seventy-three were supported by magazine exposure. Seventy-eight titles appeared in hard-copy book form, twenty-three in film, four in theatre and one on the radio.[1]

30 Title Historiography and Creative Levers

Title historiography is important as it demonstrates Ethel's monetisation drive with the number of iterations that each title was subjected to, and her draw that allowed such tremendous scalability on her titles. One title, *In Her Majesty's Service* was used just once, probably as it was not romantic fiction it did not sit well with her personal style as this became established, additionally eight 'romance' titles were also not subject to multiple marketing efforts. *The Knave of Diamonds* with twelve iterations was the largest number followed by *The Way of an Eagle* with eleven and *The Prey of the Dragon* with ten. Within this analysis the following principles for describing media have been used:

- Short story: up to 8,000 words,
- Novella: 8,000 to 20,000 words,
- Novelette: 20,000 to 40,000 words,
- Novel: over 40,000 words.

1. Title: *Repentant Rogue*:

   Genre: Short story

   1899, First Published in The Royal Magazine (UK)

   1900, First Published in Everybody's Magazine (US)

   Creative Levers: Empire, humour, sexual fantasy, female weaknesses, the Woman.

2. Title: *In Her Majesty's Service*

   Genre: Short story

   1899, First Published in The Ludgate Magazine (UK)

   Creative Levers: Empire, Military, bravery and duty.

3. **Title:** *His Heart's Desire*
   Genre: Novelette
   1905, First Published in The Novel Magazine (UK)
   1914, rights acquired back from Pearson's Magazine
   1927, First Published in Love Story Magazine (US)
   1927, Ethel file note: This story was originally titled *Death's Property*
   Creative Levers: Wealth, dysfunctional marriage.

4. **Title:** *The Hono(u)rable Burford*
   Genre: Novelette
   1906, First Published in The Novel Magazine (UK)
   1914, Rights bought back from Pearson's Magazine
   1922, First Published in McCall's Magazine (US)
   Creative Levers: Empire, effeminate/weak man, misogyny, tropical sickness, Sufiism.

5. **Title:** *The Secret Service Man*
   Genre: Novella
   1906, First Published in The Novel Magazine (UK)
   1914, Rights acquired back from Pearson's Magazine
   1921, Cassell in *Rosa Mundi: And Other Stories* (UK)
   Creative Levers: Empire, military, weak and strong women, devious and kind men.

6. **Title:** *The Deliverer*
   Genre: Novella
   1907, First Published in The Novel Magazine (UK)
   1914, Rights acquired back from Pearson's Magazine
   1921, Cassell in *Rosa Mundi: And Other Stories* (UK)
   1923, Peg's Companion Magazine (UK)

Creative Levers: Family, unattractive unintelligent but strong man.

7. Title: *The Looker On*

    Genre: Short story

    1907, First Published in The Novel Magazine (UK)

    1914, Rights acquired back from Pearson's Magazine

    Creative Levers: Empire, self-effacing hero and buffoon, shallow girl, strong silent steady man.

8. Title: *The Second Fiddle*

    Genre: Short story

    1908, First Published in The Novel Magazine (UK)

    1914, rights acquired back from Pearson's Magazine

    1927, First Published in Love Story Magazine (US)

    1928, The Sunday Circle Magazine (UK)

    Creative Levers:

    Callous woman, caring woman, disability.

9. Title: *Her Compensation*

    Genre: Novelette

    Date unknown. Entire copyrights sold to Family Herald Press

    1908, First Published in Story-Teller Magazine (UK)

    1915, Holden and Hardingham (UK)

    1932, Ernest Benn in *The Live Bait: And Other Stories* (UK)

    Creative Levers: Empire, blackmail, Christianity/prayers, woman with a past.

10. **Title:** *Her Place of Hono(u)r*

    Genre: Novelette

    1908, International rights sold to Family Herald Press

    1908, First Published in Story-Teller Magazine (UK)

    1910, UK Rights sold to The Red Magazine

    1914, Holden & Hardingham with *The Desire of his Life* (UK)

    1919, Cassell in *The Tidal Wave: And Other Stories* (UK)

    1927, Love Story Magazine (US)

    Creative Levers: Empire, small strong man, naïve woman, sexually boring marriage.

11. **Title:** *Her Freedom*

    Genre: Short story

    1908, First Published in Grand Magazine (UK)

    1921, Rights acquired back from George Newnes with *The Consolation Prize*

    1922, Cassell in *The Odds: And Other Stories* (UK)

    1922, First Published by Putnam in *The Odds: And Other Stories* (US)

    Creative Levers: Dominant man, strong-willed independent woman, marriage and love not synonymous, disabled sibling, disguise.

12. **Title:** *The Sea Urchin and the Prince*

    Genre: Novelette

    1909, UK Rights sold to The Red Magazine

    1909, First Published in The Red Magazine (UK)

    Creative Levers: Dominant handsome man, strong-willed woman.

13. **Title:** *The Place of Hono(u)r*

    Genre: Novella and film

    1909, First Published in The Novel Magazine (UK)

    1914, Copyright acquired from G.A. Pearson

    1917, T Fisher Unwin in *The Safety Curtain: And other Stories* (UK)

    1917, First Published by Putnam Grosset Dunlap in *The Safety Curtain: And other Stories* (US)

    1917, First Published by Copp Clark in *The Safety Curtain: And other Stories* (Canada)

    1920, Agreement with Stoll for global film distribution rights

    1921, Ethel confirms Stoll US distribution rights

    1922, Film from Stoll

    1923, Novel Magazine (UK)

    1925, Ethel gives Stoll instruction to destroy all negatives

    1927, Love Story Magazine (US)

    Creative Levers: Empire, small strong man, naïve woman, sexually boring marriage.

14. **Title:** *The Friend Who Stood By*

    Genre: Short story

    1909, UK Rights sold to The Red Magazine

    1909, First Published in The Red Magazine (UK)

    1909, First Published in People's Home Journal (US)

    1914, T. Fisher Unwin in *The Swindler and other Stories* (UK)

    1927, Sunday Circle Magazine (UK)

    1932, Weldon's Ladies Journal. Ethel resisted request to change the name to Fair Play (UK)

    Creative Levers: Ugly man, honesty.

15. Title: *The Virtue of Prudence*

    Genre: Short story

    1909, UK Rights sold to The Red Magazine

    1909, First Published in The Red Magazine (UK)

    Creative Levers: Narrative has not been located.

16. Title: *A Debt of Honour*

    Genre: Novella and film

    1909, UK Rights sold to The Red Magazine

    1909, First Published in The Red Magazine (UK)

    1909, First Published in Gunter's Magazine (US)

    1920, Cassell magazine Agreement with *The Prey of the Dragon* (UK)

    1921, Cassell in *Rosa Mundi & Other Stories* (UK)

    1921, Ethel withholds Stoll US film distribution rights

    1922, Film from Stoll (UK).

    1924, Berlingake Tidende for Danish & Norwegian serial rights

    Creative Levers: Empire, strong and weak men, alcohol, blackmail.

17. Title: *The Magic Circle/City*

    Genre: Short story

    1909, UK Rights sold The Red Magazine

    1910, First Published in The Red Magazine (UK)

    1913, Queen Mary's Gift Book from Hodder (UK)

    Creative Levers: Marriage faithfulness / dysfunctionality, deception.

18. Title: *The Example*

    Genre: Short story

    1909, UK Rights sold to The Red Magazine

1910, First Published in The Red Magazine (UK)

Creative Levers: Empire, military resolute men.

19. **Title:** *Where the Heart is*

    Genre: Novelette

    Publishing and Media Historiography:

    1909, UK Rights sold to The Red Magazine.

    1910, First Published in The Red Magazine (UK).

    1914, T. Fisher Unwin in *The Swindler: And Other Stories* (UK).

    Creative Levers: Unattractive girl, dull man.

20. **Title:** *Her Hero*

    Genre: Short story

    1909, UK Rights sold to The Red Magazine.

    1910, First Published in The Red Magazine (UK)

    1914, T. Fisher Unwin in *The Swindler: And Other Stories* (UK)

    1919, Weekly News Magazine (UK)

    Creative Levers: United States, strong woman, marriage.

21. **Title:** *The Consolation Prize*

    Genre: Short story

    1909, First Published in The Strand Magazine (UK)

    1909, First Published in The Strand Magazine (US)

    1921, Rights acquired from George Newnes with *Her Freedom*

    1922, Cassell in *The Odds: And Other Stories* (UK)

    1922, Putnam in *The Odds: And Other Stories* (US)

    Before 1926 in The Red Magazine (UK)

    Creative Levers: Ugly, rich, kind man.

22. **Title:** *The Right Man*

    Genre: Short story

    1909, UK Rights sold to The Red Magazine

    1910, First Published in The Red Magazine (UK)

    1914, T. Fisher Unwin in *The Swindler & Other Stories* (UK)

    1931, Illustrated Dressmaker Magazine (UK)

    Creative Levers: Ugly but sensitive man, weak heroine.

23. **Title:** *The Heart of a Tyrant*

    Genre: Novelette

    1910, First Published in The Family Reader (UK)

    1922, Story-Teller Magazine (UK)

    Creative Leavers: Narrative has not been located.

24. **Title:** *Her Weapon of Defence*

    Genre: Novelette

    1910, UK Rights sold to The Red Magazine

    1910, First Published in The Red Magazine (UK)

    Creative Levers : Narrative has not been located.

25. **Title:** *Her Own Free Will/The Chain*

    Genre: Novelette and film

    1910, UK Rights sold to The Red Magazine

    1911, First Published in The Red Magazine (UK)

    1912, *The Chain* published at 'one penny' by Hodder Williams (UK)

    1919, Hodder Williams sell rights with *The Prey of the Dragon* (UK)

    1922, Cassell in *The Odds and Other Stories* (UK)

    1924, Film from Eastern Productions

Creative Levers: Polarised feminism (submissive / recusant), physical violence, rough diamond with a heart.

26. **Title:** *The Swindler*

 Genre: Short story and film

 Publishing and Media Historiography:

 1910, UK Rights sold to The Red Magazine

 1910, First Published in The Red Magazine (UK)

 1914, T. Fisher Unwin in *The Swindler: And Other Stories* (UK)

 1919, Film from Stoll (UK)

 Creative Levers: Cheat, weak man.

27. **Title:** *The Swindler's Handicap*

 Genre: Short story

 1910, UK Rights sold to The Red Magazine.

 1911, First Published in The Red Magazine (UK)

 1914, T. Fisher Unwin in *The Swindler: And Other Stories* (UK)

 Creative Levers: American, infatuation, Catholicism, female amputation.

28. **Title:** *The Way of an Eagle*

 Genre: Novel and film

 1910, First Published from A.L. Burt (US)

 1911, First Published in The Red Magazine (UK)

 1911, Putnam Knickerbocker novel (US)

 1912, T. Fisher Unwin and Ernest Benn novel also in paperback (UK)

 1913, Watt appointed literary agent specifically for this work

 1913, First Published by Copp Clark (Canada)

 1918, Film from Samuelson (UK)

1922, The London Magazine (UK)

1922, Produced on the London stage (UK)

1926, A ninety minute reading on the radio (UK)

1929, The Girls' Mirror magazine (UK)

1936, Film from Columbia (US)

1936, Hutchinson novel (UK)

Creative Levers: Empire, disguise, humour, dysfunctional marriage, strong ugly man, lesbianism, ambivalent sexuality, religion, death, weak men, brain fever, drug addiction.

29. **Title:** *The Woman of his Dream*

   Genre: Short story and film

   1910, First Published in The Red Magazine

   1919, Cassell in *The Tidal Wave and Other Stories* (UK)

   1921, Film from Stoll (UK)

   Creative Levers: Female pupil and teacher infatuation.

30. **Title:** *Those Who Wait*

   Genre: Short story

   1911, UK Rights sold to The Red Magazine

   1911, First Published in The Red Magazine (UK)

   1917, T. Fisher Unwin in *The Safety Curtain: And other Stories* (UK)

   1917, First Published by Putnam Grosset Dunlap in *The Safety Curtain: and other Stories* (US)

   1917, First Published by Copp Clark in *The Safety Curtain: And other Stories* (Canada)

   Creative Levers: Low self-worth, suicide, a woman-less narrative.

31. Title: *The Knave of Diamonds*

    Genre: Novel, film and theatre

    1911, First Published from A.L. Burt (US)

    1911, First Published in The Red Magazine (UK)

    1913, Putnam (US)

    1913, T. Fisher Unwin (UK)

    1917, Ernest Benn (UK)

    1918, First Published by Copp Clark (Canada)

    1931, Hutchinson (UK)

    1921, Stage play (UK)

    1921, Film from Stoll

    1921, Ethel gives Stoll US distribution rights

    1921, Stage play (UK)

    1921 Grand Magazine (UK)

    1922, Stage play (UK)

    Date unknown N.J. Boon Amsterdam as Ruitenboer (Jack of Diamonds)

    Creative Levers: Swarthy man, French, cynicism, disability, asylum, American Indian, wealth, drunkenness, callous, sanity, theft, violence (marital, spiteful, sexual), drugs, marriage (duty, sanctity of), mixed-race, adoption, murder.

32. Title: *The Knight Errant*

    Genre: Novelette and film

    1911 UK Rights sold to The Red Magazine

    1912 First Published in The Red Magazine (UK)

    1914, T. Fisher Unwin in *The Swindler Other Stories* (Collection) (UK)

    1921, Ethel gives Stoll US film distribution rights

    1922, Film from Stoll (UK)

    Creative Levers: Rights for women, evil Indian, gallant older man, savage beating, gypsy romance.

33. **Title:** *The Prey of the Dragon*

   Genre: Novella and film

   1911, UK Rights sold to The Red Magazine

   1912, First Published in The Red Magazine (UK)

   1912, Penny Rights sold to Hodder & Stoughton

   1919, Rights acquired back from Hodder Williams jointly with *Her Own Free Will*

   1920, Agreement with Cassell to use in a magazine together with *A Debt of Honour*

   1921, Cassell in *Rosa Mundi: And Other Stories* (UK)

   1921, Stoll given US film distribution rights

   1921, Film from Stoll (UK)

   1924, Berlingake Agreement for Danish & Norwegian serial rights

   Creative Levers: Empire, death, female strength, character inversion, savage beating, alcohol, illness, paternal conflict.

34. **Title:** *The Nonentity*

   Genre: Novella and film

   1911, UK Rights sold to The Red Magazine

   1912 First Published in The Red Magazine (UK)

   1914, T. Fisher Unwin in *The Swindler & Other Stories* (UK)

   1920, Agreement with Stoll for UK film rights.

   1921, Ethel withholds Stoll's US distribution rights.

   1922, Film from Stoll (UK)

   Creative Levers: Empire, military, boring aristocrat officer, buffoon, bitchiness, disguise, dishonesty, sexual assault.

35. **Title:** *The Return Game*

    Genre: Novelette

    1911 UK Rights sold to The Red Magazine.

    1912 First Published in The Red Magazine (UK)

    1919 Cassell in *The Tidal Wave and Other Stories* (UK)

    Creative Levers: Empire, Irish giant of a man, lost virginity, vengeful woman.

36. **Title:** *A Question of Trust*

    Genre: Novelette and film

    1911, UK Rights sold to The Red Magazine

    1912, First Published in The Red Magazine (UK)

    1914, T. Fisher Unwin in *The Swindler: And Other Stories* (UK)

    1920, Film from Stoll (UK)

    1921, Ethel gives Stoll US film distribution rights

    Creative Levers: Alcoholism, absinthe, drugs, dominant man.

37. **Title:** *The Tidal Wave*

    Genre: Novelette and film

    1912, First Published in The Red Magazine (UK)

    1919, Cassell in *The Tidal Wave: And Other Stories* (UK)

    1919, Story-Teller Magazine (UK)

    1919, First Published by Grosset Dunlap in *The Tidal Wave: And Other Stories* (US)

    1920, Film from Stoll (UK)

    1920, Putnam (US)

    1921, Ethel gives Stoll US film distribution rights

    1921, Cassell in French and Spanish

    1931, Cassell (UK)

    Creative Levers: Slow giant of a man, manipulative man, impulsive flirt, brain fever, love vs passion.

38. **Title:** *The Experiment*

Genre: Short story and film

1912, First Published in The Novel Magazine (UK)

1917, T. Fisher Unwin in *The Safety Curtain: And other Stories* (UK)

1917, First Published by Putnam Grosset Dunlap, in *The Safety Curtain: And other Stories* (US)

1917, First Published by Copp Clark in *The Safety Curtain: And other Stories* (Canada)

1919, Novel Magazine (UK)

1919, Pearson sells rights back to Ethel for one serial issue

1919, Weekly News Magazine (UK)

1920, Agreement with Stoll for UK film movie rights

1921, Ethel withholds US film distribution rights.

1922, Film from Stoll (UK)

1935, Agreement with The Reader's Library (Oldhams) to use in *The Book of Great Love Stories*

Creative Levers: Weak flippant, flighty and foolish self-denigrating woman, fettered and unfettered in marriage.

39. **Title:** *The Penalty*

Genre: Novella

1911, UK Rights sold to The Red Magazine

1913, First Published in The Red Magazine (UK)

1913, Agreement with Paget Literary Agency for serial rights in US newspapers

1921, Cassell in *Rosa Mundi: And Other Stories* (UK)

1924, Berlingake Tidende for serial in Danish & Norwegian

Creative Levers: Empire, military, duplicity.

40. **Title:** *The Eleventh Hour*

 Genre: Novella and film

 1914, Cassell (Story-Teller Magazine) agree to publish the 20,000-word story that Ethel will write, copy to be delivered middle of September 1914. British and Colonial rights sold

 1914, First Published in The Story-Teller Magazine in a one use only deal (UK)

 1917, T. Fisher Unwin in *The Safety Curtain: And other Stories* (UK)

 1917, First Published by Putnam Grosset Dunlap in *The Safety Curtain: And other Stories* (US)

 1917, First Published by Copp Clark in *The Safety Curtain: And other Stories* (Canada)

 1922, Film from Stoll (UK)

 Creative Levers: England, unhappy single woman, lazy man, bull like gentle non-communicative farmer, men only want sex, suicide, deep love that cannot find an expression.

41. **Title:** *The Keeper of the Door*

 Genre: Novel and film

 1914, First Published in The Red Magazine (UK)

 1915, T. Fisher Unwin (UK)

 1919, Film from Stoll (UK)

 Creative Levers: Empire, cancer, drugs (their effect and addiction), male bitchiness, euthanasia, diphtheria, death, attempted murder, hereditary madness, depression, love of God related to death.

42. **Title:** *The Englishman from Heidelberg/The Man from Heidelberg*

 Genre: Short story

 1914, First Published in The Piccadilly Magazine (UK)

1914, Ethel states no further publications in Piccadilly.

1915, The Story-Teller Magazine (Cassell) UK

1917, Cassell's Penny Magazine: *The Man from Heidelberg* (UK)

Creative Levers: Narrative has not been located.

43. **Title:** *The Rocks of Valpré*

 Genre: Novel and film

 1914, First Published in The Red Magazine (UK)

 1914, T. Fisher Unwin (UK)

 1919, Film from Stoll (UK)

 1935, Film from Real Art Productions (UK)

 1937, released as a film in the US

 Creative Levers: Immaturity, adolescent sexuality, military, inability to manage money, theft, weak woman, dominant strong man.

44. **Title:** *The Desire of his Life*

 Genre: Short story

 1914, First Published by Holden and Hardingham with *Her Compensation* (UK)

 1920, First Published by A. L. Burt (US)

 1919, Cassell in *The Tidal Wave and Other Stories* (UK)

 Creative Levers: Dominant woman, maternal control, sensitive man without imagination, a cousin marriage, dominant irritable older man, strong younger woman.

45. **Title:** *The Bars of Iron*

 Genre: Novel and film

 1915, First Published in The Red Magazine (UK)

 1916, Hutchinson (UK)

1916, Hutchinson as a 6d paper back (UK)

1916, First Published by Putnam (US)

1916, #7 in Publisher's Weekly list of US bestsellers

1919, A. L. Burt (US)

1920, Film from Stoll (UK)

1921, Stoll given US distribution rights

Creative Levers: Empire, Irish, corporal punishment, alcohol, repellent child abuser, blind child, paternal violence, mood swings, miscarriage, rape, stillbirth, power of prayer, death, war, heroism.

46. **Title:** *The Safety Curtain*

    Genre: Novelette and film

    1916, First Published in The Strand Magazine (UK)

    1917, T. Fisher Unwin in *The Safety Curtain: And other Stories* (UK)

    1918, Film from Norma Talmadge Film Corporation (US)

    Creative Levers: Dominant man, weak woman, cruelty within an unconsummated marriage, Christian and Japanese gods.

47. **Title:** *The Hundredth Chance*

    Genre: Novel and film

    1917, First Published in The Red Magazine (UK)

    1917, Hutchinson (UK)

    1917, First Published by Putnam (US)

    1917, noted as #10 in US Publisher's Weekly bestsellers

    1920, Film from Stoll (UK)

    1921, Ethel gives Stoll US distribution rights

    Creative Levers: Divorce, disability, physical abuse of women, depression, drunkenness, weak women, aggressive and ugly men.

48. **Title:** *The Rose of Dawn*

   Genre: Novelette

   1917, First Published in The Strand Magazine (UK)

   1918, Ethel decides not to sell the story in the US

   Creative Levers: Narrative has not been located.

49. **Title:** *Greatheart*

   Genre: Novel and film

   1918, First Published by T Fisher Unwin (UK)

   1918, First Published by Putnam Grosset Dunlap (US)

   1918, #6 in Publisher's Weekly US bestsellers

   1921, Film from Stoll (UK) with US film distribution rights

   Creative Levers: Handicapped man, drug addiction, maternal and paternal violence, female bitchiness, callous man, bastard child.

50. **Title:** *Rosa Mundi / Sunlit Sands*

   Genre: Short story

   1918, First Published in Lloyds Magazine (UK)

   1919, First Published in Pictorial Review (US)

   1921, Cassell in *Rosa Mundi: And Other Stories* (UK)

   1931, Weldon's Ladies Home Journal title 'sunlit Sands'

   1924, Berlingake Tidende for Danish & Norwegian serial rights

   1937, Mother and Home Magazine (UK)

   Creative Levers: Empire, American, female sexual obligations.

51. **Title:** *The Lucky Number*

   Genre: Novelette

   1919, First Published in Cassell's Magazine (UK)

1925, Hutchinson in *The Passer-By and Other Stories* (UK)

1925, Serial rights to Bonnier for Scandinavia

Creative Levers: Wall Street financier, ruined investors, death, young forceful aristocrat.

52. **Title:** *The Altar of Hono(u)r*

    Genre: Novel

    1919, First Published by Hutchinson (UK)

    1928, Strand Magazine (UK) ·

    1928 Strand Magazine Colonial Edition (UK and Colonies)

    1929, First Published in McCall's magazine as *The Altar of Honor* (US)

    1930, A.L. Burt and Putnam (US)

    Creative Levers: Empire, Irish, death, violent and uncaring family, ugly sister, living off wife's money, very young lovers, lecherous middle-aged man, irrevocability of marriage, men are devils when married, weak childish woman, bastard child, bloodline issues, woman with a past, suicide, death, boredom and drug abuse.

53. **Title:** *The Lamp in the Desert*

    Genre: Novel and film

    1919, First Published by Hutchinson (UK)

    1921, Ethel gives Stoll US film distribution rights

    1922, Film from Stoll (UK)

    1923, Film from Columbia (US)

    Creative Levers: Empire, military, homoerotic, female weakness, bitchiness, plotting, and snobbishness, male violence, physical abuse to humans and animals, illegitimate marriages, murder, infant death, disease, charity, disgrace, execution, drugs.

54. **Title:** *The Odds*

    Genre: Short story

    1919, First Published in Hutchinson's Magazine (UK)

    1919, First Published in The Strand Magazine (US)

    1920, Stoll Agreement for one act stage play Coliseum Theatre London and other

    venues. The play appeared at, Shepherd's Bush Empire, Hackney Empire, Wood

    Green, Empire, Coliseum, Manchester Hippodrome and Manchester Ardwick

    Theatre

    1920, The Delineator Magazine (US)

    1922, Cassell in *The Odds: And Other Stories* (UK)

    1922, Putnam in *The Odds: And Other Stories* (US)

    1922, Stoll agrees to rights reversion for theatres

    Creative Levers: Empire, feminism and its polarity.

55. **Title:** *The Sacrifice*

    Genre: Novelette

    1919, First Published in Hutchinsons Magazine (UK)

    1921, Collier's Magazine (US)

    1922, Cassell in *The Odds: And Other Stories (Collection)* (UK)

    1922, First Published by Putnam in *The Odds: And Other Stories* (US)

    1931, Weldon's Ladies Journal Magazine (UK)

    Creative Levers: Dishonest aristocrat, marriage by blackmail, reserved and

    forceful man, sexual assault.

56. **Title:** *Where Three Roads Meet*

    Genre: Novel

    1920, First Published by Putnam (US)

    1935, First Published by Cassell (UK)

1935, First Published by Ryerson (Canada)

1936, Putnam (US)

Creative Levers: Death, lineage, child-bearing repugnance without father's love, dominant controlling man, the master builder/God, philosophy of giving not taking, forced sexual relations, egocentric, deserter, responsibility over passion.

57. **Title:** *The Tenth Point*

    Genre: Short story

    1919, Hutchinson's purchase rights to publish a story in Hutchinson Magazine, story as yet unwritten and untitled.

    1920, First Published in Hutchinson's Magazine (UK)

    1921, US rights sold to Metropolitan Magazine by Paget Agency

    1921, Metropolitan Magazine (US)

    1921, Sovereign Magazine (UK)

    1921, First Published in Metropolitan Magazine (US)

    1925, Hutchinson in *The Passer-By: And Other Stories* (UK)

    1925, Bonnier for Scandinavian serial rights

    1934, Hutchinson in *A Century of Love Stories* (UK)

    Creative Levers: Straying married women, implied lesbianism, selfish flirt, early air flight.

58. **Title:** *The Princess's Game*

    Genre: Novel

    1920, First Published by Henry Hardingham (UK)[1]

    Creative Levers: Empire, handsome strong Irishman, coquettish woman, bitchiness, lost love.

59. **Title:** *The Top of the World*

    Genre: Novel and film

1920, First Published by Putnam Grosset Dunlap (US)

1921, Ethel withholds Stoll's US film distribution rights

1925, Film from Famous Players-Lasky Corporation (US)

1926, First Published by Cassell as a popular edition (UK)

Creative Levers: Empire, scheming villainess, violent emotions, ménage à trois, virtuous and independent heroine, marriage without consummation, drugs, evil Jewish doctor, lazy Irish, untrustworthy Boer, kaffirs lazy and smelly, gay and loving vs tough South African.

60. **Title:** *Verses*

Genre: Poetry

1920, First Published by Hutchinson (UK)

1923, First Published by Putnam (US)

1923, Knickerbocker (US)

61. **Title:** *Without Prejudice*

Genre: Novelette

1920, First Published in The Strand Magazine (UK).

1922, Cassell in *The Odds: And Other Stories* (UK)

1922, First Published in Collier's Magazine (US)

1922, First Published by Putnam in *The Odds: And Other Stories* (US)

Creative Levers: Empire, marriage for the right reasons – not just because he is not objectionable, bitchiness, indomitable man, stubborn jaw, sardonic lips, women's work, one-sided demand of marriage, rustlers and thieves, honest man, 'New Women' with a pistol but who is also subservient.

62. **Title:** *The Obstacle Race*

 Genre: Novel

 1921, First Published in The New Magazine (UK)

 1921, First Published by Cassell (UK)

 1921, N.J. Boon (Amsterdam) serial rights throughout Europe

 1921, First Published by Putnam and A.L. Burt (US)

 1921, First Published by McClelland Stewart (Canada)

 Creative Levers: Disability, women do not marry to produce children, physical abuse, weak self-centred woman, ugly strong man, social inequality, suicide, woman with a past.

63. **Title:** *Death's Property*

 Genre: Novelette

 1922, First Published by Cassell in *The Odds: And Other Stories* (UK)

 1922, First Published by Putnam in *The Odds: And Other Stories* (US)

 Creative Levers: Huge fortune, unhappy marriage, feigned death to escape marriage, love.

64. **Title:** *Charles Rex*

 Genre: Novel

 1922, First Published in The Red Magazine (UK)

 1922, Hutchinson (UK)

 1922, First Published in McCall's Magazine (US)

 1922, Putnam Grosset Dunlap (US)

 1922, First Published by Ryerson (Canada)

 Creative Levers: Ugly honest, restless, self-deprecating and volatile man, disguise, sadomasochism, disability, gambling, marriage outside of social strata, feminism, sexual assault, anti-blood sports, horse racing, murder, death, divorce.

65. Title: *The Passer-By*

    Genre: Short story

    1923, First Published in McCall's Magazine (US)

    1924, First Published in Hutchinson's Magazine (UK)

    1925, Hutchinson in *The Passer-By: And Other Stories* (UK)

    1925, Bonnier serial rights for Scandinavia

    Creative Levers: Recluse, shy, bitchy humour, recluse.

66. Title: *The Unknown Quantity*

    Genre: Novel

    1923, First Published Hutchinson (UK)

    1923, First Published by Putnam and A.L. Burt (US)

    1924, The New Magazine (UK)

    Creative Levers: Manipulative ugly woman, divorce, marriage market, bitchiness, spoilt rich young woman, suicide, financial ruin, 'Electra' complex, self-effacing man, invalid, spoilt mindful child, dysfunctional marriage, hyper-compassion, lecherous man.

67. Title: *Tetherstones*

    Genre: Novel

    1923, First Published in The Strand Magazine (UK)

    1923, First Published by Hutchinson (UK)

    1923, First Published in McCall's Magazine (US)

    Creative Levers: Extreme fundamentalist Christian without mercy or humanity, Wodehouse-like character, sexual assault, blind girl, woman with a low self-esteem, torture, death, madness, determined disciplinarian man.

68. **Title:** *Tommy Rot*

   Genre: Novella

   1923, First Published in Home Magazine (UK)

   1923, First Published in McCall's magazine (US)

   1925, Hutchinson in *The Passer-By and Other Stories* (UK)

   1925, Bonnier serial rights for Scandinavia

   Creative Levers: Disabled man with little self-respect, war wounds, blindness, compassionate nurse, psychology of friendship and loss.

69. **Title:** *The Money Monster*

   Genre: Novelette

   1924, First Published in McCall's Magazine (US)

   1924, First Published in The Corner Magazine (UK)

   1925, Hutchinson in *The Passer-By and Other Stories* (UK)

   1925, Bonnier serial rights for Scandinavia

   Creative Levers: Selfless mother, hard dominant businessman, ruin or slave to unloved man, child beating, bankruptcy.

70. **Title:** *A Man under Authority*

   Genre: Novel

   1925, First Published in McCall's magazine (US)

   1925, First Published in The Royal Magazine (UK)

   1925, First Published by Cassell (UK)

   Creative Levers: Opium overdose, unattainable honest woman, teenage unpleasantness, murder, deeply Christian curate.

71. **Title:** *The Master Key*

    Genre: Short story

    1925, First Published in McCall's magazine (US)

    Creative Levers: Narrative has not been located.

72. **Title:** *Full Measure*

    Genre: Short story

    1925, First Published in McCall's magazine (US).

    1925, First Published in Hutchinson's Magazine (UK)

    1926, Our Home magazine (UK)

    1927, Cassell in *The House of Happiness and Other Stories* (UK)

    Creative Levers: Social polarity, agricultural village setting, magnanimous man.

73. **Title:** *(The) Quest*

    Genre: Novella

    1927, First Published in McCall's magazine (US)

    1932, First Published Ernest Benn in *Live Bait: And Other Stories* (UK)

    Creative Levers: Strong-willed and self-assured boy, invalid, disease, strong-willed and determined 'girl', dying man revived by long lost sister, drowning, impersonation (girl dressed as a boy).

74. **Title:** *The Real Thing*

    Genre: Novella

    1926, First Published in McCall's magazine (UK)

    1927, Cassells Magazine (UK)

    1927, Cassell in *The House of Happiness and Other Stories* (UK)

    1928, Eve's Own Stories magazine (UK)

    Creative Levers: Empire, Cynicism, effeminate man, strong proud insensitive woman, orphans, twins, rich ugly man, differing social strata, bankruptcy, judging a book by its cover, suicide.

75. Title: *The Black Knight*

Genre: Novel

1926, First Published by Cassell (UK)

1926, First Published by Grosset Dunlap (US)

1927, McCall's Magazine (US)

Creative Levers: Suicidal, gambling, sex trafficking, cocaine addiction, independent woman, military VC, invalid, fire injury, human frailty, male kindness and determination.

76. Title: *The House of Happiness*

Genre: Novel

1926, First Published Putnam Knickerbocker A.L. Burt (US)

1927, Putnam Knickerbocker A.L. Burt (US)

1927, First Published by Cassell in *The House of Happiness and Other Stories* (UK)

Creative Levers: Empire, rich older dominant man, dominant woman, flighty girl, Regency drama, disdain for tradition, language of the period, military, adultery, cuckold, torrid love affair, failed marriage, colonial religious insensitivity, suicide, extra-marital affairs as a pastime, death, extended family story over decades, bitterness, cynicism, real loneliness in a marriage without love.

77. Title: *The Good Turn*

Genre: Novelette

1926, First Published in Hutchinson's Magazine (UK)

1926, First Published in McCall's magazine (US)

1927, Cassell in *The House of Happiness and Other Stories* (UK)

1928, Eve's Own Stories magazine (UK)

Creative Levers: Monied Irish, Wodehouse-like character, military, shipwreck, inheritance, cross class relationship.

78. **Title:** *Quits*

Genre: Novella

1927, First Published in McCall's magazine (US)

1927, First Published in Hutchinson's Magazine (UK)

1930, Woman's Weekly magazine (UK)

1932, Ernest Benn in *The Live Bait: And Other Stories* (UK)

Creative Levers: Flighty married women, dull man, unhappy marriage, vindictive spinster mischief-maker, duel.

79. **Title:** *By Request / Peggy by Request*

Genre: Novel

1927, First Published by Hutchinson and T. Fisher Unwin as *By Request* (UK)

1927, First Published in The Red Magazine as *By Request* (UK)

1928, First Published by Putnam and A.L. Burt as *Peggy by Request* (US)

1928, First Published by Ryerson as *Peggy by Request* (Canada)

Creative Levers: Empire, parental death, military, social pariah, social convention, bitchiness, virginity, drugs (opium), lesbian relationship, sexual assault, extra-marital affair, dysfunctional marriage, suicide.

80. **Title:** *Live Bait*

Genre: Short story

1928, First Published in McCall's magazine (US)

1928, First Published in Cassell's Magazine (UK)

1932, Ernest Benn in *The Live Bait: And Other Stories* (UK)

Creative Levers: Gambling, integrity, poor man with a conscience, dominant controlling and abusing father, cheat, impersonation, humour.

81. **Title:** *The Gate Marked Private*
   Genre: Novel
   1928, First Published by Cassell (UK)
   1928, First Published by Grosset Dunlap (US)
   Creative Levers: Illegitimate child, adoption, mother as aunt, selfishness, resentfulness, depression, invalid, hypochondriac, teenage challenges, cynicism, prostitution.

82. **Title:** *Picnics*
   Genre: Not known
   1928, First Published in The Weekly Despatch magazine (UK)
   Creative Levers: Narrative has not been located.

83. **Title:** *The Love Master*
   Genre: Novella
   1929, First Published in All-Story Magazine (US)
   Creative Levers: Narrative has not been located.

84. **Title:** *The Silver Bride / The Silver Wedding*
   Genre: Novel
   1930, First Published by A.L. Burt (US)
   1931, Liberty Magazine (US)
   1931, Film from Metro-Goldwyn-Meyer (US)
   1931, First Published by Hutchinson (UK) as *The Silver Wedding*
   1932, Putnam (US)

Creative Levers: War injury, strong-willed children, dysfunctional marriage resolved, polarisation of unhappiness and love, war deaths, tuberculosis, extramarital affair, car accident, paralysis, appendicitis.

85. Title: *Storm Drift*

Genre: Novel

1930, First Published Hutchinson (UK)

1931, First Published in Physical Culture Magazine (US)

1938, Cassell (UK)

Creative Levers: Enteric fever, insecure man with hidden strength, idle rude man, drugs, humour, sickness, death, power of prayer, miscarriage, jealousy, egoism, marriage as an irreversible decision.

86. Title: *The Hairpin Bend*

Genre: Novel

1930, First Published in The Chicago Tribune (US)

1932, First Published by Ernest Benn in *The Live Bait: And Other Stories* (UK)

Creative Levers: Empire, invalid, motoring extremis, lapsed insurance, impersonation.

87. Title: *The Prison Wall*

Genre: Novel

1932, First Published by Cassell (UK)

1932, First Published by Ryerson (Canada)

1933, First Published by Grosset & Dunlap and Putnam (US)

Creative Levers: Empire, fraud, selfish vain and calculating woman, vamp, immature but determined young man, death, gullibility.

88. **Title:** *The Halting Place*
    Genre: Novelette
    1932, First Published in Help Yourself Annual (UK)
    1936, Hazell Watson Viney from (UK)
    Creative Levers: Narrative has not been located.

89. **Title:** *The Losers*
    Genre: Novelette
    1932, First Published by Ernest Benn in *The Live Bait: And Other Stories* (UK)
    Creative Levers: Legless man and ugly injured woman from the war now permanently veiled, the horror of war, cruel unthinking children.

90. **Title:** *The Chatelaine*
    Genre: Novelette
    1932, First Published by Ernest Benn in *Live Bait: And Other Stories* (UK)
    Creative Levers: Strong determined woman, long family line, landowner, invalid, disability, heritage, property dispute, impersonation.

91. **Title:** *The Pageant of Youth*
    Genre: Novelette
    1932, First Published by Ernest Benn in *Live Bait: And Other Stories* (UK)
    Creative Levers: Empire, youthfulness, cynic, re-kindled love.

92. **Title:** *Misunderstanding*
    Genre: Novelette
    1932, First Published by Ernest Benn in *Live Bait: And Other Stories* (UK)
    Creative Levers: Vamp, gambling, bitchiness, a failed marriage.

93. **Title:** *The Serpent in the Garden*
    Genre: Novel
    1932, First Published Hutchinson (UK)
    1938, First Published Doubleday Doran (US)
    Creative Levers: Gangster, spies / secret service, dying beauty, innocent girl, sexual assaults, extreme physical violence, acid attack, death, sex slaves.

94. **Title:** *Dona Celestis*
    Genre: Novel
    1933, First Published by A.L. Burt Putnam (US)
    1933, First Published by Ernest Benn (UK)
    Creative Levers: Empire, female weaknesses and strengths, drug use, same-sex relationships.

95. **Title:** *The Electric Torch*
    Genre: Novel
    1934, First Published by Cassell (UK)
    1934, Good Needlework magazine (UK)
    1934, First Published by Putnam Doubleday Doran (US)
    1934, First Published by Ryerson (Canada)
    Creative Levers: Empire, drugs, marriage consummation.

96. **Title:** *Honeyball Farm*
    Genre: Novel
    1937, First Published by Putnam (US)
    1937, First Published by Ryerson (Canada)
    1937, Grosset Dunlap (US)
    1938, First Published by Hutchinson (UK)

Creative Levers: Violent father figure, hypochondriac, forward cold girl, dirty cantankerous old man, alcohol, drugs, underage sexual vulnerability, sexual assault, slavery in marriage, murder, mentally challenged youth.

97. Title: *The Juice of the Pomegranate*

Genre: Novel

1938, First Published in All-Story Magazine (US)

1938, First Published Cassell (UK)

1938, Doubleday Doran 1 (US)

1938, First Published by Ryerson (Canada)

Creative Levers: Empire, New Woman, sexual assault, alcohol, man without a moral compass, rape, lost virginity, pregnancy out of wedlock, good strong man, sex before marriage, suicide, spy, drugs, physical violence, fatal car accident, power of prayer, miscarriage.

98. Title: *Sown among Thorns*

Genre: Novel

1939, First Published in Woman's Weekly magazine (UK)

1939, Cassell (UK)

Creative Levers: Driven insensitive man, dominant woman, tolerant husband, poor colonel with no connections, child death and mourning, mentally challenged lady, selfless heroine, parental death, lack of inherited wealth, class struggle, hardworking lower social class man who is in fact a true gentleman.

31. American Magazine Story Environments

Mccall's November 1925

Ethel's *A Man Under Authority* appeared along with other fiction writers and an article on the travels of then Prince of Wales with *Through Africa With The Prince of Wales.*

Love Story Magazine July 23, 1927

Ethel's *His Heart's Desire*, appeared alongside Ruby M. Ayres' *The Tragedy Girl.*

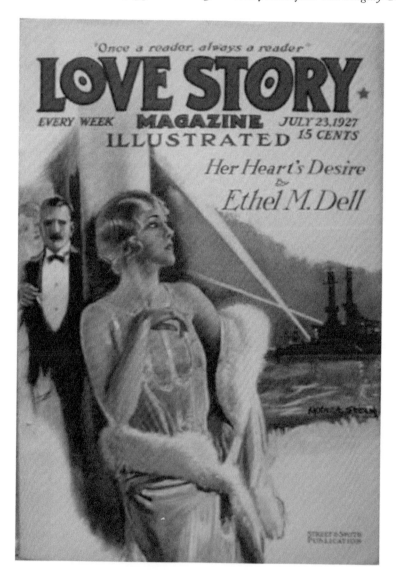

McCall's August 1929

A front cover promotion of the serialisation of Ethel's *The Altar of Honor*

McCall's September 1929

Highbrow literary acceptance with a joint Kipling and Dell cover.

Physical Culture March 1931

Ethel's serialised *Storm Drift* appeared along with an Edgar Wallace story.

Physical Culture June 1931

Ethel's serialised *Storm Drift* appeared along with other romantic fiction writers:
Zane Grey's *Tales of the South Seas*, and Warwick Deeping's *The Ten Commandments*.

32. Film Productions

Title: *The Way of an Eagle*

Release date: 1918 in the UK

Screenplay by: G.B. Samuelson. Essentially the same as the published narrative

Director: G.B. Samuelson

Producer: G.B. Samuelson

~

Title: *The Safety Curtain*

Release date: July 1918 in the US

Screenplay by: Sidney Franklin, a deviation from the published narrative

Director: Sidney Franklin

Producer/Actor: Norma Talmadge Film Corporation

~

Title: *The Keeper of the Door*

Release date: March 1919 in the UK

Screenplay by: R. Byron-Webber

Director: Maurice Elvey

Producer: Stoll Picture Productions

~

Title: *The Rocks of Valpré*

Release date: June 1919 in the UK

Screenplay by: R. Byron-Webber, a deviation from the published narrative

Director: Maurice Elvey

Producer: Stoll Picture Productions

~

Title: *The Swindler*

Release date: December 1919 in the UK

Screenplay by: Kate Gurney, a deviation from the published narrative

Director: Maurice Elvey

Producer: Stoll Picture Productions

~

Title:	*The Hundredth Chance*
Release date:	June 1920 in the UK
Screenplay by:	Sinclair Hill
Director:	Maurice Elvey
Producer:	Stoll Picture Productions

~

Title:	*A Question of Trust*
Release date:	August 1920 in the UK
Screenplay by:	Sinclair Hill, not the published narrative
Director:	Maurice Elvey
Producer:	Stoll Picture Productions

~

Title:	*The Tidal Wave*
Release date:	1920 in the UK and the US
Screenplay by:	Sinclair Hill, essentially the same as the published narrative
Director:	Sinclair Hill
Producer:	Stoll Picture Productions

~

Title:	*Bars of Iron*
Release date:	November 1920 in the UK
Screenplay by:	Unknown
Director:	F. Martin Thornton
Producer:	Stoll Picture Productions

~

Title:	*Greatheart*
Release date:	June 1921 in the UK
Screenplay by:	Mrs. Sidney Groome, loosely based on the published narrative
Director:	George Ridgwell
Producer:	Stoll Picture Productions

~

Title:	*The Place of Honour*
Release date:	June 1921 in the UK
Screenplay by:	William J. Elliott
Director:	Sinclair Hill
Producer:	Stoll Picture Productions

~

Title:	*The Knave of Diamonds*
Release date:	June 1921 in the UK
Screenplay by:	Leslie Howard Gordon and Frank Miller
Director:	René Plaissetty
Producer:	Stoll Picture Productions

~

Title:	*The Woman of his Dream*
Release date:	July 1921 in the UK
Screenplay by:	Leslie Howard Gordon, very loosely based on the published narrative
Director:	Harold M. Shaw
Producer:	Stoll Picture Productions

~

Title:	*The Prey of the Dragon*
Release date:	September 1921 in the UK
Screenplay by:	Leslie Howard Gordon, not the published narrative
Director:	F. Martin Thornton
Producer:	Stoll Picture Productions

~

Title	*The Lamp in the Desert*
Release date:	January 1921 in the UK
Screenplay by:	Leslie Howard Gordon
Director:	F. Martin Thornton
Producer:	Stoll Picture Productions

~

Title:	*The Experiment*
Release date:	September 1922 in the UK
Screenplay by:	William J. Elliott, very loosely based on the published narrative
Director:	Sinclair Hill
Producer:	Stoll Picture Productions

~

Title:	*A Debt of Honour*
Release date:	1922 in the UK
Screenplay by:	Unknown, not the published narrative
Director:	Maurice Elvey
Producer:	Stoll Picture Productions

~

Title:	*The Eleventh Hour*
Release date:	1922 in the UK
Based on:	The Eleventh Hour
Screenplay by:	Leslie Howard Gordon
Director:	George Ridgwell
Producer:	Stoll Picture Productions

~

Title:	*The Experiment*
Release date:	September 1922 in the UK
Screenplay by:	William J. Elliott, very loosely based on the published narrative
Director:	Sinclair Hill
Producer:	Stoll Picture Productions

~

Title:	*The Nonentity*
Release date:	November 1922 in the UK
Screenplay by:	Sinclair Hill, very loosely based on the published narrative
Director:	Sinclair Hill
Producer:	Stoll Picture Productions

~

Title:	*The Knight Errant*
Release date:	1922 in the UK
Screenplay by:	Leslie Howard Gordon and Mrs. Sydney Groome, loosely based on the published narrative
Director:	George Ridgwell
Producer:	Stoll Picture Productions

~

Title:	*The Lamp in the Desert*
Release date:	January 1923 in the US
Screenplay by:	Unknown
Director:	Unknown
Producer:	Columbia Pictures

~

Title:	*Her Own Free Will*
Release date:	20 July 1924 in the US
Screenplay by:	Gerald C. Duffy. South Africa is replaced by South America, but essentially the same as the published narrative
Director:	Paul Scardon
Producer:	Eastern Productions

~

Title:	*The Top of the World*
Release date:	9 February 1925 in the USA
Screenplay by:	Jack Cunningham, similar to the published narrative
Director:	George Melford
Producer:	Famous Players-Lasky Corporation

~

Title:	*The Rocks of Valpré*
Release date:	January 1935 in the UK, January 1937 in the USA
Screenplay by:	H. Fowler Mear, very loosely based on the published narrative
Director:	Henry Edwards
Producer:	Julius Hagan, Real Art Productions

~

Title:	*The Way of an Eagle*
Release date:	1936 in the US
Screenplay by:	Unknown
Director:	Unknown
Producer:	Columbia

33. Photographs and Illustrations

Ethel and Ella

This photograph of Ethel and Ella by the Eton-based society photographer Alfred Douglas Kissack was almost certainly taken before *The Way of an Eagle* was published, which saw the start of Ethel's reclusiveness.

A very sombre and exhausted looking Ethel. Reportedly taken at Chattern House, Ashford on the day that *The Way of an Eagle* was published in the UK in 1912 when she was thirty-one years old.

'You have your dog, but I have my baby': Ella with Penelope Dell and Ethel
with her dog Jimmy in 1920.

Ethel with Nora and Gerald Savage

Ella and her Alberts[1]

The Dell Gypsy

Drawing by Penelope Dell as she remembered Ella on holiday

Ella Dell's gypsy caravan

Family members

Ethel's brother Reggie Dell

Ethel's aunt, Sister Alphonsine Dell O.S.B.

The Friends

Violet Ebsworth, Ethel's secretary

Violet Vanburgh, the actress

Edith de Wolf with the deep growly voice

Violet Ebsworth and Mary Bastard with Penelope Dell aged 3 or 4

Edwardian Parlour Games

No.	Score	Trumps.	Partner	No.	Score	Trumps.	Partner
1		**"The Knave of Diamonds," by Dell.** *Diamonds Trumps for four hands.*		13		**"The Dark Mile," by Broster.** *Spades Trumps for four hands.*	
2		Winner of trick containing King of Diamonds scores double.		14		Deal four cards to each player, then draw in turn from stock after each round. Trick winner draws first.	
3		Winner of trick containing Queen of Diamonds scores double.		15		Winner of trick containing King of Spades scores three extra.	
4		Winner of trick containing Knave of Diamonds scores three extra.		16		Winner of trick containing Queen of Spades scores two extra.	
5		**"Famine Alley," by Miss Prudence O'Shea.** *Clubs Trumps for four hands.*		17		**"Les Miserables," by Dumas.** *Misere. No Trumps. Score opponents' tricks.*	
6		No score for tricks taken by Aces.		18		*No Trumps.* No score for tricks taken by Kings.	
7		No score for tricks taken by Kings.		19		*No trumps.* Score opponents' tricks.	
8		No score for tricks taken by Queens.		20		Plain round. *No trumps.*	
9		**"Good Companions," by Priestley.** *Hearts Trumps for four hands.* Winning couple and losing couple of deal 9 continue to play together for deals 10, 11, 12. *Hearts Trumps.*		21		**"The Heart of Midlothian," by Scott.** *Hearts Trumps for four hands.*	
				22		If trick taken with King of Hearts score three extra.	
10		As above.		23		If trick taken with Queen of Hearts score two extra.	
11		As above.					
12		As above.		24		If trick taken with Knave of Hearts score one extra.	

Name ....   *Begin at Table No.* ....

Forward ....   *TOTAL* ....

"PUZZLING PASTIMES."

Other highly amusing Games of a similar character, viz. :

Games marked A are Easy.   B Medium.   C Advanced.

Number			Number		
A	13	The Game of a Puzzling Man	C	135	Disjointed Insects
B	31	Buried Christian Names (Women)	B	144	Disguised Dogs
			A	160	Who Knows ?
B	32	Buried Christian Names (Men)	C	161	More Slogans
C	37	Try to Guess Us	B	173	The Animals Went in one by one
B	41	Is it "It"? it is!	A	188	Careless Cars
A	51	The Life History of Kate	A	189	A Schoolboy's Outfit
B	66	Half-an-Hour in a Fairy World	C	195	Un"author"ised Editions
			B	196	Do you know
C	73	The Old, Old Story	C	216	Books, Plays, Operas and Authors
A	74	A Grocer's Mistakes	A	221	Names of Favourite Cars
C	90	The Game of Tantalising Towns	B	222	Good Afternoon
B	100	An Artful Game	C	223	Mixed Pins
A	101	A Muddle Headed Greengrocer	B	224	Mine Ease at Mine Inn
B	109	Chrysanthemums	B	225	Hint the Tint
C	112	Off with their Heads	A	226	Finish it Off
B	126	Tantalising Tors	B	227	O, for a Word!
C	132	A Wireless Wail	C	228	'Umming Along
A	133	Mo'or Cars		229	Rhyme in Time

Eight Games of one sort in a Box.
Price 1/- per Box.
To be obtained of all Stationers.

Published by
G. DELGADO, Ltd., LONDON, N.1.

UN "AUTHOR" ISED EDITIONS.

No. 195

UN"AUTHOR"ISED EDITIONS.

A young librarian was told to make a set of covers for some dilapidated library books. Unfortunately, he mislaid the catalogue, and having labelled the covers with the book titles, he proceeded to attach the authors' names from memory, with the following strange result. Can you put him right ?

1 The Cathedral by Compton Mackenzie

Example :
BY HUGH WALPOLE.

2 The Rosary by E. M. Dell ...

3 The Crimson Circle by Conan Doyle

4 The Mighty Atom by Hall Caine

5 She Stoops to Conquer by Sheridan

6 Keeping up Appearances by Bernard Shaw

7 Little England by Rudyard Kipling

8 Bulldog Drummond by John Buchan

9 Robert Elsmere Mrs. Henry Wood

10 The Last of the Barons by Scott

11 King Solomon's Mines by Zangwill

12 Uncle Tom's Cabin by Mrs. Hodgson Burnet

13 The Water-Babie by Barrie ...

14 The Constant Nymph by Michael Arlen

15 The Hundredth Chance by Ian Hay

16 Sard Harker by John Galsworthy

17 Dodo by H. G. Wells ...

18 The Keeper of the Door by Hugh Walpole

19 Red Wagon by J. Masefield ...

20 The Old Wives Tale by Stephen Mackenna

21 Our Mutual Friend by Ouida ...

22 Roper's Row by Charles Dickens

23 The Four Feathers by W. J. Locke

24 The White Monkey by Compton Mackenzie

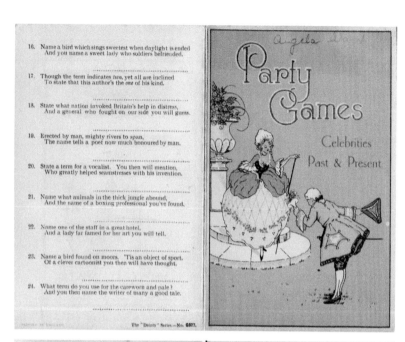

16. Name a bird which sings sweetest when daylight is ended
And you name a sweet lady who soldiers befriended.

17. Though the term indicates two, yet all are inclined
To state that this author's the one of his kind.

18. State what nation invoked Britain's help in distress,
And a general who fought on our side you will guess.

19. Erected by man, mighty rivers to span,
The name tells a poet now much honoured by man.

20. State a term for a vocalist. You then will mention,
Who greatly helped seamstresses with his invention.

21. Name what animals in the thick jungle abound,
And the name of a boxing professional you've found.

22. Name one of the staff in a great hotel,
And a lady far famed for her art you will tell.

23. Name a bird found on moors. 'Tis an object of sport,
Of a clever cartoonist you then will have thought.

24. What term do you use for the careworn and pale?
And you then name the writer of many a good tale.

The "Dainty" Series.—No. Q977.

CELEBRITIES. Past and Present.

The answers supply the names of
well-known persons.

1. Here's a riddle to solve. Let those guess it who can
What great poet's name would suggest a tall man?

2. Though strongly suggestive of wig and court,
A political leader to light now is brought.

3. Give the name for a valley where green mosses grow,
And you name, too, an authoress, whom you all know

4. Name a person employed to prepare food for you,
And you name a great sailor and explorer too,

5. Name a track through a stream, which on foot you may
tread, And the name of a motor magnate you have said.

6. Though the name indicates one in clerical gown,
Yet a person so called is a noted film clown.

7. State a dish often seen on the breakfast table,
And you mention an essayist, witty and able.

8. Though paternity doubtless by this we imply,
Yet an artist so called made "Ole Bill" never die.

9. A good make of underwear, cosy and light,
Tells of a King's favourite, who fell from that height.

10. Name a bird, which for food will on other birds prey,
And you name too, a cricketer, living to-day.

11. Name a county in Wales, with a town of the same,
And you then name a man of Egyptian tomb fame,

12. What does cook add to gravy to make it look brown?
Now you mention a poet whose poems are well-known

13. State a term, quite well-known to men fond of the race,
And you name a peer who in the House takes his place,

14. Name a painful growth on the joint of a toe,
And a man's name you have who dreamed dreams,
long ago.

15. State a term for the moon when we see it grow less,
And an artist of pussy cat fame you will guess.

Ethel's Major Titles:
An Indication of Volume Output

- *The Way of an Eagle: Fifty-two* editions in six languages held by 217 libraries worldwide.
- *The Top of the World: Thirty-one* editions held by 172 libraries worldwide.
- *The Bars of Iron:* First published in 1916. Hutchinsons reported that they had printed 721,000 copies by 1929. Twenty-five editions in four languages held by forty-seven libraries worldwide.
- *The Hundredth Chance:* First published in 1917. Hutchinsons reported that they had printed 641,000 copies by 1929. Twenty-three editions in three languages held by 140 libraries worldwide.
- *Greatheart:* Twenty-two editions in four languages held by 148 libraries worldwide.
- *The Black Knight*: Nineteen editions in three languages held in 132 libraries worldwide
- *The Lamp in the Desert*: First published in 1919. As reported in Truth newspaper (1.10.1916) the first edition print run was 60,000. Hutchinsons reported that they had printed 313,000 copies by 1929. Seventeen editions in two languages held by 137 libraries worldwide.
- *The Swindler and Other Stories*: Fifteen editions held by 132 libraries worldwide.
- *Rosa Mundi and Other Stories*: Fourteen editions held by 181 libraries worldwide.
- *Charles Rex:* First published in 1922. Hutchinsons reported that they had printed 190,000 copies by 1929.
- *Tetherstones:* First published in 1923. Hutchinsons reported that they had

printed 125,000 copies by 1929.

- *The Unknown Quantity:* First published in 1923. Hutchinsons reported that they had printed 93,000 copies by 1929.
- *The Passer-By:* First published in 1925. Hutchinsons reported that they had printed 42,000 copies by 1929.
- In 1920 Hutchinson and Hurst & Blackett sold over 1 million of their 3s 6d fiction series featuring Ethel M. Dell, Arnold Bennett.[1]

INDEX

BIBLIOGRAPHY

Primary Data

Author's Private Collection

Banger, Jean. letters and interview transcripts.

Barnwell A. letters

Bowra, E.V. letters

Brown, Faith letters

Dell Irene Elizabeth letters

Dell R. J. Handwritten genealogy notes for the Dell family undated but used for *Nettie and Sissie* with Penelope Dell annotations. Therefore, written about 1975 when Penelope Dell commenced writing *Nettie and Sissie*, before his death in 1977 and the publication of *Nettie and Sissie.*

Dell, Ethel M., Letters

Dell, Poppy, letters

Evershed, Mary, letters

Pawson, Chris, emails

Penelope Dell Adoption Order

Penelope Dell Agreement to Adopt

Philips, Patsy, (Churchill) letters

Redemptionist convent letters to and from Poppy Dell

Savage, E. Louise, letters

Savage, Mary Evelyn, letters

Savage. John Col., letters

Talbot, (Nursie), letters

Tanner R., letters

Tanner R., questionnaire completed June 2012.

The Equitable Life Assurance Society letter dated 27th February 1975 signed
   G.A. Wadey secretary concerning Vincent Dell
The Equitable Life Assurance Society letter dated 8th February 1975 signed
   G.A. Wadey secretary concerning Vincent Dell

Other Collections:

British Film Institute

British Library Manuscripts

Buckinghamshire Parish Register, Aylesbury, UK.

Devon County Council, UK

Hampshire UK, Record Office archives

New York Public Library James B Pinker correspondence

Margaret Herrick Museum, Los Angeles

Oscars Library, Los Angeles

Northwestern University Library, Illinois, Charles Deering McCormick
   Library of Special Collections, Papers of the Pinker Literary, Artistic,
   Dramatic, and Film Agency,

University of North Carolina, A.P. Watt Records Collection Reference 11036

University of North Carolina, Michael Sadler's Papers Reference 11033

Online Resources

www.ebay.com

www.amazon.com

www.britishnewspaperarchives .com

www.newspapers.com

The Orlando Project, Cambridge University Press

www.WomenandSilentBritish cinema.com

www.arosebooks.com

www.bookfinder.com

www.measuringworth.com

The Standard Index of Short Stories, 1900–1933, Special Reference Departments, Boston Public Library, Massachusetts

http://www.philsp.com/homeville/fmi/q253.htm

Sheffield Hallam blog

www.worldcat.org

Published Data

Aldington R., 'Lawrence of Arabia, A Biographical Enquiry': Collins, London, 1955.

Anderson, R., 'The Purple Heart Throbs': Hodder and Stoughton, London, 1974.

Appignanesi L., 'Mad Bad and Sad, A History of Women and the Mind Doctors from 1800 to the Present': Virago, London, 2008.

Atkins, K., 'Victorian women on Drugs, Parts 1 & 2': www. Pointsandhs.com 2012.

Aikens K., 'A Pharmacy of her own: Victorian Woman and the Figure of the Opiat': Ann Arbor, Pro Quest, 2008.

Barry, I., 'Lets go to the Pictures': Chatto & Windus, London 1926.

Batchelor, J., 'The Edwardian Novelists': Duckworth, London, 1982.

Beauman, N., 'A Very Great Profession: The Woman's Novel 1914–39': Virago, London, 1983.

Bell, M., Williams, M., Ed. 'British Women's Cinema': Routledge, Abingdon, 2010.

Bloom, C., 'Popular fiction since 1900': Palgrave Macmillan, 2002.

Bowra, C.M. 'Memories': Widenfeld & Nicholson, London, 1966

Burke, P. 'Reflections on Cultural History' in 'Interpretation and Cultural History', (eds.).

Pittock, J, and Wear A.: New York: St. Martin's Press, 1991.

Byatt, A.S., 'The Ferocious Reticence of Georgette Heyer: Sunday Times, Magazine, 5 October 1975.

Cartland B., Daily Express, 14 July 1977.

Chambers Biographical Dictionary of Women, Edinburgh, 1996.

Cloud, H., 'Barbara Cartland. Crusader in Pink': Weidenfeld and Nicholson, London, 1979.

Colman, A., 'Drugs and the Addiction Aesthetic in Nineteenth Century Literature': Palgrave Macmillan, Cham Switzerland, 2019.

Coward, N., 'Three Plays', Vintage Press, Knopf Doubleday, New York, 1999.

Cox, H., and Mowatt, S., 'Revolutions from Grub Street', Oxford University Press, Oxford, 2014.

Daly, N., 'Modernism, Romance, and the Fin de Siecle: Popular Fiction and British Culture, 1880–1914': Cambridge University Press, 1999.

Diniejko, D., 'Victorian Drug Use': The Victorian Web, 2002.

Dell, E. M., 89 titles have been referenced.

The following titles have not been located:

'The Virtue of Prudence', 1909.

'The Heart of the Tyrant', 1910.

'Her Weapon of Defence', 1910.

'The Englishman from Heidelberg', 1915.

'The Rose of Dawn', 1917.

'The Master Key', 1925.

'Picnics', 1928.

'The Love Master', 1929.

'The Halting Place', 1932.

Dell, P., 'Nettie and Sissie': Hamish Hamilton, London 1977.

Ervine, St. J., The Times Newspaper 25 April 1922.

Fernandez, H., and Libby, T., 'Heroin: Its History, Pharmacology and Treatment': Minnesota, Hazeldon, 2011.

Fitzgerald, Z., 'save me the Waltz': Vintage Books, London, 2001.

Franzen, J., 'A Rooting Interest. Edith Wharton and the problem of sympathy': The New Yorker, February 13 & 20, 2012.

Fussell, R., 'George Orwell', Sewanee Review, vol. 93, No.2 (Spring 1985): The John Hopkins University Press.

George, R.M., 'Homes in the Empire, Empire in the Home': Cultural Critique, No.26 (Winter, 1994–1994).

Greenberger, A., 'The British Image of India: A Study in the Literature of Imperialism': 1880–1960. London, Oxford University Press, 1969.

Graves, R., 'The Cost of Letters', Horizon, Vol. XIV No. 81 September 1946.

Griest, G.L., 'Mudie's Circulating Library and the Victorian Novel': David and Charles, Indiana University Press, 1970.

Harrison, J., 'The Centauri Device': London, Doubleday, 1974.

Hammond, M., 'Reading, Publishing and the Formation of Literary Taste in England': Ashgate, Aldershot, 2006.

Hayter, A. 'Opium and the Romantic Imagination,: Berkley and Los Angeles: University Press, 1968.

Heyer, G., 'The Infamous Army': William Heinemann, London, 1937.

Hodge, J., 'The Private World of Georgette Heyer: London: The Bodley Head, 1984.

Hughes, R., 'In Hazard' London: Penguin Vintage Classic Books, 2002.

Hunter, J., 'Edwardian Fiction': Harvard University Press, Cambridge, Mass., 1982.

Hyde, F. E., Markham, F., 'A History of Stony Stratford': McCorquodale & Co, Derby, 1948.

James, W., The Principles of Psychology, Cosmo Classics, New York, 1985.

Kelley, T., 'History of Public Libraries in Great Britain 1845–1975': The Library Association, London 1975.

Kemp, S., Mitchell. C., Trotter, D., 'The Oxford Companion to Edwardian Fiction': Oxford University Press, Oxford, 1977.

Kloester, J., 'Georgette Heyer Biography of a Bestseller': William Heineman, London, 2011.

Mailer, N., 'Marilyn a Biography'. Spring books, London, 1988.

Mason, A.E.W., 'Sapphire': Hodder and Stoughton, London, 1933.

McAleer, J., 'Passion's Fortune. The Story of Mills and Boon: Oxford University Press, Oxford, 1999.

McCormack, K., 'George Eliot and Intoxication: Dangerous Drugs for the condition of England': Saint Martin's, New York, 2000.

McVeigh, J., 'In Collaboration with British Literary Biography': Palgrave McMillan Springer Nature, Cham Switzerland, 2017.

Milford, N., 'Zelda Fitzgerald, A Biography': The Bodley Head, London, 1970.

Mitchel, G., 'The Saltmarsh Murders': London, Gollanz, 1932.

Miller, J. E. 'Rebel Woman: Feminism, Modernism and the Edwardian Novel': Virago London, 1994.

Morris, N., 'An Eminent British Studio: The Stoll Film Companies and British Cinema 1918–1928', Thesis Submitted for the degree of Doctor of Philosophy in the School of Film of Television Studies, University of East Anglia, May 2009.

Morris, N., 'Pictures, Romance and Luxury: Women and cinema in the 1910s and 1920s', in Bell M. and Williams M, 'eds., 'British Women's Cinema': Routledge, Abingdon, 2010.

Orwell, G., 'In Defence of the Novel', 1936, reprinted in The Collected Essays, Journalism and Letters of George Orwell, Volume One, An Age Like This, 1920–1940: (Secker & Warburg, London, 1968), p. 284 in Penguin Edition, 1970.

Orwell, G., 'Keep the Aspidistra Flying': Alfred A. Knopf, New York, London, Toronto, 2011.

Orwell, G., 'The Cost of Letters', Horizon, Vol. XIV No. 81 September 1946.

Pappas, S., 'Opioid Crisis Has Frightening Parallels to Drug Epidemic of Late 1800s': www.LiveScience.com, 29 September 2017.

Pearce, D.H., 'sherlock Holmes, Conan Doyle and Cocaine': Journal of the History of the Neurosciences: Basic and Clinical Perspectives, 3 (4), 1994, 227–232.

Perrin, A., 'East of Suez': Chatto & Windus , London, 1906.

Priestley, J.B., ' Modern English Novelists: Joseph Conrad: The English Journal , Vol. 14, No. 1 National Council of Teachers of English Jan., 1925.

Sayers, D., 'The Unpleasantness at the Bellona Club': London, Ernest Benn, 1928.

Shelton, J., 'Bad Girls: Gerty, Cissy, and the Erotics of Unruly Speech': James Joyce Quarterly, Vol. 34, No.1/2, Joyce's Women: (Fall, 1996 – Winter, 1997), University of Tulsa Press.

Simpson, John., 'Strange Places, Questionable People': London, Pan Macmillan, 2008.

Skinner, C., 'Our Hearts were Young and Gay': New York, Dodd, Mead & Co., 1942.

Spain, N., 'The Way of Ethel M. Dell': The Saturday Book, Ed. John Hadfield, Hutchinson, London, 1955.

Symondson, K., The Times Literary Supplement, 6 January 2017.

Tanner, D., 'E M Dell and the Tosh Horse': The Persephone Biannually No. 29 Autumn/Winter 2021–22.

Tanner, D., 'Literary Success and Popular Romantic Fiction: Ethel M. Dell, a Case Study' in The Book World, Selling and Distributing British Literature, 1900–1940, edit. Nicola Wilson: Brill, Leiden 2016.

Tanner, R. and D., 'Burma 1942, Memories of a Retreat': The History Press, Stroud 2009.

Thompson, E., 'The other side of the Medal': Hogarth, London, 1925

Thompson, F., 'Ethel M. Dell and Winchester, A memory of the Best Selling Author and her Home on Sleeper's Hill': Hampshire Life, 1986.

Todd, J., Dictionary of British Women Writers, Routledge, London, 1989.

Trodd, A., 'A Reader's Guide to Edwardian Fiction': Harvester, Brighton, 1991.

Unwin, S. Sir.   'The Truth about a Publisher': George Allen and Unwin, London, 1960.

Watson, W., 'Miss Pettigrew Lives for a Day': First published 1938, London Persephone Classics, 2000.

Wearing, J.P.,   'The London Stage 1920–1929, Calendar of Productions, Performers and Personnel': Rowman and Littlefield, United States, 2014.

West, R., 'The Tosh Horse': The New Statesman July 12th, 1922.

Wilde, O., 'The Complete works of Oscar Wilde': Geddes & Grosset, New Lanark 2001.

Wodehouse, P.G., 'The Inimitable Jeeves': Herbert Jenkins, London, 5th Printing.

Wodehouse, P.G., 'Carry on Jeeves': Arrow, London, 7th Printing.

Wodehouse, P.G., 'Uncle Dynamite': Penguin, Harmondsworth, 1966.

Woolf, V., 'The Waves': A Project Gutenberg of Australia eBook, 2002.

Woolf, V., 'Orlando': A Project Gutenberg of Australia eBook, 2015.

Woolf, V., 'To The Lighthouse': A Project Gutenberg of Australia eBook, 2001.

Wolpert, S., Journal of Asian Studies, Vol. 29 No. 4 August 1970, Review: Greenberger, A, 'The British Image of India: A Study in the Literature of Imperialism', 1880–1960. London, Oxford University Press, 1969.

Kean H., 'The Great Cat and Dog Massacre': CUP Press Chicago and London, 2017

Yule, H., Burnall A., 'Hobson-Jobson Anglo-Indian Dictionary': Wordsworth Editions, Ware 1996.

NOTES AND SOURCES

Preface
1.   Hutchinson's publicity material in The Altar of Honour 1929.

Chapter 1. Background to a Recluse
1.   Mary Hammond, Reading, Publishing and the Formation of Literary Taste in England (Aldershot, Ashgate, 2006), p. 163.

Chapter 2. The Biographical Environment
1.   Craig Brown. Nothing is real. The slippery art of biography, (Times Literary Supplement. 10th September 2021), p. 3.
2.   Janet McVeigh. In Collaboration with British Literary Biography, (Cham, Palgrave Macmillan Springer, 2017), p. 208.
3.   See Craig Brown. Nothing is real. The slippery art of biography, (Times Literary Supplement. 10th September 2021), p. 3.
4.   Barbara Cartland, Daily Express, July 14th 1977.
5.   Jane Hodge, The Private World of Georgette Heyer, (Bath, Chivers, 2008), p. 65.
6.   Penelope Dell letter to Dame Joan McLoughlin August 25 1975. Author's collection.
7.   Norman Mailer, Marilyn a Biography, (London, Spring Books, 1988), p. 18.
8.   Richard Aldington, Lawrence of Arabia, a Biographical Enquiry, (London, Collins, 1955), p. 18.
9.   Chambers Biographical Dictionary of Women, Edinburgh, 1996.
10.   Exeter University: 2022/23 Course EAS3225 - 'Reader, I Married Him': The Evolution of Romance Fiction from 1740 to the Present.
11.   Pamela Regis, A Natural History of the Romance Novel, (Philadelphia, University of Pennsylvania Press, 2003), p. 116.
12.   Clive Bloom, Popular Fiction Since 1900, (Basingstoke, Palgrave Macmillan, 2002), p. 34.
13.   Henry Cloud, Barbara Cartland. Crusader in Pink, (London Weidenfeld & Nicholson, 1979), p.23.
14.   Ethel M. Dell, The Unknown Quantity, (London, Hutchinson, 1923), p. 272.
15.   Victoria Sherrow, Encyclopedia of Hair: A Cultural History (Westport, Greenwood Press, 2006), p. 70.

Chapter 3. Peer Envy, Perhaps

1.   George Orwell, The Cost of Letters, Horizon X1V (September 1946).
2.   Stanley Unwin, The Truth about a Publisher, (London, Allen & Unwin, 1960), pp. 93–94.
3.   Nicola Beauman, A Very Great Profession, (London, Virago, 2004), (London, Persephone Books), 2008, p. 5.
4.   George Orwell, Keep the Aspidistra Flying, (New York, Knopf, 2011), pp. 259–261.
5.   George Orwell, In Defence of the Novel, 1936, in The Collected Essays, Journalism and Letters of George Orwell, eds. Sonia Orwell and Ian Angus 4 Vols. (London, Secker & Warburg, 1968), 1:281.
6.   Ibid., 1:284.
7.   Paul Fussell, George Orwell, Sewanee Review, vol. 93.2, No.2 (1985), pp. 234, 235.
8.   P.G., Wodehouse, Carry on Jeeves, (London, Herbert Jenkins, 1925), 7th Printing, pp. 211, 218.
9.   P.G., Wodehouse, The Inimitable Jeeves, (London, Herbert Jenkins, 1923) 5th Printing, pp. 18–19, 239–240.
10.   P.G., Wodehouse, Uncle Dynamite, (Harmondsworth, Penguin books, 1966), p. 191.
11.   P.G., Wodehouse, Uncle Dynamite, (Harmondsworth, Penguin books, 1966), p. 237.
12.   Noel Coward, Three Plays, (Vintage Books, Knopf Doubleday, 1999), introduction.
13.   Ethel M. Dell, The Electric Torch, (London, Cassell, 1934), p. 185.
14.   Jen Shelton, Bad Girls: Gerty, Cissy, and the Erotics of Unruly Speech, James Joyce Quarterly, Vol. 34, No.1/2, Joyce's Women (Fall, 1996 Winter, 1997), University of Tulsa Press.
15.   A. S. Byatt, The Ferocious Reticence of Georgette Heyer, Sunday Times, (5 October 1975), Magazine, pp. 28–31, 33–4, p. 36, p. 38.
16.   Rebecca West, Notes on Novels, The New Statesman 19, 16 September 1922.
17.   Janet McVeigh, In Collaboration with British Literary Biography, (Palgrave Macmillan Springer, Chaud Switzerland, 2017), p. 205.
18.   Jonathan Franzen, A Rooting Interest. Edith Wharton and the problem of sympathy, The New Yorker, February 13 & 20, 2012. p. 60.
19.   T.S. Eliot, Yeats from the first annual Yeats Lecture, delivered to the Friends of the Irish Academy at the Abbey Theatre, Dublin, in 1940. Subsequently published in Purpose.

20.   Elinor Glyn, Romantic Adventurer : Being the Autobiography of Elinor Glyn, (New York, Dutton 1937), p. 131.

21.   Ethel M. Dell, The Passer By, (London, Hutchinson, 1925), pp. 12–30

Chapter 4. A Remarkably Driven Novelist

1.   Ethel M. Dell to A. P. Watt 19th February 1932. University of North Carolina, A.P. Watt Records ref. 11036.

2.   Ethel M Dell, The Electric Torch, (London, Cassell, 1934), p. 185. Penelope Dell, Nettie and Sissie, (London: Hamish Hamilton, 1977), pp. 140–141. www.http://orlando.cambridge, Penelope Dell to Dame Joan McLoughlin 25 August 1975. Author's collection.

3.   Ethel M Dell, The Secret Service Man, in Rosa Mundi and Other Stories, (London, Cassell, 1921), p. 227.

4.   Ethel M. Dell to A.P. Watt dated 14th August 1918. University of North Carolina, Chapel Hill, A. P. Watt Records Collection ref. 11036.

5.   Ethel M. Dell, Storm Drift, (London, Hutchinson, 1930), p. 97.

6.   Laurel Brake, Star Turn? Magazine, Part-Issue and Book Serialisation, Victorian Periodicals Review, Vol. 34. No.3 (2001).

7.   This number includes serialised stories and is the total discovered by the date of this publication.

8.   Ethel M. Dell, Greatheart, ref. 56M 86M/3 Hampshire County archives.

9.   Ethel M. Dell to A.P. Watt letter dated 21st February 1913.

10.   Mary Ann Gillies, The Professional Literary Agent, (Toronto, University of Toronto Press, 2007), p. 37.

11.   University of North Carolina, A. P. Watt Records ref. 11036.

12.   Ethel M. Dell, to the Society of Authors, 4th July 1912, British Library MS 56510.

Chapter 5. A Cloistered, Conflicted and Wealthy Family

1.   Ethel M. Dell, The Keeper of the Door, (London, T. Fisher Unwin, 1915), p. 377.

2.   Vi Sharpe (née Philipps) to Penelope Dell 13th February 1975. Author's collection.

3.   Vi Sharpe (née Philipps) to Penelope Dell 7th July 1977. Author's collection.

4.   Ethel M. Dell to A.P. Watt 12th April 1919. University of North Carolina, A. P. Watt Records ref. 11036.

5.   Ethel M. Dell to A.P. Watt 12th April 1919. University of North Carolina, A. P. Watt Records ref. 11036.

6.   Lisa Appignanesi, Mad Bad and Sad, a History of Women and the Mind Doctors from 1800 to the Present, (London, Virago, 2008), p. 239.

7.   Ethel M. Dell to James B. Pinker 4th December 1901. University of North Carolina, A. P. Watt Records ref. 11036.

8.   First published 28th June 1890 in the Scots Observer.

Chapter 6. The Sibling's Stimuli

1.   Ethel M. Dell, The Rocks of Valpré, (London, T. Fisher Unwin, 1914), p. 260.

2.   Maurice Bowra, (C.M.), Memories, (London, Weidenfeld & Nicholson, 1966), pp. 35–36.

3.   Ethel M. Dell, The Lamp in the Desert, (London, Hutchinson, 1919), pp. 170–175.

4.   Ethel M. Dell, The Rocks of Valpré, (London, T. Fisher Unwin, 1914), p. 156.

5.   Maurice Bowra, (C.M.), Memories, (London, Weidenfeld & Nicholson, 1966), p. 39.

6.   Ethel M. Dell, The Losers, (Ernest Benn, London), p. 314.

Chapter 7. Relationships and Wealth

1.   Ethel M. Dell, The Tidal Wave, in the Red Magazine, London, assumed between 1911 and 1912, p. 11.

2.   Ethel M. Dell, Storm Drift, (London, Hutchinson, 1930), p. 276.

3.   Ethel M. Dell, The Hundredth Chance, (New York, Grosset & Dunlap, 1917), p. 159.

4.   MISS ETHEL M. DELL'S WILL (in left hand draw in safe in Office)' University of North Carolina, Chapel Hill, A. P. Watt Records Collection ref. 11036; File 196.02.

5.   Ethel M. Dell, Storm Drift, (London, Hutchinson, 1930), p. 253.

6.   £5,037.14.1d. England & Wales, National Probate Calendar (Index of Wills and Administrations). Values converted at www.measuringgrowth.com.

7.   Penelope Dell, Nettie and Sissie, (London, Hamish Hamilton), p. 43.

8.   Penelope Dell letter to Ella Dell 29th October 1929. Author's collection.

9.   £3,472. England & Wales, National Probate Calendar (Index of Wills and Administrations). Values converted at www.measuringgrowth.com.

10. Maude Ebsworth to Penelope Dell 23rd July 1977. Author's collection.

11. Ethel M Dell, Greatheart, (London, T. Fisher Unwin, 1919) hand written inscription on the flysheet. Author's collection.

12. Adoption Agreement dated 7 March 1919. Author's collection.

13. Ethel M. Dell, Bars of Iron, (London, Hutchinson, 1954), p. 88.

14. Ethel M. Dell, Knave of Diamonds, (London, Ernest Benn, 1954), p. 177.

15. Ethel M. Dell, Sea Urchin and the Prince, (London, The Red Magazine, 1909), p. 371.
16. The London Gazette 31 Jan. 1919, published in the Supplement to the Edinburgh Gazette 5 February 1919, p. 865.
17. Penelope Dell to I. E. Dell on Oakdene PNEU school notepaper, 1932. Author's collection.
18. Ibid undated 1932 and 12 March 1932.
19. Diana Hunt letter to Penelope Dell 25th July 1975. Author's collection.
20. Chris Pawson email to the author 30th January 2017.
21. Patsy Churchill (née Philipps) to Penelope Dell undated letter in the 1970s. Author's collection.
22. A Barwell (Ethel's chauffeur) to Penelope Dell letter dated 20th January 1978. Author's collection.
23. Madge Philipps to Patsy Churchill undated. undated letter in the 1970s. Author's collection.
24. Gielgud, John. An Actor and His Time, (London, Sidgwick and Jackson, 1979), p. 115.

Chapter 8. Health, Sickness and Drugs

1. Ethel M. Dell, The Lamp in the Desert, (London, Hutchinson, 1919), p. 292.
2. Ethel M. Dell, The Way of an Eagle, (London, Fisher Unwin, 1914), p.19.
3. Ethel M. Dell, The Keeper of the Door, (London, T. Fisher Unwin, 1915), p.120.
4. Ibid., p. 188.
5. Ibid., p. 186.
6. Queenie D. Leavis, Fiction and the Reading Public, (London, Chatto and Windus 1965), p. 53.
7. Ethel M. Dell, The Black Knight, (London, Cassell,) pp. 268–269.
8. Ethel M. Dell, The Lamp in the Desert, (London, Hutchinson, 1919), p. 115.
9. Ethel M. Dell, Storm Drift, (London, Hutchinson, 1930), p. 97.
10. Ethel M. Dell, The Serpent in the Garden, (London, Cassell, 1932), p. 321.
11. Ethel M. Dell, The Juice of the Pomegranate, (London, Cassell, 1954), p. 281.
12. Lisa Appignanesi, Mad Bad and Sad, A History of Women and the Mind Doctors from 1800 to the Present', (Virago, London, 2008).
13. Andrzej Diniejko, Victorian Drug Use, The Victorian Web, 2002.
14. Kristina Aikens, A Pharmacy of her own: Victorian Woman and the Figure of the Opiat, Ann Arbor, Pro Quest, 2008.
15. Ethel M. Dell, to Mrs. Edward Blakeney July 9th 1936. British Library call reference BL MS.63085.
16. Alison Flood, The Guardian, 23rd September 2008.

Chapter 9. Dislike of Adventure, Kind and Socially Naïve

1.   Ethel M. Dell, The Passer-By, (London, Hutchinson, 1925), p. 12.
2.   Ethel M. Dell, Without Prejudice in The Odds and Other Stories, (London, Cassell, 1922), p. 29.
3.   Ethel M. Dell, Where Three Roads Meet, (London, Cassell, 1935), p. 257.
4.   Ibid., p. 334.
5.   Ethel M. Dell, The Passer-By, (London, Hutchinson, 1925), p.12.
6.   Ibid., p. 23.
7.   Ibid., p. 30.
8.   Ibid. p. 185.
9.   Ethel M. Dell, The Juice of the Pomegranate, (London, Cassell, 1954), p. 53.
10.   Ibid., p. 56.
11.   Maurice Bowra (C. M.), Memories, (London, Weidenfeld & Nicholson, 1966), pp. 35–36.
12.   Nancy Spain, The Way of Ethel M. Dell, ed. John Hadfield (London, Hutchinson, 1955) as published in the Saturday Book 1966, pp. 73–78.
13.   Ethel M. Dell to Lady Smithers, 23rd January 1922. Author's collection.
14.   Nancy Spain, The Way of Ethel M. Dell ed. John Hadfield (London, Hutchinson, 1955) published in the Saturday Book 1966, pp. 73–78.
15.   Nursie Talbot, interviews with Penelope Dell in the 1970s Author's collection.
16.   Philip Waller, Writers, Readers, & Reputations, Literary Life in Britain 1870–1918 (Oxford, Oxford UP, 2006), p. 374.
17.   Nursie Talbot, interviews with Penelope Dell in the 1970s. Author's collection.
18.   Faith Brown, Dell's cook in 1938, questionnaire and letter dated November 1975. Author's collection.

Chapter 10. The Lampooned Style

1.   Ethel M. Dell, The Hundredth Chance, (New York, Grosset & Dunlap, 1917), p. 51.
2.   Mary Hammond, Reading, Publishing and the Formation of Literary Taste in England, 1880–1914 (Aldershot: Ashgate, 2006).
3.   Nicola Beauman, A Very Great Profession: The Woman's Novel 1914–39, (London, Virago, 2004), p. 183.
4.   News Chronicle, 19 September 1939, p. 5. On Dell's death this paper reported her earnings as at £25,000 a year. This figure has been extrapolated

to today's values using an historical calculator available at www.http:// measuringworth.com.

5. George Orwell, The Cost of Letters, Horizon X1V (September 1946).

6. Robert Graves, The Cost of Letters, Horizon X1V (September 1946).

7. Antony Alpers, The Stories of Katherine Mansfield Review by W.H. New, Journal of New Zealand Literature, No. 3 (1985).

8. John Simpson, Strange Places, Questionable People, (London, Pan Macmillan, 2008), p. 235.

9. Nancy Spain, The Way of Ethel M. Dell ed. John Hadfield (London, Hutchinson, 1955) as published in the Saturday Book 1966, pp. 73–78.

10. Ethel M. Dell, Her Compensation, (London, Holden and Hardingham), p. 37.

11. George Macdonald. Phantastes: A Faerie Romance for Men and Women. (London, Smith and Elder 1858).

12. Stanley Unwin, The Truth about a Publisher, (London, Allen & Unwin, 1960), pp. 93–94.

13. Audrey C. Peterson, Brain Fever in the Nineteenth Century: Fact or Fiction,. Victorian Studies, vol. 19, no.4, (Jun., 1976) Indiana University Press, pp. 445–464.

14. Stanley Unwin, The Truth about a Publisher, (London, Allen & Unwin, 1960), pp. 93–94.

15. Nancy Spain, The Way of Ethel M. Dell ,ed. John Hadfield (London, Hutchinson, 1955) as published in the Saturday Book 1966, pp. 73–78.

16. Ethel M. Dell, The Passer-By, (London, Hutchinson, 1925), p. 12.

17. Ethel M. Dell, Knave of Diamonds, (London, Ernest Benn, 1954), p. 41.

18. Ethel M. Dell to A.P. Watt. 22nd May 1931. University of North Carolina, A.P. Watt Records ref. 11036.

19. Ethel M. Dell to A.P. Watt. 19th February 1932. University of North Carolina, A.P. Watt Records ref. 11036.

20. Ethel M. Dell to A.P. Watt. 4th February 1937. University of North Carolina, A.P. Watt Records ref. 11036.

21. Ethel M. Dell, The Passer-By, (London, Hutchinson, 1925), p. 7.

22. Ibid., p. 21.

23. Alice Kelly, The Field of Honour and unknown First World War story by Edith Wharton, (The Times Literary Supplement 6th November, 2015), p. 16.

24. Ethel M. Dell, Greatheart, (London, T. Fisher Unwin, 1919) p. 39.

25. Ethel M. Dell, The Hundredth Chance, (New York, Grosset & Dunlap, 1917), p. 306.

26.   Ethel M. Dell, Bars of Iron, (London, Hutchinson, 1954), p.19. Greatheart, (London, T. Fisher Unwin, 1919), p.148.
27.   Ethel M. Dell, Storm Drift, (London, Hutchinson, 1930), p. 141.
28.   Ethel M. Dell, Bars of Iron, (London, Hutchinson, 1954), p. 211.
29.   Ethel M. Dell, The Knave of Diamonds, (London, Ernest Benn, 1954), p. 28.
30.   Ethel M. Dell, The Full Measure (McCall's Magazine, 1925), p. 317.
31.   Ethel M. Dell, Bars of Iron, (London, Hutchinson, 1954), p. 19.
32.   Ethel M. Dell, The Way of an Eagle, (London, Fisher Unwin, 1914), p. 10.
33.   Ibid., p. 10.
34.   Ethel M. Dell, The Knave of Diamonds, (London, Ernest Benn, 1954), p.94.
35.   Ibid., p.25.
36.   Ethel M. Dell, The Keeper of the Door, (London, T. Fisher Unwin, 1915), p.133.
37.   Ethel M. Dell, The Swindler's Handicap, (London, T. Fisher Unwin, 1914), p. 52.
38.   Ibid., p.47.
39.   Ethel M. Dell, The Passer-By, (London, Hutchinson, 1925), p. 7.
40.   Ethel M. Dell, The Rocks of Valpré, (London, T. Fisher Unwin), p. 286.
41.   Ethel M. Dell, Where Three Roads Meet, (London, Cassell, 1935), p. 29.
42.   Ethel M. Dell, Her Own Free Will, (London, Cassell, 1922), p. 130
43.   Ethel M. Dell, The Knight Errant in The Swindler and Other Stories, (London, T. Fisher Unwin, 1914), p. 262.
44.   Ibid., p. 274.
45.   Ibid., p. 313.
46.   Ethel M. Dell, The Odds in The Odds and Other Stories, (London, Cassell, 1922), p. 4.
47.   Ethel M. Dell, Without Prejudice in The Odds and Other Stories. (London, Cassell, 1922). p. 42.
48.   Ethel M. Dell, Death's Property in The Odds and Other Stories. (London, Cassell, 1922). p. 227.
49.   Ethel M. Dell, The Lamp in the Desert, (London, Hutchinson, 1919), p. 30.
50.   Ethel M. Dell, Where Three Roads Meet, (London, Cassell, 1935), p. 21.
51.   Ethel M. Dell, The Juice of the Pomegranate (London, Cassell, 1954), p. 99.
52.   Ibid., p. 195.
53.   Ethel M. Dell, Honeyball Farm, (London, Hutchinson, 25th Thousand), p. 102.
54.   Ethel M. Dell, The Lamp in the Desert, (London, Hutchinson, 1919), p. 41.
55.   Ibid., p. 290.

56. Ibid., p. 285.
57. Ethel M. Dell, A Debt of Honour, (London, The Red Magazine, 1909), p. 283.
58. Ethel M. Dell, A Debt of Honour, (London, The Red Magazine, 1909), p. 319.
59. Ethel M. Dell, Storm Drift, (London, Hutchinson, 1930), p. 166.
60. Ethel M. Dell, The Swindler's Handicap, (London, T. Fisher Unwin, 1914), p. 31.
61. Paul Fishman, The Fatal absence of Self Doubt, www.fishmandeville, commenting on Graham Greene, The Dark Backward' (London, Vintage, 1994), and Selina Hastings, Evelyn Waugh, The Ordeal of Gilbert Pinfold, (London, Harmondsworth: Penguin, 1957).
62. The Furrow, Vol. 26, No.5 (May 1975), 294–296. Review of The Abdication by Desmond Forrestal.
63. Queenie D. Leavis, Fiction and the Reading Public, (London, Chatto and Windus 1965), p. 62.
64. Victoria Stewart, The Woman Writer in Mid-Twentieth Century Middlebrow Fiction: Conceptualizing Creativity. Journal of Modern Literature, Volume 35, Number 1 Fall 2011, University of Indiana Press, p. 27.
65. Queenie D. Leavis, Fiction and the Reading Public, (London, Chatto and Windus 1965), p. 232.
66. The Rorschach test is a psychological test in which subjects' perceptions of inkblots are recorded and then analysed using psychological interpretations.
67. Ethel M. Dell, The Black Knight (Cassell, London, 1926), p. 9.
68. Ibid., p. 197.

Chapter 11. An Understanding of Ethel's Writing

1. J.A. Passmore, The Dreariness of Aesthetics: Mind, New Series, Vol. 60, No. 239 (Jul., 1951), pp. 318–335.
2. Kate Symondson, Times Literary Supplement, January 6th 2017, p. 13.
3. J.A. Passmore, The Dreariness of Aesthetics: Mind, New Series, Vol. 60, No. 239 (Jul., 1951), pp. 318–335.
4. Michael Joseph, The Commercial Side of Literature, (London, Hodder and Stoughton, 1925), p. 15.
5. Ethel M. Dell, The Way of an Eagle, (London, Fisher Unwin, 1914), p. 251.
6 Ibid., p. 62.
7. Ibid., p. 366.
8. Ethel M. Dell, The Knave of Diamonds, (London, Ernest Benn, 1954), p. 179.

9.   Ethel M. Dell, The Safety Curtain and Other Stories (London, Fisher Unwin, 1917), p. 34.

Chapter 12. Ethel and the New Woman

1.   Ethel M. Dell, The Gate Marked Private, (London, Cassell, 1928), pp. 146–147.
2.   Ménie M. Dowie, Gallia, (London, Metheun & Co., 1895), p.113.
3.   Herbert G. Wells, Ann Veronica, (London, Weidenfeld & Nicholson, 2010), p. 151.
4.   Ibid., p. 219.
5.   Rebecca West Book Review of 'Marriage' by H.G. Wells, The Freewoman, Vol. 2, No. 44, September 19, 1912, pp. 346–348.
6.   Sarah Grand, The New Aspect of the Woman Question, The North American Review 158, no. 4 48 (1894), pp. 270–76.
7.   Jad Adams review of Jill Liddington's Vanishing for the Vote. Times Literary Supplement (Manchester University Press September 2014), p. 30.
8.   Ethel M. Dell, The Rocks of Valpré, (London, T. Fisher Unwin, 1914), p. 299.
9.   Ethel M. Dell, The Black Knight, (Cassell, London, 1926), pp. 71 & 107.
10.   Ethel M. Dell, The Gate Marked Private, (London, Cassell, 1928), pp. 146–147.
11.   Ethel M. Dell, The Juice of the Pomegranate, (London, Cassell, 1954), p. 14.
12.   Queenie D. Leavis Fiction and the Reading Public ,(London, Chatto and Windus 1965), p. 289.
13.   Nickianne Moody, Elinor Glyn and the Invention of 'IT', Critical Survey 15, no. 3 (2003), pp. 92–104.
14.   David Warren Maurer, Language and the Sex Revolution: World War I through World War II, American Speech 51, no. 1/2 (1976).

Chapter 13. The Humour

1.   Ethel M. Dell, The Knave of Diamonds, (London, Ernest Benn, 1954), p. 29.
2.   Ethel M. Dell, The Way of an Eagle, (London, Fisher Unwin, 1914), p. 65.
3.   Ethel M. Dell, The Lamp in the Desert, (London, Hutchinson, 1919), p. 148.
4.   Ethel M. Dell, Bars of Iron, (London, Hutchinson, 1954), p. 18.
5.   Ethel M. Dell, The Passer-By, (London, Hutchinson, 1925), p. 15.
6.   Ethel M. Dell, The Knave of Diamonds, (London, Ernest Benn, 1954), p. 9.
7.   Ethel M. Dell, The Lamp in the Desert, (London, Hutchinson, 1919), p. 28.
8.   Ethel M. Dell, Pageant of Youth, (Ernest Benn, 1932), p. 240.
9.   St. John Ervine, The Times newspaper 25th April 1922.
10.   Nancy Spain, The Way of Ethel M. Dell ed. John Hadfield (London, Hutchinson, 1955) as published in the Saturday Book 1966, pp. 73–78.

11.   Francisco P. Tosti, The second verse of Goodbye (1908):

Hush! A voice from the faraway!

Listen and learn, it seems to say,

All tomorrows shall be as today.

All tomorrows shall be as today.

The chords is frayed the cruse is dry,

The link must break, and the lamp must die.

Good-bye, to Hope! Good-bye, Good-bye!

Good-bye, to Hope! Good-bye, Good-bye!

12.   Ethel M. Dell, The Good Turn (London, Cassell, 1927), p. 125.

13.   Ibid., p. 141.

14.   Ibid., p. 124.

15.   Ethel M. Dell, The Black Knight (Cassell, London, 1926), p. 10.

16.   Ethel M. Dell, Honeyball Farm, (London, Hutchinson, 25th Thousand), pp. 142/3.

17.   Ethel M. Dell, The Serpent in the Garden, (London, Cassell, 1938), p. 42.

18.   Ethel M. Dell, The Safety Curtain and Other Stories (London, Fisher Unwin, 1917), p. 104.

19.   Ethel M. Dell, The Juice of the Pomegranate, (London, Cassell, 1954), p. 93.

Chapter 14. The Empire and Notions of Masculinity

1.   Alan Greenberger, The British Image of India: A Study in the Literature of Imperialism, 1880–1960. (London, Oxford University Press, 1969), and Ethel M Dell, The Safety Curtain in The Safety Curtain and Other Stories, (London T. Fisher Unwin, London. 1917.

2.   Ethel M. Dell, The Keeper of the Door, (London, T. Fisher Unwin, 1915), p. 310.

3.   Ethel M. Dell, The Lamp in the Desert (London: Hutchinson, 1919), p. 169.

4.   Edward John Thompson, The Other Side of the Medal (London: Hogarth, 1925), p. 114.

5.   Ibid., p. 15.

6.   Ibid., p. 162.

7.   Ethel M. Dell, The Unknown Quantity. (London, Hutchinson, 1923), p. 158.

8.   Allen Greenberger, The British Image of India: A Study in the Literature of Imperialism, 1880–1960, (London, Oxford University Press, 1969).

9.   Stanley Wolpert, Journal of Asian Studies, Review: Greenberger, A, The British Image of India: A Study in the Literature of Imperialism, 1880–196, (London, Oxford University Press, 1969), p. 956.

10. Edmund Candler, Abdication, Studies: an Irish quarterly Review, vol.12, no.45 (mar. 1923), pp 157–158 by W. D. Irish Province of the Society of Jesus.

11. Bithia M. Croker, Diana Barrington: A Romance of Central India, 3 vols. (London: Ward and Downey, 1888), 3: 63.

12. Allen Greenberger, The British Image of India: A Study in the Literature of Imperialism, 1880-1960 (Oxford, Oxford UP, 1969), p. 12.

13. Ethel M. Dell, The Way of an Eagle (London, Fisher Unwin, 1914), p. 187.

14. Ibid., p. 86, and Ethel M. Dell, The Safety Curtain and Other Stories (London, Fisher Unwin, 1917), p. 49.

15. Allen Greenberger, British Image of India, (see above, n. 242), p. 12.

16. Ethel M. Dell, A Question of Trust, in The Red Magazine, London, 1911, p. 334.

17. Ethel M. Dell, Bars of Iron, (London, Hutchinson, 1954), pp. 15, 124.

18. Ethel M. Dell, The Keeper of the Door, (London, T. Fisher Unwin, 1915), p. 367.

19. Ethel M. Dell, The Way of an Eagle, (London, T. Fisher Unwin, 1914), p. 27.

20. Rosemary M. George, Homes in the Empire, Empire in the Home, Cultural Critique 26(1993/4), pp. 95–126.

21. Yule, H & Burnall A. C, 'Hobson-Jobson Anglo-Indian Dictionary' first published in 1886. Accessed edition: Wordsworth Editions, Ware 1996.

22. Ethel M. Dell, The Electric Torch, (London, Cassell, 1934), p. 173.

23. Ethel M. Dell, The Lamp in the Desert,(London, Hutchinson, 1919), p. 22.

24. Ethel M. Dell, The Electric Torch, Bath, (Lythway Press Ltd., 1971), p. 74.

25. Ethel M. Dell, The Lamp in the Desert,(London, Hutchinson, 1919), p. 16.

26. Ethel M. Dell, The Way of an Eagle, (London, T. Fisher Unwin, 1914) p. 31.

27. Alfred E.W. Mason, Sapphire, (London, Hodder and Stoughton, 1932).

28. Allen Greenberger, The British Image of India: A Study in the Literature of Imperialism, 1880-1960. (London, Oxford University Press, 1969), p. 39.

29. Rosemary M. George . Homes in the Empire, Empire in the Home, Cultural Critique, No.26 (Winter, 1994–1994), p. 119.

30. Ibid., p. 161.

31. Ethel M. Dell, The Keeper of the Door, (London, T. Fisher Unwin, 1915), p. 299.

32. Dell, Ethel M. The Secret Service Man, in Rosa Mundi and Other Stories, (Cassell, London, 1971), p. 240.

Chapter 15. Violence, Sexuality and Male and Female Roles

1. Ethel M. Dell, The Hundredth Chance, (New York, Grosset & Dunlap, 1917), p. 101.

2.   Ethel M. Dell, The Knight Errant in The Swindler and Other Stories, (London, T. Fisher Unwin, 1914), p. 322.

3.   Ethel M. Dell, The Knave of Diamonds, (London, Ernest Benn, 1954), pp. 258–259.

4.   Ethel M. Dell, Death's Property in The Odds and Other Stories, (London, Cassell, 1922), p. 259.

5.   Ethel M. Dell, The Lamp in the Desert,(London, Hutchinson, 1919), p. 33.

6.   Ethel M. Dell, The Desire of his Life with Her Compensation, (London, Holden and Hardingham, 1914), p. 37.

7.   Ethel M. Dell, The Hundredth Chance, (New York, Grosset & Dunlap, 1917), p. 163.

8.   Ethel M. Dell, Storm Drift, (London, Hutchinson, 1930), p. 63.

9.   Ethel M. Dell, Bars of Iron, (London, Hutchinson, 1954), p. 13.

10.   Ibid., p. 260.

11.   Ethel M. Dell, A Question of Trust in The Red Magazine, London, 1911, p. 379.

12.   Ethel M. Dell, Greatheart, (London, T. Fisher Unwin, 1919), p. 291.

13.   Nicola Beauman, A Very Great Profession, (London, Persephone Books, 2008), p.175, quoting J. Montgomery, The Twenties. Allen & Unwin, 1975, p. 216.

14.   Ethel M. Dell, Storm Drift, (London, Hutchinson, 1930), p. 314.

15.   Ethel M. Dell, The Electric Torch, (Bath, Lythway Press Ltd., 1971), p.2 1.

16.   Ibid., p. 213–218.

17.   Ethel M. Dell, The Sacrifice, in The Odds: And Other Stories, (London, Cassell, 1922), p. 312.

18.   Ethel M. Dell, The Electric Torch, (Bath, Lythway Press Ltd., 1971), p. 23.

19.   Ethel M. Dell, The Hundredth Chance, (New York, Grosset & Dunlap, 1917), p. 121.

20.   Ibid., p. 101.

21.   Ethel M. Dell, The Rocks of Valpré, (London, T. Fisher Unwin, 1914), p. 202.

22.   Ethel M. Dell, The Desire of his Life with Her Compensation, (London, Holden and Hardingham, 1914), p. 6.

23.   Ethel M. Dell, Bars of Iron, (London, Hutchinson, 1954), p. 245.

24.   Ethel M. Dell, The Experiment in The Safety Curtain: And other Stories, (London, T. Fisher Unwin, 1917), pp. 125–127.

25.   Ethel M. Dell, Bars of Iron, (London, Hutchinson, 1954), p. 150.

26.   Ethel M. Dell, The Lamp in the Desert,(London, Hutchinson, 1919), p. 89.

27.   Ethel M. Dell, The Tidal Wave, in the Red Magazine, London, assumed between 1911 and 1912, p. 42.

28.   Ethel M. Dell, The Knave of Diamonds, (London, Ernest Benn, 1954), p. 81.

29.   Ethel M. Dell, Without Prejudice in The Odds and Other Stories. (London, Cassell, 1922), p. 54.

30.   Ethel M. Dell, The Hundredth Chance, (New York, Grosset & Dunlap, 1917), p. 121.

31.   Ethel M. Dell, Greatheart, (London, T. Fisher Unwin 1918), p. 215.

32.   Ibid., p. 245.

33.   Ethel M. Dell, The Safety Curtain, www.Classic Reader.com. p. 47.

34.   Ethel M. Dell, The Unknown Quantity. (London, Hutchinson, 1923), p. 151.

35.   Ethel M. Dell, The Rocks of Valpré, (London, T. Fisher Unwin, 1914), p. 49.

36.   Ibid., p. 38.

37.   Ethel M. Dell, The Tidal Wave, in the Red Magazine, London, assumed between 1911 and 1912, p. 21.

38.   Ethel M. Dell, Where Three Roads Meet, (London, Cassell, 1935), p. 51.

39.   Ethel M. Dell, The Electric Torch, (Bath, Lythway Press, 1971), p. 267.

40.   Ethel M. Dell, Death's Property in The Odds and Other Stories, (London, Cassell, 1922), p. 230.

41.   Ethel M. Dell, Bars of Iron, (London, Hutchinson, 1954), p. 169.

42.   Ibid., p. 263.

43.   Ethel M. Dell, Bars of Iron, (London, Hutchinson, 1954), p. 216.

44.   Ethel M. Dell, The Hundredth Chance, (New York, Grosset & Dunlap, 1917), pp. 89–91.

45.   Ethel M. Dell, The Way of an Eagle, (London, T. Fisher Unwin, 1914), p. 114.

46.   Ethel M. Dell, The Tidal Wave, in The Red Magazine, London, assumed between 1911 and 1912, p. 46.

47.   Sheffield Hallam University's 'Readerships and Literary Cultures 1900–1950 Special Collection' blog. . Melodrama, Ethel M. Dell and 'The Tosh Horse' posted on April 9, 2013.

48.   Ethel M. Dell, The Tidal Wave, in the Red Magazine, London, assumed between 1911 and 1912, pp. 19, 27, 28.

49.   Ethel M. Dell, Bars of Iron, (London, Hutchinson, 1954), p. 214.

50.   Ethel M. Dell, Greatheart, (London, T. Fisher Unwin 1918), pp. 25, 91, 215, 273, 279.

51.   Ethel M. Dell, Tetherstones, (London, Hutchinsons, 1923), pp. 51–52.

52.   Ethel M. Dell, The Black Knight (Cassell, London, 1926), pp. 118, 141–142, 262.

53.   Ethel M. Dell, Honeyball Farm, (London, Hutchinson, 25th Thousand), p. 121.

54.   Ethel M. Dell, The Juice of the Pomegranate (London, Cassell, 1954), p. 296.
55.   Ethel M. Dell, The Lamp in the Desert,(London, Hutchinson, 1919), p.121.
56.   Ibid., pp. 178–180.
57.   Ethel M. Dell, Without Prejudice in The Odds and Other Stories, (London, Cassell, 1922), p.57.
58.   Ethel M. Dell, The Unknown Quantity, (London, Hutchinson, 1923), p. 34.
59.   Ethel M. Dell, Quits, (London, Ernest Benn, 1932), pp. 195, 216,
60.   Ethel M. Dell, Pageant of Youth, (London, Ernest Benn, 1932), p. 235.
61.   Ethel M. Dell, Charles Rex, (London, Hutchinson, 1922), p. 167.
62.   Ethel M. Dell, Misunderstanding, (Ernest Benn, 1932), p. 263.
63.   Ethel M. Dell, The Black Knight, (Cassell, London, 1926), pp. 168, 170.
64.   Ethel M. Dell, Honeyball Farm, (London, Hutchinson, 25th Thousand), pp. 36, 146, 209.
65.   Ethel M. Dell, The Juice of the Pomegranate, (London, Cassell, 1954), pp. 19, 95.
66.   Naomi Wolf, Sex and Intellect, Times Literary Supplement 24 December 2017, p. 15.

Chapter 16. Religion and Moral Musings

1.   Ethel M. Dell, The Rocks of Valpré, (London, T. Fisher Unwin, 1914), p. 442.
2.   Ethel M. Dell, The Bars of Iron, (London, Hutchinson, 1954), p. 58.
3.   Religious references are analysed in Ethel's narrative, with the exception of Sufiism and Judaism. In The Honourable Burford,(Novel Magazine 1906) the Sufi and Jewish phrase 'This, too, will pass' is quoted.
4.   Ethel M. Dell, The Swindler's Handicap, (London, T. Fisher Unwin, 1914), p. 56.
5.   Ethel M. Dell, The Keeper of the Door, (London, T. Fisher Unwin, 1915), p. 546.
6.   Ethel M. Dell, The House of Happiness, (London, Cassell, 1926), p. 78.
7.   Ethel M. Dell, The Rocks of Valpré, (London, T. Fisher Unwin, 1914), p. 298.
8.   Ethel M. Dell, The Way of an Eagle, (London, T. Fisher Unwin 1912), p. 129.
9.   Ethel M. Dell, Tetherstones, (London, Hutchinsons, 1923), p. 223.
10.   Ethel M. Dell, The Keeper of the Door, (London, T. Fisher Unwin 1915), p. 520.
11.   Ethel M. Dell, The Bars of Iron, (London: T. Fisher Unwin 1912), p. 129.
12.   Ethel M. Dell, The Way of an Eagle, (London, T. Fisher Unwin 1912), p. 153.

13.   Ethel M. Dell, Greatheart, (London, T. Fisher Unwin 1918), p. 164.

14.   Ethel M. Dell, Greatheart, (London, T. Fisher Unwin 1918), p. 220.

15.   Ethel M. Dell, The Lamp in the Desert, (London, Hutchinson, 1919), p. 24.

16.   Ethel M. Dell, The Lamp in the Desert, (London, Hutchinson, 1919), p. 253,

17.   Ethel M. Dell, The Keeper of the Door, (London, T. Fisher Unwin 1915), p. 115.

18.   Ethel M. Dell, The Bars of Iron, (London, T. Fisher Unwin 1912), p. 290.

19.   Ibid., p. 44.

20.   Ethel M. Dell, The Bars of Iron, (London, T. Fisher Unwin 1912), p. 320.

21.   Ethel M. Dell, Storm Drift, (London, Hutchinson, 1930), p. 323.

22.   Ethel M. Dell, The Keeper of the Door, (London, T. Fisher Unwin 1915), p. 115.

23.   Ethel M. Dell, The Rocks of Valpré, (London, T. Fisher Unwin, 1914), p. 442.

24.   Ethel M. Dell, The Unknown Quantity. (London, Hutchinson, 1923), pp. 126, 197–199.

25.   Ethel M. Dell, The Knave of Diamonds (London, Ernest Benn, 1954), p. 201.

26.   Ethel M. Dell, The Bars of Iron, (London, T. Fisher Unwin 1912), pp. 47–48, 83.

27.   Ethel M. Dell, The Hundredth Chance, (New York, Grosset & Dunlap, 1917), pp. 403–404.

28.   Ethel M. Dell, Greatheart, (London, T. Fisher Unwin 1918), p. 3.

29.   Ethel M. Dell, The Rocks of Valpré, (London, T. Fisher Unwin, 1914), p. 332.

30.   Robert Southey, The Curse of Kehama, (London, Printed for Longman, Hurst, Rees, Orme & Brown by J. Ballantyne, 1812.)

31.   Ibid., Preface.

32.   Ethel M. Dell, Storm Drift (London, Hutchinson, 1930), p. 69.

Chapter 17. Ethel's Hidden Philosophies

1.   Ethel M. Dell, Storm Drift, (London, Hutchinson, 1930), p. 34.

2.   Ethel M. Dell, The Obstacle Race, (London, Cassell, 1923), p. 108.

3.   Ethel M. Dell, The House of Happiness (London, Cassell, 1926), pp. 45 and 67.

4.   Ethel M. Dell, The Losers, (London, Ernest Benn), p. 326.

5.   Ibid.

6.   Ethel M. Dell, Greatheart, (London, T. Fisher Unwin 1918), p. 113.

7.   Ethel M. Dell, Charles Rex, (London, Hutchinson, 1922), p. 13.

8.   Ibid., p. 210.

9.   Ethel M. Dell, The Unknown Quantity. (London, Hutchinson, 1923), p. 221.

10.   Ethel M. Dell, The Chatelaine, (Ernest Benn, London, 1932), p. 62.

11.   Ethel M. Dell, Charles Rex, (London, Hutchinson, 1922), p. 131.

12.   Ibid., p. 33.
13.   Ethel M. Dell, The Knave of Diamonds, (London, Ernest Benn, 1954), p. 8.
14.   Ethel M. Dell, Charles Rex, (London, Hutchinson, 1922), p. 276.
15.   Ibid., p. 14.
16.   Ethel M. Dell, The Knave of Diamonds, (London, Ernest Benn, 1954), p. 134.
17.   Ibid., p. 66.
18.   Ethel M. Dell, Charles Rex, (London, Hutchinson, 1922), p. 214.
19.   Ethel M. Dell, The Bars of Iron, (London, T. Fisher Unwin 1912), p. 139.
20.   Ibid., p. 184.
21.   Ethel M. Dell, The Altar of Honour, (London, Hutchinson, 1929), p. 12.
22.   Ibid., p. 28.
23.   Ethel M. Dell, The Rocks of Valpré, (London, T. Fisher Unwin, 1914), pp. 226–227.
24.   Ethel M. Dell, Charles Rex, (London, Hutchinson, 1922), p. 110.
25.   Ethel M. Dell, The Knave of Diamonds, (London, Ernest Benn, 1954), pp. 67–68.
26.   Ibid., p. 8.
27.   Ibid., p. 211.
28.   Ethel M. Dell, The Obstacle Race, (London, Cassell, 1923), pp. 52–53.
29.   Ethel M. Dell, The Unknown Quantity. (London, Hutchinson, 1923), p. 221.
30.   Ethel M. Dell, Charles Rex. (London, Hutchinson, 1922), p. 104.
31.   Ibid. p. 123
32.   Ethel M. Dell, Tetherstones, (London, Hutchinson, 1923), p. 8.
33.   Ethel M. Dell, The Black Knight (Cassell, London, 1926), p. 103.
34.   Ethel M. Dell, The Real Thing, (London, Cassell, 1927), p. 181.

Chapter 18. The Reading Public and Reading Environment

1.   Ethel M. Dell, Greatheart, (London, T. Fisher Unwin, 1918), p.106. [In 1894, Mudie's Select Library and W.H. Smith's, the largest of the private circulating libraries, issued simultaneous announcements detailing the new terms on which they would buy novels from publishers: They would pay no more than four shillings per volume, on volumes that bore a nominal price of ten and sixpence. Publishers suddenly found that their dependence on the circulating libraries significantly less profitable.]
2.   A.P. Watt archives UNC11026 record of telephone conversation on 1932 December 2 that Weldon's 'did not usually care to publish stories that had been published previously in magazines that cost less the 1/- each to buy'. But they did eventually publish.

3. George Orwell, Bookshop Memories (1936), quoted in Nicola Humble, The Feminine Middlebrow Novel 1920s to 1950s (Oxford: Oxford UP, 2001), p. 12.
4. Thomas Kelly, History of Public Libraries in Great Britain 1845–1975 (London, The Library Association, 1975), p. 518.
5. Ibid.
6. Thomas Kelly, History of Public Libraries in Great Britain 1845–1975 (London, The Library Association, 1975), p. 215.
7. Nickianne Moody, presentation at Authors, Publishers and Readers: Selling and Distributing Literary Cultures, 1880–1940, seminar, Reading University, March 2012.
8. Jeaneatte Foster, An approach to Fiction through the Characteristics of Its Readers. The Library Quarterly, vol. 6, No. 2, Apr.' 1936, p.131. The University of Chicago Press.
9. 165.8M books borrowed x 50% for women readers x 10% for Ethel's readers.
10. Philip Waller, Writers, Readers, & Reputations, Literary Life in Britain 1870–1918, (Oxford, OUP, 2006), p. 679.
11. Orwell, G, Bookshop Memories, 1936, reprinted in The Collected Essays, Journalism and Letters of George Orwell, Volume One, An Age Like This, 1920–1940 (Secker & Warburg, 1968), 244, in Penguin Edition, 1970.
12. Analysis of all UK regional newspapers up to the time of Ethel M. Dell's death.
13. Ronald F. Batty, How to run a Twopenny Library, (London: Gifford, 1938), pp. 11, 91.
14. Mary Ann Gillies, The Professional Literary Agent (Toronto, University of Toronto Press, 2007), p. 38.
15. Stanley Unwin, The Truth about a Publisher, (London, Allen & Unwin, 1960), pp. 93–94.
16. Guinevere. L. Griest, Mudie's Circulating Library and the Victorian Novel (David and Charles, Indiana University Press, 1970), p. 142.
17. Western Mail 15th June 1921 p. 4 Bequest in Appreciation of her novels.
18. Dorothy L. Sayers, The Unpleasantness at the Bellona Club, (London, Ernest Benn, 1928) p. 159.
19. Bulletin of the American Library Association, Vol. 24, No. 9, Proceedings of the Fifty Second Annual Conference (September, 1930), pp. 427–433.
20. Bulletin of the American Library Association, Vol. 21, No. 10, Papers and Proceedings: Forty-Ninth Annual Conference 1927 (October 1927), p. 376.
21. Bulletin of the American Library Association, Vol. 27, No. 4 (April, 1933), p. 190.

22.   V. Dora, The English Journal, Vol. 26, No. 2 (Feb., 1937), p. 111.
23.   Seeing the Old through the New Marion Emory ,The English Journal, Vol. 24, No. 6 (Jun., 1935), pp. 462–466.
24.   Bulletin of the American Library Association, Vol. 26, No. 9 (September, 1932), p. 723.
25.   Jeannette Howard Foster, An Approach to Fiction through the Characteristics of Its Readers, The Library Quarterly, Vol. 6, No. 2 (Apr. 1936), pp. 124–174.
26.   Alice P. Hackett, Fifty Years of Best Sellers 1895–1945 (New York, R. R. Bowler 1945); quoted in L. Carnowsky, Library Quarterly 16.2 (1946). p. 175.
27.   Bulletin of the American Library Association, Vol. 15, No. 4, Papers and Proceedings of the Forty-Third Annual Meeting of the American Library Association (July 1921), p. 178.
28.   Philip B. Eppard: The Journal of Library History (1974–1987), Vol. 21, No. 1, Libraries, Books, & Culture I (Winter, 1986), p. 248.
29.   Harrison Smith, Twenty-Five Years of Best-Sellers: The English Journal, Vol. 33, No. 8 (Oct., 1944).

Chapter 19. Poetry

1.   Ethel M. Dell, Verses (London, Hutchinson, 1920, Putnam and Knickerbocker Press New York 1923), p. 10.
2.   Evelyn Waugh, Literary Style in England and America, (Chicago, The Thomas More Association 1955).
3.   Michael Joseph, The Commercial Side of Literature, (London, Hutchinson, 1925), p. 49.
4.   Ethel M. Dell, Verses (London, Hutchinson, 1920, Putnam and Knickerbocker Press New York 1923).
5.   Ibid., p. 10.
6.   Ralph Waldo Emerson, Early Poems of Ralph Waldo Emerson. (New York, Boston, Thomas Y. Crowell & Company, 1899).
7.   Barbara Cartland, Lines on Love and Life, (London, Hutchinson, 1972), p. 11.
8.   Ethel M. Dell Greatheart, (London, T. Fisher Unwin, 1918), p. 319.
9.   Barbara Cartland, Lines on Love and Life, (London, Hutchinson, 1972), p. 27.

Chapter 20. Literary Influences

1.   Ethel M. Dell, The Rocks of Valpré, (London, T. Fisher Unwin, 1914), p. 213.
2.   George Macdonald, Phantastes: A Faerie Romance for Men and Women, (London, Smith and Elder, 1858) p. 179.

3.   Ethel M. Dell, The Lamp in the Desert, (London, Hutchinson, 1919) p. 153.
4.   Ralph Waldo Emerson, Early Poems of Ralph Waldo Emerson, New York, Hurst & Company: 1899) p. 97.
5.   Robert Southey, The Curse of Kehama (London, Printed for Longman, Hurst, Rees, Orme & Brown by J. Ballantyne, 1812).
6.   Ibid., Preface.
7.   Ethel M. Dell, Storm Drift, (London, Hutchinson, 1930), p. 69.
8.   Rudyard Kipling's Verse, Inclusive Edition, 1885–1918. Garden City: Doubleday, Page, 1922; Bartleby.com, 2013.
9.   Ethel M. Dell, The Eleventh Hour, (London, T. Fisher Unwin, 1917), p. 19.
10. Ethel M. Dell, The Keeper of the Door, (London, T. Fisher Unwin, 1915), p. 245.
11. Ibid., p. 47.
12. Ethel M. Dell, The Rocks of Valpré, (London, T. Fisher Unwin, 1914), p. 213.
13. Ethel M. Dell, The Way of an Eagle, (London, T. Fisher Unwin 1912), p. 4.
14. Ethel M. Dell, The Keeper of the Door, (T. Fisher Unwin, London, 1915), p. 329.
15. Ethel M. Dell, The Hundredth Chance, (New York, Grosset & Dunlap, 1917), p. 260.
16. Ethel M. Dell, The Keeper of the Door, (T. Fisher Unwin, London, 1915), p. 347.
17. Ethel M. Dell, Peggy By Request, (London, Ernest Benn, 1954), p. 242.
18. Ethel M. Dell, The Knave of Diamonds, (London, Ernest Benn, 1954), p. 239.
19. Ethel M. Dell, The Hundredth Chance, (New York, Grosset & Dunlap, 1917), p. 194.
20. Ethel M. Dell, The Keeper of the Door, (London, T. Fisher Unwin, 1915), p. 36.
21. Ethel M. Dell, The Hundredth Chance (New York, Grosset & Dunlap, 1917), p. 233.
22. Ethel M. Dell, The Altar of Honour, (London, Hutchinson, 1929), p.1 96. The pre-Raphaelite artist Edward Byrne-Jones' 1884 painting of the scene of the legend illustrates the heroine's self-image well.
23. Ethel M. Dell, Charles Rex, (London, Hutchinson, 1922), p. 277
24. https://www.dartmouth.edu/~library/rauner/exhibits/power-honor-authority.html.
25. Ethel M. Dell, The Knave of Diamonds, (London, Ernest Benn, 1954), p. 80.
26. Ethel M. Dell, Death's Property in The Odds and Other Stories, (London, Cassell, 1922), p. 247
27. Ethel M. Dell, The Bars of Iron, (London, T. Fisher Unwin 1912), p. 199.

28.   A.P. Watt to Hodder letter 21st October 1913. University of North Carolina, A. P. Watt Records ref. 11036.
29.   Barbara Cartland. Daily Express, 14 July 1977, p. 17.
30.   Jennifer Kloester, Georgette Heyer Biography of a Bestseller, (London, William Heineman 2011), pp. 15, 83.
31.   Sayaka Nakagomi, English middle-class girls' high schools and 'domestic subjects' 1871–1914. PhD thesis. University of London. April 2016.
32.   Sir Cecil Maurice Bowra, English classical scholar, literary critic and academic. He was warden of Wadham College, Oxford and served as a vice-chancellor of Oxford University.

Chapter 21. Marketing and Selling

1.   Ronald F. Batty, How to Run a Twopenny Library, (London: Gifford, 1938), p. 11.
2.   Multiple source bibliographical data: http://www.philsp.com/homeville; Author's private collection; University of North Carolina, Chapel Hill, A. P. Watt Records Collection ref. 11036; www.britishnewspaperarchive.co.uk; New York Public Library, The Berg Collection, James B. Pinker correspondence.
3.   Christopher Hilliard, The Twopenny Library: The Book Trade, Working-Class Readers, and "Middlebrow" Novels in Britain, 1930–42, Twentieth-Century British History 25.2 (2014), there pp. 199–200.
4.   Iris Barry, Lets go to the Pictures (London, Chatto & Windus, 1926), p. 59.
5.   Annette Kuhn, 'Cinema-going in Britain in the 1930s: Report of a Questionnaire Survey,' Historical Journal of Film, Radio and Television 19: 4 (1999), pp. 531–543.
6.   Denis Gifford, 'The Early Memories of Maurice Elvey,' Griffithiana: Journal of Film History   60/61 (1997), 117–119.
7.   Nathalie Morris, 'An Eminent British Studio: The Stoll Film Companies and British Cinema 1918–1928', PhD thesis, University of East Anglia, 2009.
8.   Thomas Kelly, A History of Public Libraries in Great Britain, 1845–1975 (London: The Library Association, 1975), p. 518.
9.   Ronald F. Batty, How to Run a Twopenny Library (London: Gifford, 1938), p. 11.
10.   Ibid., p. 91.
11.   Hackett Alice Payne Fifty Years of Best Sellers 1895–1945, New York, R. Bowker as reviewed in The Library quarterly: Information, community, Policy, Vol. 16 No.2 (Apr., 1946), there 175–176. The University of Chicago Press.

Chapter 22. The Marketing Mix and Magazines

1. Watt to Hodder Williams quoting Ethel. April 3, 1918. University of North Carolina, A.P. Watt Records ref. 11036.
2. Pictorial Review, MagazineArt.org.
3. 'Pictorial Sold'. Time Magazine. 11 January, 1932.
4. Love Story Magazine, Newsstand: 1925.
5. Matt Vaughn, The University of Tulsa pulpmags.org
6. The Modernist Journals Project, Brown University and the University of Tulsa Periodical Directory 1890–1922.
7. https://victorianfictionresearchguides.org/cassells-family-magazine.

Chapter 23. Films

1. Iris Barry, Lets go to the Pictures (London: Chatto & Windus, 1926), p. 59.
2. Ibid.
3. Annette Kuhn, Cinema-going in Britain in the 1930s: Report of a Questionnaire Survey, Historical Journal of Film, Radio and Television 19.4 (1999), pp. 531–43.
4. Alexis Weedon, Elinor Glyn's System of Writing, Publishing History 60 (2006), pp. 31–50.
5. The Film World, The Times newspaper June 14th 1920, col. A, p. 18.
6. Cummings, Denise K; Annette Kuhn. Elinor Glyn. In Jane Gaines, Radha Vatsal, and Monica Dall'Asta, eds. Women Film Pioneers Project. Center for Digital Research and Scholarship. New York, NY: Columbia University Libraries.
7. Denis Gifford, 'The Early Memories of Maurice Elvey,' Griffithiana: Journal of Film History 60/61 (1997), pp. 117–19.
8. Nathalie Morris, 'An Eminent British Studio: The Stoll Film Companies and British Cinema 1918–1928' (PhD thesis, University of East Anglia, 2009).
9. Thomas Kelly, A History of Public Libraries in Great Britain, 1845–1975 (London: The Library Association, 1975), p. 518.
10. Denis Gifford, The Early Memories of Maurice Elvey, Griffithiana: Journal of Film History 60/61 (1997), p. 119.
11. Watt to Ethel November 6, 1924. University of North Carolina, A.P. Watt Records ref. 11036.
12. Watt to Ethel November 24, 1924. University of North Carolina, A.P. Watt Records ref. 11036.

Chapter 24. The Theatre

1.   Ethel M. Dell, The Rocks of Valpré, (London, T. Fisher Unwin, 1914), p. 466.
2.   The Manchester Guardian, 9 May 1923, p. 11.
3.   The Illustrated London News, 1 July 1922, p. 30.
4.   The Observer, 24 April 1921, p. 14.

Chapter 25. An Invisible yet successful Catharsis

1.   Virginia Woolf, Orlando, A Project Gutenberg of Australia eBook, 2015, p. 21.
2.   Virginia Woolf, To the Lighthouse, A Project Gutenberg of Australia eBook, 2015, p. 12.
3.   Virginia Woolf, The Waves, A Project Gutenberg of Australia eBook, 2015, p. 118.
4.   Mary Hammond, The Great Fiction Bore: Free Libraries and the Construction of a Reading Public in England, Libraries and Culture, 37.2, p. 95.
5.   Simon Frost, A Trade in Desires: Emigration, A.C. Gunter and the Home Publishing Company – calls for a user-oriented model. In The Book World, Selling and Distributing British Literature, 1900–1940, edit. Nicola Wilson, Brill, Leiden 2016.
6.   Michelle Lovric, Women's Wicked Wisdom: From Mary Shelley to Courtney Love The Creative Urge, Chicago Review Press, Chicago, 2004, p. 133.
7.   Benjamin Lefebvre, Edit., The L.M.Montgomery Reader, Life in Print, Vol.1, Toronto, Toronto University Press, 2013, p. 3.
8.   Queenie. D. Leavis, Fiction and the Reading Public (London, Chatto and Windus 1965), p. 35.
9.   Rachel Anderson, The Purple Heart Throbs, London, (Hodder and Stoughton, London, 1974), p. 148.
10. Rachel Anderson in Twentieth Century Romantic and Gothic Writers, Ed. James Vinson, Macmillan Surrey 1982, p. 209.
11. Emily Maitlis Internet Blog accessed 23/05/2019.
12. Rachel Anderson in Twentieth Century Romantic and Gothic Writers, Ed. James Vinson, Macmillan Surrey 1982, p. 209.
13. Ethel M. Dell, The Black Knight (Cassell, London, 1926), p. 239

Chapter 29. Ethel's Forty-one year output

1.   This data has been compiled from multiple sources including the correspondence and contractual archives in the University of North Carolina, the British Library, global book and magazine sellers, eBay, www.bookfinder.com, and from the author's personal collection.

Chapter 30. Title Historiography and Creative Levers

1. The Penelope Dell archives show this as being published by Wright and Brown known as a major printer for lending libraries. No publication date has been located.

Ella and her Alberts

1. Author's collection. The Albert was a light car designed by A.O. Lord. The cars were expensive, boasting a radiator similar to that of the Rolls-Royce. The body was mainly made of aluminium and most were four-seat tourers. About 1900 vehicles were manufactured, the last being in 1929.

Ethel's Major Titles: An Indication of Volume Output

1. Joseph McAleer, Passion's Fortune. The Story of Mills and Boon, (Oxford, Oxford University Press), p. 43.

About the Author

David Tanner holds a degree from the School of Oriental and African Studies (London University), and has lived in the United States, East Africa, Japan and the Philippines and has worked in over 40 countries. He has published military history (*Burma 1942, Memories of a Retreat*) and an historical novel of the Great Game and the Russian threat to British India in 1904 (*Cossacks at the Door*). His analysis of Dell and her work (*Literary Success and Popular Romantic Fiction: Ethel M. Dell, a Case Study*) appeared in The Book World Selling and Distributing British Literature 1900-1940.